SOFTWARE QUALITY INSTITUTE SERIES

Constructing Superior

Software

Paul C. Clements, Editor

Len Bass
Les Belady
Alan W. Brown
Paul C. Clements
Peter Freeman
Scott Isensee
Rick Kazman
Herb Krasner
John D. Musa
Shari Lawrence Pfleeger
Karel Vredenburg
Tony Wasserman

MACMILLAN
TECHNICAL
PUBLISHING
U·S·A

Constructing Superior Software

Copyright © 2000 by Macmillan Technical Publishing

International Standard Book Number: 1-57870-147-3

Library of Congress Catalog Card Number: 99-61797

Printed in the United States of America

First Printing: November, 1999

03 02 01 00 99   7 6 5 4 3 2 1

Interpretation of the printing code: The rightmost double-digit number is the year of the book's printing; the rightmost single-digit number is the number of the book's printing. For example, the printing code 99-1 shows that the first printing of the book occurred in 1999.

Trademarks

Warning and Disclaimer

Publisher
David Dwyer

Executive Editor
Alan Bower

Managing Editor
Sarah Kearns

Development Editor
Jill Bond

Project Editor
Linda Seifert

Technical Editor
Ian Lawthers

Indexer
Lisa Stumpf

Proofreader
Jennifer Mahern

Compositor
Wil Cruz

Contents at a Glance

Table of Contents

About the Authors

Len Bass is a senior software engineer at the Software Engineering Institute of Carnegie Mellon University (CMU). He has written or edited six books and numerous papers in a wide variety of areas of computer science, including software engineering, human-computer interaction, databases, operating systems, and theory of computation. His most recent book, *Software Architecture in Practice* (co-authored with Paul Clements and Rick Kazman), received Software Development Magazine's Productivity Award. He was the primary author of the Serpent User Interface Management System, which was widely cited for its innovativeness and influence. He organized a group that defined a user-interface software reference model that is an industry standard, and headed a group that developed a software architecture for flight training simulators that has been adopted as a standard by the U.S. Air Force. He also headed a group that developed a technique for evaluating software architectures for modifiability. He is currently working on techniques for the analysis of software architectures, and techniques for the development of software architectures for product lines of systems. He is the representative of the ACM to the International Federation of Information Processing technical committee on Software: Theory and Practice. Before joining CMU in 1986, he was professor and chair of the Computer Science Department at the University of Rhode Island. He received his Ph.D. in computer science in 1970 from Purdue University.

Les Belady is the Executive Director of the Austin Software Council, a non-profit organization representing the Central Texas region of the software industry and for those whose business success is tied to software. He is the retired Chairman and CEO of Mitsubishi Electronic Information Technology Center. Les has over three decades of experience in conducting and managing research. During 23 years with IBM, he led the software engineering effort at the T.J. Watson Research Center (1975–1981), was responsible for software technology at corporate headquarters (1981–1982), and established the software research program at the Japan Science Institute (1982–1984). Prior to joining Mitsubishi Electric Research Labs, he was the vice president of the Microelectronics and Computer Technology Corporation, where he founded and headed the Software Technology Program. His groundbreaking paper on virtual systems became a Citation Index Classic in 1983 as the most referenced article published in the field of software in two decades.

Les is an IEEE Fellow and recipient of the 1990 J.D. Warnier Prize for Excellence in Information. From 1979–1983, he was the editor-in-chief of the IEEE Transactions on Software Engineering.

Alan W. Brown, Ph.D., serves as Chief Technology Officer for Sterling Software's Applications Development Group (ADG), where he is responsible for research activities across the organization. He advises on specifications for new software products and the future direction of enterprise application and component-based software development products. He has published over 40 papers, edited three books, and is the author of four books in the areas of object-based systems, CASE tools, and software engineering practices.

Paul Clements is a senior member of the technical staff at the Software Engineering Institute at Carnegie Mellon University, where he specializes in the study of software architecture and software product line production.

He is co-author of *Software Architecture in Practice* (Addison Wesley Longman, 1998), and three forthcoming books on software product lines, software architecture evaluation, and software architecture documentation. Prior to coming to the SEI, he worked for the U. S. Naval Research Laboratory in Washington, D.C., where he specialized in software engineering methods for real-time systems. He holds Masters and Doctoral degrees in computer science from the University of North Carolina at Chapel Hill and the University of Texas at Austin, respectively.

Peter Freeman is the Dean of the College of Computing at Georgia Institute of Technology. He served on the faculty of the Department of Information and Computer Science at the University of California, Irvine for almost 20 years before going to Georgia Tech in 1990. He has been a member of the Board of Directors of the Computing Research Association since 1988, member of review committee of IRS and FAA Air-Traffic Control modernization efforts, and Chair of the Visiting Committee, Schlumberger Austin Research. He was recently named a Fellow of the IEEE and AAAS and is a faculty member of the Omicron Delta Kappa National Leadership Honor Society.

Peter is the author of *Software Perspectives: The System Is the Message* (AW 1987), *Software Systems Principles* (SRA, 1975), and numerous technical papers. He is the founding editor of the McGraw-Hill Series in Software Engineering and Technology and serves on several editorial boards. He is the past Chair of the IEEE/CS Technical Committee on Software Engineering and is an active consultant to industry and government.

Scott Isensee is a lead usability developer at BMC Software in Austin, Texas. He previously served as team leader of the corporate user interface architecture group at IBM. He also led the cross-company UI team that developed the Common Desktop Environment, the graphical user interface for UNIX. He is a member of ISO, ANSI, and W3C committees, writing software user interface and usability standards. He has 17 years experience designing application software, hardware, and operating system user interfaces. Scott holds Masters degrees in industrial psychology and computer science. He is a Certified Professional Ergonomist. He holds 20 patents and is an author of 62 publications on UCD topics, including the books *Designing for the User with OVID: Bridging User Interface Design and Software Engineering* and *The Art of Rapid Prototyping*. He is a frequent presenter at industry conferences and is widely recognized as an authority on user interface design methodology and prototyping.

Rick Kazman is a senior member of the technical staff at the Software Engineering Institute of Carnegie Mellon University and adjunct professor at the Universities of Waterloo and Toronto. His primary research interests are software engineering (software architecture, design tools, and software visualization), human-computer interaction (particularly interaction with 3D environments), and computational linguistics (information retrieval). He is the author of over 50 papers, and co-author of several books, including *Software Architecture in Practice*, which was written along with Len Bass and Paul Clements. Kazman received a B.A. and M.Math from the University of Waterloo, an M.A. from York University, and a Ph.D. from Carnegie Mellon University.

Herb Krasner is an independent software systems management consultant specializing in troubleshooting problem projects and products, and in coaching organizations to become excellent producers of superior software. With over 26 years of experience in computing/information systems and software engineering in both industrial and academic settings, he is considered to be a world-class expert in:

- Strategies for competitive production of superior software products and services: better, faster, and cheaper.

- Software systems assessment, audit, certification, and evaluation methods.

- Software and systems engineering disciplines, and related technologies.

- Software project and process management approaches.

- Establishing effective software quality and process improvement programs.

- Software quality techniques.

- Complex software systems in various application domains.

- Appraisal of organization/project systems and software engineering capabilities.

- Establishment of successful TQM, TBM, and business process re-engineering programs.

- Legal implications of software project failures and related issues.

Herb has helped many companies achieve results-oriented improvement of software capabilities using a number of models/standards, including: SEI's CMM for Software, ISO 9000-3, ISO 9126, MBNQA, Motorola's QSR/Six-Sigma, and SEI's SE CMM. Several of his clients have successfully climbed the SEI CMM ladder to the highest levels of process maturity, and thereby realized significant business benefits. As a Master Lead Assessor, he has successfully led over 40 SEI CMM-based assessments since being trained and certificated at the SEI in 1988. Krasner Consulting has had successful client engagements with: Gateway 2000, SSA, Hartmarx, Arthur Andersen, Schlumberger, Motorola, 3M, Tracor, Lockheed Martin, SEMATECH, GCS Inc., Litton Industries, TRW, Xerox, CSC, Intel, Lotus Development Corp., Compubahn Inc., Reliant Data Systems, Tandem Computers, Austin Ventures, Precision Robots, Inc., Plasma Materials & Technology, EMC Automation, State of Texas, University of Texas, Applied Research Laboratory (UT), U.S. General Accounting Office, and InfoGlide.

Herb is the founder of the Austin Software Process Improvement Network, Past Chairman of the Software Quality Institute at the University of Texas, and has been keynote speaker at several international conferences. He teaches the body of knowledge class for the ASQ Certified Software Quality Engineer program. He has published over 66 papers, reports, and book sections on a variety of software subjects, and has presented in many professional forums. Prior to initiating his successful consulting business in 1991, he held positions as: Division Manager, SAIC; Chief Software Technologist, Lockheed R&D; Project Leader, MCC Empirical Studies of Software; Senior Software Scientist, Harris Corporation; Asst. Professor of Computer Sciences, Clemson University; Computer Systems Architect, various contract projects; Chief Programmer, Unitravel PAX Res; Database Administrator, Medicaid Claims IS—South Carolina DISD. He is active in professional societies: ACM (26 years), IEEE Computer Society (20 years), ASQ (8 years); and has served as Chairman of several international conferences, Director of the ACM Scholastic Student Programming Contest, and on a number of industry-wide task forces on software issues and concerns. He holds academic degrees in Computer Science from the University of Missouri at Rolla: BS ('73), MS ('75), and ABD/Ph.D. ('79).

John D. Musa is one of the creators of the field of software reliability engineering and is widely recognized as the leader in reducing it to practice. He is currently a senior international consultant with a wide variety of clients. He has more than 30 years diversified practical experience as software practitioner and manager. He was formerly Technical Manager of Software Reliability Engineering (SRE) at AT&T Bell Laboratories, Murray Hill, NJ. Musa is a Fellow of the IEEE, and an international leader in software engineering listed in *Who's Who in America* and *American Men and Women of Science*. He has published 100 papers and given more than 175 major presentations. He is principal author of the widely acclaimed pioneering *Software Reliability: Measurement, Prediction, Application* and author of the new book *Software Reliability Engineering: More Reliable Software, Faster Development and Testing*.

Shari Lawrence Pfleeger is president of Systems/Software, Inc., a consulting firm specializing in software quality issues. She is also a senior researcher at the University of Maryland and former director of Howard University's Center for Research in Evaluating Software Technology. She is the author of *Software Engineering: Research and Practice* (Prentice Hall, 1998), *Software Metrics: A Rigorous and Practical Approach* (with Norman Fenton, International Thomson Press, 1997), and *Applying Software Metrics* (with Paul Oman, IEEE Computer Science Press, 1997). Her next book, *Solid Software* (with Les Hatton and Charles Howell, Macmillan Technical Publishing), will be published in 2000. Pfleeger has been associate editor-in-chief of *IEEE Software* and editor of the Quality Time column. She is now associate editor of *IEEE Transactions on Software Engineering*.

Karel Vredenburg is the architect and corporate champion for User-Centered Design (UCD) at IBM. He has responsibility for the development of IBM's UCD approaches, methods, and tools, and for the deployment of them company-wide. He also leads IBM's team of UCD practitioners. Karel joined IBM in 1988 after having done graduate studies, research, and teaching at the University of Toronto. He introduced UCD at IBM in 1993 and assumed his present role in 1995. He has written over 50 conference and journal publications. Karel is a regular speaker at industry conferences and runs a workshop/tutorial series entitled, "Practical UCD: How to Introduce, Deploy, and Optimize User-Centered Design" at conferences such as UPA, International HCI, and HFES. He is a member of the ISO committee that develops standards such as the Human-Centered Design of Interactive Systems (#13407) International Standard, the National Institute for Standards and Technology (NIST) working group developing a Common Industry Format (CIF) for Usability Test Reports, and serves on the National Research Council education committee representing HCI and UCD.

Tony Wasserman founded Software Methods & Tools in 1997, after spending the previous 14 years at Interactive Development Environments, Inc. (IDE), a company he founded and where he served as president, CEO, and chairman. Prior to starting IDE, Tony was a University of California professor. His User Software Engineering project introduced the concepts of rapid prototyping of user interfaces as an early form of what is now known as Joint Application Development.

He is a Fellow of the ACM and a Fellow of IEEE.

About the Technical Reviewer

Ian Lawthers is a senior consultant at the Centre for Software Engineering in Dublin, and is currently project manager of the ESPINODE-Ireland project, which is aimed at providing support in Software Process Improvement to the software industry within Ireland, both North and South. He also runs the Software Process Improvement Network (SPIN) group in the Dublin area.

Previously, he provided training and consultancy in ISO 9000 and software process improvement to small- and medium-sized companies in Ireland, the UK, and Eastern Europe, and was involved in the implementation of a Business Process Re-engineering project with a large multinational organisation.

Ian has also worked at Shorts-Bombardier in Belfast, where he was involved in all parts of the software lifecycle.

He holds a BSc Hons. degree from Queen's University, Belfast.

Tell Us What You Think!

As the reader of this book, *you* are our most important critic and commentator. We value your opinion and want to know what we're doing right, what we could do better, what areas you'd like to see us publish in, and any other words of wisdom you're willing to pass our way.

As the Executive Editor for the Software Quality Institute series at Macmillan Technical Publishing, I welcome your comments. You can fax, email, or write me directly to let me know what you did or didn't like about this book—as well as what we can do to make our books stronger.

Please note that I cannot help you with technical problems related to the topic of this book, and that due to the high volume of mail I receive, I might not be able to reply to every message.

When you write, please be sure to include this book's title and author, as well as your name and phone or fax number. I will carefully review your comments and share them with the author and editors who worked on the book.

Fax: 317-581-4663

Email: softwareengineering@mcp.com

Mail: Alan Bower
          Executive Editor
          Software Quality Institute series
          Macmillan Technical Publishing
          201 West 103rd Street
          Indianapolis, IN 46290 USA

The Software Quality Institute Editorial Board

COLLEGE OF ENGINEERING

THE UNIVERSITY OF TEXAS AT AUSTIN

Software Quality Institute · Center for Lifelong Engineering Education · www.sqi.utexas.edu
PRC MER R9800 · Austin, Texas 78712-1080 · (512) 471-4874 · FAX (512) 471-4824

November 1, 1999

Constructing Superior Software is the first of a series of books for software professionals sponsored jointly by the Software Quality Institute and Macmillan Technical Publishing. This book provides an overview of leading issues impacting the production and deployment of quality software.

The emphasis of this series is solutions to real-life problems based on actual experience. The books in the series are written by practitioners for practitioners.

The Software Quality Institute is a multidisciplinary partnership between The University of Texas at Austin and software and information systems organizations. Its mission is to inform and educate software producers and users about issues vital to the production and application of high-quality software. The Institute is a unit within the College of Engineering under The Center for Lifelong Engineering Education. It offers a wide range of educational programs, and the series that this book initiates is a significant addition to The Institute's program offerings.

Sincerely,

Alfred G. Dale

Chair, Editorial Board

Software Quality Institute

Introduction

Les A. Belady and Paul C. Clements, Austin Texas

This is a book about constructing high-quality software systems. Achieving high product quality, while at the same time meeting time-to-market and cost goals, has emerged as a critical priority for software development companies because quality is often the greatest, most visible product differentiator. Quality means a satisfied customer community, increased market share, and a solid basis from which to launch new product initiatives.

Our emphasis on quality is no accident, because this is the first book in a series produced by the Software Quality Institute (SQI) at the University of Texas at Austin. The books will discuss high-leverage problems and offer strategies for improving software quality and software business practices. They will be written by experienced practitioners who understand and can help solve the problems facing real-life software professionals.

This flagship book in the SQI series was cooperatively written by members of the editorial board overseeing the series. (And we have also invited a few others to join us as well.) As such, it offers a unique combined perspective on what some of the finest and most practical writers of software engineering today consider keys to producing quality products.

The Qualities of "Quality"

Whatever you mean by "quality," it can probably be phrased in terms of constituent "qualities" that can be measured and analyzed independently. Qualities can be divided into three broad categories:

- Qualities of systems

- Qualities of design that lead to those systems

- Qualities of projects that produce the systems

Dividing qualities into these categories is helpful, because different skills and techniques can be brought to bear with each one.

Achieving project quality is largely a matter of technical management, while achieving system or product quality is more a matter of software engineering skill. Achieving design quality takes perhaps a little of both. The organization of this book reflects that structuring.

System qualities include those that can be measured by observing the end product run. Performance, reliability, functionality, security, and usability all fall under the banner of system qualities. Chapters in Part I explore

- The importance of taking the system view in a development effort so that all the requirements (including quality requirements) are met coherently

- Engineering for reliability, which is a crucial factor in customer-perceived product quality; and

- Ensuring that you produce a highly usable system by adopting user-centered development as primary paradigm.

Design qualities measure those aspects of the design that lead to the system desired by the customer. Some design qualities are independent of system qualities: An elegant design may lead to a poorly running system, while an all-but-incomprehensible design might spawn a performance winner (but likely a maintenance loser). Either may take too long or be too expensive for the project to support. Design is therefore high-quality with respect to how well it allows the system and the developing project to in turn meet their respective quality goals. Chapters in Part II treat

- The importance of software architecture as the central design concept to achieve a system's required function and qualities;

- The practice of rationalizing a design—that is, making a design look coherent and complete after the fact, even if it didn't start out that way; and

- How to base your design on already-existing components so that you can take advantage of high-quality work already done.

Finally, project qualities are those that can be analyzed by observing the development project. Project quality is reflected in how well the development effort is managed, how effective the teams are that staff, and how self-aware the project is—that is, how much it can tell about itself in terms of how well it is doing with respect to preplanned goals. Chapters in Part III discuss

- How to facilitate effective teamwork in your development project;

- How to build a cost-effective, goal-oriented measurement effort; and

- How to select the appropriate tools to serve as the foundation of the development project.

Our goal was not to write a book in which these important topics were covered exhaustively. You will notice that the book is not nearly thick enough to satisfy that ambition. Rather, our purpose was to write a book that would serve as a gentle reminder to a project manager or developer as to what must not be forgotten or forsaken if your goal is to deliver a high-quality system—on time and within budget. Think of this book as a checklist for project sanity, a whisperer in your ear of what's really important.

The Mother of All Qualities: Simplicity

One of the first things we would whisper in your ear, if we could, is "Work very hard to keep everything as simple as you can." Of all the principles articulated in this book, simplicity is the broadest and perhaps the most fundamental.

We all have an intuitive notion of simplicity. We recognize it in clear and easy to understand speaking and writing; in the elegant solution of a tough problem; in uncluttered forms; in a good teacher's explanations; in the physicist's insight in formulating the laws of nature; or in a leader's setting of goals and strategies. As we quickly grasp simple statements and forms, we can easily use them as building blocks for our thoughts and activities in work and play.

We also recognize that the world around us is complex and human activities increase this complexity. We often suspect that some of this complexity is inherent and we can do nothing about it. We can also easily see that some complexity can be reduced without penalizing usefulness but with a net gain in elegance and quick understanding. Many of these intuitive ideas can be applied to programming as well. Simple programs are easier to use, review, document, and modify, with the result of significantly reduced cost in all phases of the process.

Paradoxically, achieving simplicity sometimes requires extra work. An example of this may be seen in Chapter 5, "Rationalize Your Design," in which software documentation is discussed. This chapter points out that documentation written from the point of view of the writer is not nearly so useful as documentation written from the point of view of the reader. Achieving the reader's perspective requires more work, but results in a document that is vastly simpler to understand, to reference, to use, than one that results from an author's stream of consciousness. Blaise Pascal (1623–1662) understood this perfectly when he wrote "I have made this letter a rather long one, only because I didn't have the leisure to make it shorter." Edsger Dijkstra, the inventor of many of the software engineering principles we now take for granted, once said that he would happily spend two hours pondering how to make a single sentence clearer. He reasons that if the paper is read by a couple of hundred people—a decidedly modest estimate for someone of Dijkstra's caliber and reputation—and he can save each reader a minute or two of confusion, then it's well worth the effort. We admire simplicity wrought from complexity precisely because we realize that it is an achievement both worthwhile and difficult, and not everyone can do it.

Software is the means by which we delegate human thought to an agent of very limited intelligence, the computing machine. Some human thoughts are well formalized and thus easy to delegate, but others assume a vast amount of context and background that computers are unable to provide on their own. One way, therefore, to view the task of the programmer is bridging the gap between the simplicity of the machine and the complexity of the human mind.

Simplicity and Information Theory

Information theory expresses information-carrying capability of an artifact in terms of the number of two-state bits required to represent the data, and the probability distribution of each bit being in one of two possible states. The more bits there are and the more uniform the a priori probability of being in either of the states, the more information can be conveyed. For example, two bits (each of which is true with 50 percent probability) can carry more information than three bits where, for instance, one bit is always "false" and the two others each have less than 50 percent probability of being in one state. The concept is expressed in the mathematical formula of *entropy* as the measure of information.

Entropy fits the intuitive notion of "surprise." If we know in advance the outcome, we are not surprised at all and do not receive any information when that outcome in fact comes to pass. In contrast, if we don't know anything in advance and everything is equally likely, we are maximally surprised by a specific outcome. If we have a hint that the odds are higher for one of the two states, however, then we are less surprised if most of the time we see the most likely outcome, but more surprised when we see the exception.

Complexity—and its opposite, simplicity—are strongly related to information and also can be measured by entropy. Simply put, the less information needed to describe a thing, the simpler it is. For example, it is simpler to cope with two equally difficult situations if one of them occurs relatively infrequently (that is, with low probability) than to keep switching our attention from one to the other. When writing this prose, for example, it was more comfortable to arrange the frequently needed reference material on the desk and keep the rest in the library than to have a very large desk covered with all the necessary (but mostly seldom-used) material.

Therefore, the twin of simplicity is predictability. Simple artifacts are predictable artifacts.

Think about how this principle can be applied in software development. For every artifact that is built—a programming language, a user interface, a document, a piece of software—someone will act as its consumer. Just as documents should be written for their readers, artifacts should be built for their consumers. And once those consumers are identified, we should do what we can do make the artifacts predictable. So, for example:

- A simpler user interface is one that matches the user's intuition about what will happen next.

- A simpler project plan is one that matches the expectations of the customer, the manager, and the workers.

- A simpler program is one that is easy to understand because it contains no surprise gimmicks, or because it uses a well-known pattern or algorithm, or because it obeys simple coding standards.

- A simpler programming language is one that provides a single way to carry out a given task.

- A simpler architecture is one that uses the same few interaction mechanisms throughout its infrastructure.

It is worth pointing out that software developers frequently deal with information theory by trying to cram as much information into as few bits as possible, usually to increase network bandwidth. We want to emphasize that we are here counseling the opposite tack: With information theory applied to software development artifacts, less is more. The less information conveyed by an artifact, the simpler it is.

This is illustrated by one of the most fundamental and widely applied software design principles in our field today. First articulated by Parnas in 1972, *information-hiding* holds that a software component (which he called a module) consists of an interface and an implementation. The interface is the sum of everything that a user of the module may safely assume about it; the implementation consists of everything else, and is subject to change. By using a module only via the facilities on its interface, consumers insulate themselves from the inevitable changes that occur to its implementation. The interface facilities are abstract; that is, they are the same no matter which of an endless variety of implementations back them up. Because the implementation details are hidden, the interface is simpler—conveys less information—than the hidden programs. Information-hiding is the basis of today's object-oriented design, and its name is no accident. Hiding information—reducing the information available to the consumer of a module and thus making it simpler— pays enormous dividends in terms of increased programmer productivity and maintainability of software.

To summarize, simplicity can be gained by limiting the information made available to the consumers of an artifact. Tell them what they need to know, and no more.

This may be the fundamental desideratum for simplicity. It applies to all of the principles manifested by chapters in this book. It applies to

- Writing effective, easy-to-use documentation (see Chapter 5, "Rationalize Your Design").

- Large-scale design with minimally interconnected components (see Chapter 4, "Software Architecture and Quality") whose behavior can be predicted and whose interactions can be managed, resulting in a more reliable system (see Chapter 2, "Engineer the Reliability").

- User interfaces and tools that help, not hinder, the user (see Chapter 3, "User-Centered Design and Development, and Chapter 9, "Select Tools to Fit the Tasks").

- Formation of effective teams and with streamlined team interactions (see Chapter 7, "Teamwork Considerations for Superior Software Development").

- Deciding on measures to collect that are revealing, and not simply statistical clutter (see Chapter 8 "Use Realistic, Effective Software Measurement").

- Choosing components to import that do not require in-depth understanding of a plethora of internal details (see Chapter 6, "Building Systems from Pieces with Component-Based Software Engineering")

- Forming a clear picture of the goals of the system as a whole (see Chapter 1, "The System Is the Key").

How can you tell if you've crafted a simple artifact or created a monster? Try this heuristic: A program artifact is intolerably complex if an average fix takes increasingly more effort as the artifact ages.

We hope that this passage has given motivation for simplicity in software development. Programs and the artifacts that accompany them are written for people, not only for giving instructions to machines. Someone once remarked to Fred Brooks how timeless his classic book *The Mythical Man Month* had remained over time. He smiled and replied, "That's because it's a book about people, and not computers." Software engineering is also, in large part, about rendering artifacts readable and usable by people as well as (if not more so than) machines. If we could remember that, we could go a long way toward constructing truly superior software.

Conclusion

Many years ago, San Francisco tour guides used to point out a particular segment of one of the city's elevated freeways. This segment featured a short spur that went straight ahead for about thirty yards and came to an abrupt, barricaded halt, whereas the rest of the freeway had curved gracefully to the right and gone on its way to the Bay Bridge and Oakland. The dead-end spur, the guides said, came about because the construction crew was merrily going about its work when someone thought to look at the plans. They discovered that the freeway should have veered right about thirty yards back. One can only imagine the chagrin of the supervisors at having to report this little diversion to the holders of the purse strings.

Software projects can be like that. Sometimes we get so involved in pouring the next pier or laying the next coat of asphalt that we forget the destination we set out to reach. Very few project plans or work breakdown structures include the task "Sit down, take a deep breath, and reevaluate your situation with respect to the project's original goals."

The goal of this book is to help you do that, by reminding you of the broad principles you probably already knew when the project began, but might have forgotten as the pressures of deadlines, implacable customers, and impossible managers have conspired to divert you from the right path. Above all, this is a book for the practitioner, written for people who spend their working days designing, building, and fixing software-intensive systems for a living. It is to these people we respectfully offer the advice within.

PART I

Quality Systems

CHAPTER 1

The System Is the Key

Peter A. Freeman, College of Computing, Georgia Institute of Technology

So, you got that big promotion you told me about when you visited campus last month to recruit. That's great! It's always rewarding to hear that my former students are doing well.

You say that you are in charge of leading the overall development of your company's new product? The one that will integrate your current, mainline, cash-cow product with a new, embedded information system? That really is a first-rate opportunity for you!

What's that? You say that the development group you are taking over has never done a project like this? They don't use all the latest tools and methods and techniques that we introduced you to in SE101? And, you don't have the time or budget to undertake a big process improvement program before getting the project underway? You say the project is already behind schedule and that your management isn't very clear on the objectives for the project? Well, I guess I'm not surprised.

Would I consult with you? I'm afraid I'm already overloaded and I have some friends that can probably do a better job with some of the details anyway. In fact, they've recently written some very useful essays on the pragmatics of constructing superior software that I would highly recommend.

But, if you have a few minutes, let me tell you what I think the single most important success factor will be for you—taking a *system's view* of what you are doing. You're interested? Good! (Umm, too bad she didn't listen to this lecture when she was in SE101.) I'll try to be succinct because I've only got a few minutes before I go see the dean to argue for a better raise this year.

I assume that you understand that a system is a "set of parts coordinated to accomplish a set of goals."[1] I further assume that you understand, at least intuitively, that it is the coordination of the parts that is the ultimate determiner of success of any system. I imagine that you also have a ready stock of horror stories about systems that fail, and perhaps even a few success stories of those (few, it seems) that succeed.

If I'm correct that you intuitively understand what a system is—and I sincerely hope that you do—then why in the world is it important for you to listen to the rest of this?

For the simple reason that in my several years of helping build systems, of teaching about systems, and of studying systems, I have never seen a development situation in which just a little more attention paid to the system would not have greatly improved the result. If that is sufficient to hold your attention for a few more minutes, let's proceed!

Systems, Systems, Systems!

There are, of course, lots of systems that you deal with every day, both explicit and implicit.

You are about to undertake the development of an explicit system composed of your company's device and the new embedded information system that you and your team will develop. The relationship between the device and the embedded information system is extremely important.

Likewise, you will have (sub)systems including the control system, the computer hardware system, and, of course, the software system(s). The ways in which these various explicit systems fit together (or, don't) most likely will determine the success of the overall project in the last analysis. As the manager of the overall product development, you will need to focus very carefully on these explicit systems and their interrelationships.

And, don't forget that the people and equipment environment in which the new product will be used, coupled with the product, also form a system. This system, usually considered an implicit one because it is rarely designed, constructed, measured, and managed in the same way that an explicit system (such as the software subsystem) is treated, is nonetheless a real system.

Indeed, it is precisely these implicit systems that will cause you the most trouble! The reason should be obvious: While they definitely form a system, we don't create and manage them with the same attention to the definition of the parts and the relationships between them. As a result they quite often wind up as suboptimal systems. For example, just think about a queuing situation often encountered in retail establishments in which the flow of people waiting to be served has not been designed or managed with the resulting inefficiency for the customers (and, sometimes, the employees as well).

The primary thing I want you to think about as you put together your team for this project is that you are creating an important, implicit system—the system that will develop the new product!

A Simple Message

Let's get right to the point:

> "The various elements that impinge upon the creation of any piece of software—the procedures, tools, people, and so on—themselves form a system. Everything that you know about the kinds of systems that you work with daily—the importance of balance, interfaces, clear objectives, measurements, etc.—apply just as much to this system. We call this a 'system-development system' (SDS)" [2]

This may seem obvious. However, experience tells me that most people, most of the time, are focused on performing a task, not thinking about how they are performing it. The field of meta-mathematics, for example, studies how mathematics is done. The field itself is not widely studied and, furthermore, it often is "Greek" to some of the most innovative mathematicians.

It is not unusual, for example, to find programmers focused on creating code to carry out some set of functions which may ultimately not be needed at all in the system. If a development process was employed that uncovered such redundancies earlier, then the team could avoid the wasted work. But, the programmers are busy doing their job and neither they nor anyone else is focused on the process they are following.

The activity of "software process improvement" that has grown from almost nothing 10 years ago to an activity today in which thousands of people are engaged is all about improving the SDS. Typical process improvement activities focus not only on improving specific elements of the SDS, such as finding a better testing tool or utilizing a more relevant design method, but also on ensuring that the parts fit together well. For example, by making sure that appropriate tools are available to support the chosen design method.

One thing I hope to impress on you is that it is useful to "go up a level" and to think explicitly about the SDS with which you work. My second objective, then, should be clear: To help you derive some immediate use from this perspective and to help you understand that my colleagues' chapters in this book describe different aspects of the SDS.

Let's briefly consider just what I mean when I talk about a "system development system," the nature of the parts of the SDS, and some useful ramifications of this point of view. I want to provide some perspective on this kind of system and in so doing, provide some perspective on the other chapters in this book.

What Is a Software Development System? (SDS)

You know that a system is a "set of parts coordinated to accomplish a set of goals." For the purpose of thinking about the system being used to create software, the following six general categories of parts cover everything:

- Objectives

- Policies

- People

- Procedures

- Tools

- Information

Everything that impacts the development of software in a particular situation, and over which you have some control to cause them to interact in coordinated ways, falls into one of these six categories. This, then, follows the definition of a system.[3]

These are general categories, of course. There is little direct benefit in trying to define precisely what we mean by each; your intuitive understanding, augmented by the following comments, will suffice. Furthermore, while you certainly have some informal understanding of how they can be and are coordinated in practice to achieve practical results, that, too, is left for later explication in some of the essays in this volume.

Objectives for a Specific Development Activity

In this section I discuss the objectives for the SDS as an organizational entity. Presently, I am focusing on the objectives that exist in a specific instance of the

SDS, taking (from the environment) an understanding of what is to be produced and then producing it, such as the following:

- Produce a system to provide real-time inventory information to all our sales associates.

- Create the software needed to control the new Model XXY widget-floozer.

- Do whatever marketing needs.

The activity of needs analysis, which may be a part of a specific SDS, is concerned with getting the development objectives well-stated so that technical development of the software can proceed.

You need to understand that in many cases the most important overall factor in achieving software development success is to have clear objectives. There are two simple reasons for this: First, good objectives provide focus, which, in turn, energizes everyone. Second, without clear objectives, there is a strong risk that whatever is produced fails to satisfy the ultimate customer.

Because most organizations do not pay sufficient attention to obtaining clear objectives, I provide the following:

> **Suggestion:** Ask appropriate questions about the objectives for a specific project and as a matter of professional ethics, attempt to clarify them as appropriate.

Appropriate questions about an objective include the following:

- Is the objective achievable?

- Does it resolve conflicts among users/purchasers?

- Does it place emphasis on quality?

- Is it testable?

- Does it relate to the objectives of the larger environment?

- Is it clear and unique?

- Is it reasonable?

- Does it match the capabilities of the rest of the SDS?

In most situations, your SDS ultimately will have to do its best to meet the stated objectives. As in any professional situation, however, you have a responsibility to at least communicate to those setting the objectives your professional opinion about their obtainability.

Policies

If you think of the SDS as being like a computer, then the policies that govern its behavior are like the microcode that governs the way in which specific instructions are to be interpreted. Policies, of course, are intangible and most of them are implicit. Yet, they are still extremely important to the overall functioning of the SDS.

Consider the following examples:

- Explicit development process policies

- Rules and guidelines on hiring and promotions

- Staff development, vacation rules, and so on that set the tone

- Capital investment rules

- Choice of computing platform, language, middle-ware, and so on

Software process maturity assessment [4] typically addresses the first example in the preceding list, but the others (and many more) may actually further impact the end-result.

Thus, I have found the following useful:

> **Suggestion:** Think carefully about all of the policies, explicit and implicit, that are a part of your SDS and ask how they relate to the effective functioning of the system. Keep in mind that just because a policy seems onerous, that doesn't mean that it doesn't serve a useful and appropriate role relative to the SDS overall.

One of the basic facts of life of any system is that what may seem suboptimal in a local context, may actually contribute to optimal *system* operation. The converse—that local optimization may lead to suboptimal global operation—also may be true, so remember to always evaluate policies in the proper, global context.

People

People play many roles in the SDS, including: programmers, systems analysts, managers, secretaries, technicians, and so on. We all know and, at least pay, lip service to the maxim that you want to engage the best people possible in the SDS. Many books have been written about how to organize and manage a group of people, most of which boil down to the following in the case of making an SDS effective:

Suggestion: Think of the preceding list of SDS categories as an ordered list in which each dominates the one that follows it (objectives should dictate policies that dictate the type of people needed, and so on). Make sure that the people of the SDS properly fit the dictates of objectives and appropriate policies and ensure that everything else supports the people.

You may object that policies and objectives also should be subservient to the people, and in some instances you are right. This certainly is the case in that an enlightened organization will not impose arbitrary objectives and policies and, therefore, will not drive away (or, worse, throw away) good people. However, in the context of attempting to create rational organizations of people and other resources to achieve some objectives, it is normal for objectives and policies to dominate.

Some simple examples should make this clear. If the objective of a particular SDS is to create embedded control software for aircraft, it clearly wouldn't be a service to the organization to hire people whose sole experience and training was in creating financial software for mainframes. Likewise, while the people in an organization might prefer to work on a schedule they set for themselves, it is not unreasonable to have a policy that dictates that everyone must be on-site during certain core hours, especially if they must interact face-to-face with co-workers

That said, let me reiterate the importance of making sure that the objectives, policies, and people are well-matched. In most successful organizations, at least in the short-term, people do in fact take precedence.

Procedures

Procedures in an SDS are explicit or implicit. You undoubtedly are familiar with a number of explicit procedures that pertain to the creation of software, such as object-oriented methods, testing techniques, design-review steps, and so on. Several of the chapters in this book address what I call explicit procedures. Continuing the analogy between a computer and an SDS, you can view procedures as the "programs" to be executed by the people in an SDS. Their importance should not be underestimated.

Nonetheless, the implicit procedures used by the people in an SDS almost always dominate. These include the basic problem-solving and design procedures, or techniques, that everyone has when they are hired and that may over time be augmented through on-the-job training (both explicit and implicit). It should not be a surprise to note that often we do not pay sufficient attention to the implicit procedures that are operative in an SDS.

The implications of this predominance of implicit procedures actually pertain more to ensuring that you have appropriate people in your organization because that is how you actually acquire the implicit procedures. Nonetheless, the following may be useful:

> **Suggestion:** In choosing explicit procedures for use in an SDS (for example, a particular design method), the chance of a procedure making a significant difference will depend in part on ensuring that the implicit procedures utilized by people are supportive of the method.

If a design method is based on formal, mathematical techniques, for example, then it is essential that the people expected to use the method have some degree of mathematical maturity. Furthermore, it is possible for the existing implicit procedures of an organization to hinder any new procedures adopted for usage. For example, if the culture of the organization dictates that communication between different groups (such as. marketing and engineering) must all go through a hierarchy, then the success of using a design-walkthrough procedure based on direct communication among all parties may be severely limited.

Tools

The tools of an SDS are the artifacts that support the procedures and people such as compilers, workstations, consistency-checkers, data base systems, and so on. In the dominance hierarchy suggested earlier, tools must be chosen to support the adopted procedures. Of course, it is fairly common to adopt a tool *because* it forces people to use a particular procedure. When done intelligently and as part of a planned change of the SDS, this practice is fine.

The problem is that tools are sometimes not chosen so carefully.

> **Suggestion:** Ideally, the tools selected for an SDS are selected after the procedures are adopted. Because in practice this may not happen, at least make sure that the chosen tools do not unduly restrict the choice of appropriate procedures.

One of the myths that many people have believed is that if the right tools are selected, huge gains in productivity and control of a software process will result automatically. Tools used properly—starting with being well-matched to appropriate procedures—can provide such benefits. Unfortunately, if not well-chosen, they also can have the opposite effect.

Information

Information, of course, is what software development is all about, so why include it as an explicit part of the SDS? Simply, so that you will recognize its importance and different forms and thus be better able to manage it.

Following are three important forms of information in the SDS:

- External technical information

- Measurements

- The software itself (in all its manifestations)

"External technical information" is the totality of information about computers, software, the application domain, and so on. Obviously, it is important; however, rarely does an SDS take explicit steps to ensure that the appropriate information for the project at hand is present. Imagine an SDS in which the people knew how to program, but knew nothing of standard algorithms for sorting, searching, and so on. This clearly is not a desired situation. To prevent this from happening, a good SDS will include policies, procedures, and tools for ensuring that relevant information is present.

"Measurements" also is a broad category, including measurements on the software being produced as well as on the operation of the SDS itself. Obtaining those measurements and using them is the province of the procedures of the SDS, but it is important to think of the results as information to be managed as part of the SDS so it is not lost.

The "software itself" may include everything from executable binary code to design notes. Again, procedures and policies apply, but in thinking about what constitutes an SDS, it is useful to think explicitly about this category of information. This especially is important as reuse of various forms of software becomes more prevalent and one must devise new procedures to produce or acquire that information.

Each of these forms of information (and others as well) are different, but share the characteristic of being potentially quite voluminous.

> **Suggestion:** Focus on the most important information in each area for your SDS and develop procedures for managing it and keeping it current. Next, develop procedures for augmenting the generalized information with specifics pertinent to each particular project undertaken by the SDS.

Much of this happens implicitly, either through the adoption of specific procedures that dictate certain forms of information or by the people involved keeping their personal information-base current. This implictiness is fine, but as an SDS becomes more complex, paying explicit attention to the information in the SDS and how it relates to the other parts of the SDS will lead to enhanced performance.

So, these are the categories of the SDS. Nothing sophisticated or mysterious. They form a set of categories whose interactions can be modeled, studied, and improved to improve the performance of your SDS. In short, to do software process improvement.

Before turning to some issues relating to the entire SDS, let me note what I hope is obvious: Different tasks may require different SDSs. For example, in your situation of developing a complex, embedded system, you will need a number of tools, design processes, verification policies, and so on that would never be needed in developing a large mainframe financial application. On the other hand, in the mainframe situation you might need configuration management tools, access policies, data base tools, and other items not needed in the embedded system development.

You are appropriately focused right now on your specific situation. However, in a year or so when you get your next assignment, remember that you may well need to construct a new SDS for that situation.

Broader System Issues

It is helpful to view five basic aspects of a system:

1. The total system objectives and the performance measures to be applied

2. The system's environment, including constraints

3. The resources of the system

4. The parts of the system, including the objectives for each, functions, and measures of performance

5. The management of the system

I have already sketched out the nature of the parts. Many books have been written on each of these topics, but you don't need to read them all to utilize them in thinking more clearly about software development. A few comments will illustrate my point.

Objectives for the Entire SDS

It should be clear that the various actors in the drama of software development may have different objectives for the SDS. The objective of a software professional for the SDS, for example, might well be that it "provide a satisfying and rewarding environment for his or her professional satisfaction and advancement." On the other hand, the objective of the owner of the company might be something like "maximize my profit with minimal management aggravation."

> **Suggestion:** You should be aware that there are multiple objectives as well as be prepared to accept and accommodate that fact. Depending on your position, be prepared to negotiate a mutually acceptable set of objectives.

A second observation about objectives that I hope is no surprise to you is that there may be a difference between stated objectives (such as "Our software department always strives to deliver the highest quality product.") and observed objectives (such as "In 9 of the last 10 product deliveries, shipment was made to meet promised delivery dates even though the shipped product had known, major defects.").

> **Suggestion:** If you are in charge of running the SDS, try to determine what the underlying objectives are and don't be confused by the stated objectives.

Environment

The environment in which an SDS exists can be difficult to define when one tries to define it carefully. For example, is the current state of the art in software technology part of the environment in which the SDS operates?

Churchman [1] suggests a simple test: Ask the following two questions: Can I do anything about it? Does it matter relative to the system's objectives? If the answer to the first question is "no" and to the second question is "yes," then "it" is in the environment.

Thus, the question of whether the state of the art of software technology is part of the environment of an SDS generally is "yes," unless the SDS has the objective of changing the state of the art, in which case the answer is "no." Additionally, there typically are three other major factors in the environment of any SDS and with which we must contend: finances, organizational culture, and type of application.

As noted, an SDS can easily establish the objective of adding to the supply of software technology, removing (at least partially) the software technology factor from the environment and putting it under the control of the SDS. But, one does so only at a clear cost.

Finances generally are a given that clearly impacts how an SDS operates, but over which the SDS has no control. As the SDS successfully produces revenue-generating products, the external finances might improve; but, in the majority of situations, the finances available to sustain the SDS will always remain under the control of external forces.

Organizational culture, outside the SDS, might change over a long period of time based on the effect of the SDS, but in the timeframe of trying to understand an SDS, it is best to consider it as being external to the SDS. Can you imagine changing the culture of the U.S. Department of Defense to improve the operation of its software development activities? Hardly! A more specific example is the fact that IBM has largely left alone the operations of several companies it has acquired so as to not impose an organizational culture that would be detrimental to the SDS of those companies.

The type of application with which an SDS deals clearly may change, but it is not under the control of the SDS. If it is, then the SDS has become something more than just a software develop framework

> **Suggestion:** Be sure you are clear about the factors in the environment of your SDS, and their relationship to it. Change those that should and can be changed and accept and cope with the rest.

Resources

The resources of the SDS are just the amounts available of the various parts for a specific project. In the case of people or tools, the supply of resources is an obvious concept. You need to make sure you have an adequate supply. Objective function maximization (usually profit) dictates that you have just enough of each.

The supply of information also is fairly obvious, although less easy to quantify. To complicate things, the relationship between the amount of information available and the success of a particular project is, at best, poorly understood. That is one reason I strongly suggest that you pay explicit attention to the information resource.

When we turn to objectives, policies, and procedures, the concept of the "amount" of each such resource is, indeed, unclear. While a rudimentary conceptualization is clear (such as having no policies at all), anything more precise is largely unattainable.

Suggestion: Develop informal guidelines for your SDS that specify what it means to have sufficient amounts of all resources. Experience will serve you well in establishing measures for the less-quantifiable resources.

In the case of objectives researchers are trying to establish objective measures of sufficiency. However, I know of no efforts to quantify policies or procedures in the sense of sufficiency.

Management

You must create an SDS by choosing its various components, establishing objectives for each, ensuring that the components are well-matched and are present in sufficient supply, establishing appropriate objectives for the SDS, and making sure that it all runs smoothly. Broadly speaking, that is the role of management.

Be aware, however. Something that those of us in the software field have experienced all too often is the danger of just letting "management" control all aspects of the SDS, or, conversely, of having no management involved in the SDS. The essential truth from my perspective is to have an effective integration of organizational management and technical expertise.

Suggestion: Ideally, every part of the SDS should have both a technical and an organizational management aspect. For some, even many, parts, this will be hard to see and perhaps excessive. Thus, strive to obtain an overall integration of technical and management concerns throughout the SDS.

Using the Key

I assume that you are a person of action, not content to just study something like an SDS in the abstract. So, you will be very unsatisfied without under-standing how to use the concept of an SDS.

In fact, your intuitive understanding of what makes for a good system and your newly acquired understanding of the essential elements of an SDS are all that you need.

View your SDS and ask Churchman's five questions:

1. What are the objectives of your SDS and how can you measure them?

2. What are the important factors that constrain the environment in which development takes place?

3. What resources do you have available?

4. What is the nature of the parts of your SDS?

5. How is the SDS managed?

The stated and observed objectives should be commensurate. If not, take steps to bring them in line. Be especially careful to make sure the objectives attainment can be objectively determined.

Try to identify as many factors as possible in the environment that might prevent the SDS from achieving success. Study of similar situations in other organizations might be helpful.

Understand first the nature of the parts of your SDS. Are they balanced in the sense of tools supporting procedures that support people? Do the policies address the overall objectives? Is needed information provided for? Then look to the supply of resources. Are there enough people with the right backgrounds and experience? Are enough resources devoted to tools? Have a sufficient set of policies been established?

Finally, is the management structure focused on the effective operation of the SDS, or is it focused on things that are irrelevant? Is it given the information it needs to manage? Are there appropriate controls in place? Above all, is there proper integration between the technical and organizational aspects of the system?

There are many other specific applications of the SDS, but I trust that this brief introduction to the concept of a system-development system and its application to analyze and improve your SDS will suffice to improve it. In that context, you look to the other chapters in this book to provide more detailed information on both the parts and the overall organization of an effective SDS.

Summary

You probably understand the importance of looking at the parts of a system and how they relate to each other when you are trying to improve the performance of that system. In exactly the same way, it is possible to view as a system the categories of things that go into the process of building a system. This "system development system," or SDS, can then be studied, understood, and improved. I have outlined the nature of this SDS in this chapter both as a framework for understanding many of the things you will find in later chapters in this book and as a practical tool for your efforts to improve your SDS.

References

1. *The Systems Approach*, C. West Churchman, 1979, Dell Publishing (paper-back). This book by Wes Churchman, one of the founders of the modern "systems approach," is an excellent introduction to some of the thinking about systems in general.

2. *Software Perspectives*, Peter Freeman, 1987, Addison-Wesley. This book was written for a broad audience whose members might want to understand (and improve) the business of developing software. Presumably you do also.

3. See [Freeman, 1987, Chapter 4] for more detail. For those of you that are trying to be (too) precise, it is true that I have made some arbitrary exclusions in this definition. For example, the quality of the office space used by the people may have great impact and it may well be under your control. It doesn't neatly fall into one of these categories, however (unless you want to consider it a 'tool').

4. See *Managing the Software Process*, Watts Humphrey, 1987, Addison-Wesley, or various publications from the Software Engineering Institute at Carnegie-Mellon University.

CHAPTER 2

Engineer the Reliability

John D. Musa, Software Reliability Engineering and Testing Courses

The most important software development problem facing us today, and likely to be with us for the foreseeable future, is how to manage the following three conflicting demands:

- The need for adequate reliability or availability of a released software product.

- The need for decreasing the time required to deliver to market new software products or new releases of existing software products.

- The need to reduce development cost.

When these demands are not well managed, you may distribute an unreliable or unavailable (in the sense of service) product that results in many angry customers. Reliability and availability are generally the highest priority customer concerns. Other possibilities include missing schedules and overrunning costs. All these situations lead to loss of market share. Because profitability is very sensitive to market share, there is overwhelming pressure impinging on software engineers and managers to solve the problem I have described.

When I speak of a software product, I should really say "software-based product," because pure software cannot function. I say this to highlight the fact that software and hardware development cultures clearly are too far apart. In establishing and discussing software development principles, we should always be thinking of total systems that also contain hardware, and often, human components.

The principle I propose to engrain in software development culture is "engineer the reliability." By this I mean that we need to plan and design the reliability of a software-based system, making tradeoffs with delivery time and life-cycle cost. We then need to plan the strategies needed to achieve it, and we need to measure reliability as development and particularly test proceed. Essential to measuring reliability is the quantitative characterization of how users will employ a system. The principle "engineer the reliability" is a three-word description of the technology and practice of *software reliability engineering* (SRE). Hence, in dissecting the principle, I will be outlining this field.

In this chapter, we first will examine what SRE is, why it works, and its current status as a practice. We then will examine the SRE process, using a single consistent example throughout.

I will outline and illustrate each of the six activities of the process. The chapter concludes with a list of resources so you can explore this field further.

Software Reliability Engineering

First, we will look at some basic terms and definitions you will need to know to continue on in this chapter. Then, we will consider what software reliability engineering is and why it works. Finally, we will examine the current state of software reliability engineering: a proven, standard, widespread best practice. This is important to all of you who will be using it.

Basic Definitions

Reliability is the probability that a system or a capability of a system functions without failure for a specified time or number of natural units in a specified environment. The concept of natural units is relatively new to reliability, so let's take a look at it. A *natural unit* is a unit other than time that is related to the output of a software-based product, such as pages of output, transactions, telephone calls, or jobs. *Availability* is the probability at any given time that a system, or a capability of a system, functions satisfactorily in a specified environment. For a given average down time per failure, availability implies a certain reliability. There is one last term that is used in the field of software reliability engineering, *failure intensity* is simply the number of failures per natural or time unit. Because of its simplicity, we often use failure intensity rather than reliability in the software reliability engineering world.

We deliberately define software reliability in the same way as hardware reliability, so that we can determine system reliability from hardware and software component reliabilities, even though the mechanisms of failure are different.[1]

What SRE Is and Why It Works

Let's look a little more in-depth now at just what SRE *is*. SRE is a practice for *quantitatively* planning and guiding software development and test, with emphasis on reliability and availability. It is a practice that is backed with a lot of science and technology. SRE simultaneously does the following three things:

- Ensures that product reliability and availability meet user needs.

- Delivers your product to market faster.

- Increases productivity, lowering product cost.

In applying SRE, you can vary the relative emphasis you place on these three improvements.

How does SRE work? SRE is based on two principles:

- Improve all of a product's major quality characteristics (reliability, availability, delivery time, and life-cycle cost) by quantitatively characterizing the expected use of the product and applying this information to make product development and test more efficient.

- Quantify the major quality characteristics of the product and match them more precisely to user needs.

There are several ways in which you can employ quantitative use information to make product development and test more efficient, as in the following:

- **Reduce the number of operations you implement, by finding alternatives to implementing low use, *noncritical* functions, a concept called *Reduced Operation Software* (ROS).** This concept is the software analog of Reduced Instruction Set Computing (RISC) in hardware. With ROS, you may implement some operations as combinations of more frequently used operations, or you may not implement some operations at all, arranging for manual handling of their functions. You will still, however, implement all critical operations.

- **Focus on developing operations rather than modules, and schedule their development so that the most used operations are developed first. This concept is very competitive and is called *operational development.*** Operations are immediately viable and can be released and sold to customers. In most cases, a small percentage of operations (for example, 10 percent) represent a large percentage of use (for example, 90 percent) of a product. With operational development, you develop just these operations for release 1, providing your customers with 90 percent of the use of the product several months before your competitors. These customers are now committed to your product and are unlikely to switch unless you dissatisfy them severely. You can deliver the other 90 percent of the operations that are used 10 percent of the time several months later than you normally would have, and still have happy customers!

- **Precisely focus resources on the most used and/or critical functions or modules.** You can use this focusing in allocating time to operations or modules in requirements development, design, coding, requirements and design reviews, code inspection, and unit test. You can use it to determine where to concentrate on searching for opportunities for reuse that will be most profitable. And currently, use information is being employed for triage for the Year 2000 problem.

Finally, you can make the test phase more effective and efficient by creating a test environment that realistically represents field conditions.

The second basic principle, quantifying product major quality characteristics and matching them with user needs, really primarily involves quantifying reliability and availability. We have set delivery times and budgeted software costs for software-based systems for some time. It is only relatively recently that the technology for setting and tracking reliability and availability objectives for software has developed.[1] In addition to setting objectives, SRE involves engineering project strategies to meet those objectives. During system test, you track reliability against each objective as one of the release criteria.

A Proven, Standard, Widespread Best Practice

Software reliability engineering is a proven, standard, widespread best practice. As one example of the proven benefit of SRE, AT&T applied SRE to two different releases of a switching system, International Definity PBX. They found that customer-reported problems decreased by a factor of 10, the system test interval decreased by a factor of 2, total development time decreased 30 percent, and there were no serious service outages in 2 years of deployment of thousands of systems in the field.[2]

SRE has been an AT&T Best Current Practice since May 1991. To become a
est Current Practice, a practice must have substantial application (typically
at least 8 to 10 projects) and this application must show a strong, documented
benefit-to-cost ratio. In the case of SRE, this ratio was 12 or higher for all
projects. The practice undergoes a probing review by two boards, at third and
fourth levels of management. More than 70 project managers or their representatives reviewed the SRE proposal. There were more than 100 questions and
issues requiring resolution, a process that took several months. In 1991, SRE
was one of five practices that were approved, out of 30 that were proposed.

SRE is also a standard practice. McGraw-Hill published an SRE handbook in
1996.[2] SRE has been a standard of the American Institute of Aeronautics and
Astronautics since 1993, and IEEE standards are currently under development.

Finally, SRE is a widespread practice. As of 1997, there were over 50 published
articles by *users* of SRE, and the number was growing rapidly.[3] Because
practitioners do not typically publish very frequently, the actual number of
users is probably many times more than 50.

Users include Alcatel, AT&T, Bellcore, CNES (France), ENEA (Italy), Ericsson
Telecom, Hewlett-Packard, Hitachi, IBM, Jet Propulsion Laboratory, Lockheed-
Martin, Lucent Technologies, Microsoft, Mitre, Nortel, Saab Military Aircraft,
Tandem Computers, the U.S. Air Force, and the U.S. Marine Corps.

Tierney reported the results of a survey taken in late 1997 that showed that
Microsoft has applied software reliability engineering in 50 percent of its software development groups, including projects such as Windows NT and Word.[4]
The benefits observed were increased test coverage, improved estimates of
amount of test required, useful metrics that helped them establish ship criteria,
and improved specification reviews.

SRE is widely applicable. From a technical viewpoint, you can apply SRE to
any software-based product, starting at the beginning of any release cycle.
Developers have applied it to a variety of projects.[3,5] From an economic
viewpoint, you also can apply SRE to any software-based product, except
for very small components, perhaps those involving a total effort of less than
two staff months. If a small component such as this is used for several projects,
then it probably will be feasible to use SRE.

The cost of implementing SRE is not large. There is an investment cost of not
more than three equivalent staff days per person in the organization, which
includes a two-day course for everyone and planning with a much smaller

number. The operating cost over the project life cycle typically varies from 0.1 to 3 percent of total project cost. The largest cost component is the cost of developing the operational profile.

SRE Process and Fone Follower Example

Let's now take a look at the SRE process. There are six principal activities that you must perform, as shown in Figure 2.1. We show the software development process side by side with the SRE process, so that you can relate the activities of one to those of the other. Both processes follow spiral models, but for simplicity, we don't show the feedback paths. In the field, we collect certain data and use it to improve the SRE process for succeeding releases.

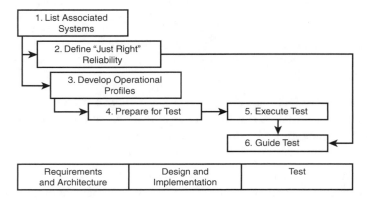

FIGURE 2.1   *The SRE process.*

The List Associated Systems, Define "Just Right" Reliability, Develop Operational Profiles, and Prepare for Test activities all start during the Requirements and Architecture phases of the software development process. They all extend to varying degrees into the Design and Implementation phase, as they can be affected by it. The Execute Test and Guide Test activities coincide with the Test phase.

We will illustrate the SRE process with Fone Follower, an example adapted from an actual project at AT&T. I have changed the name and certain details to keep the explanation simple and protect proprietary data. Subscribers to Fone Follower call and enter, as a function of time, the phone numbers to which they want to forward their calls. Fone Follower forwards a subscriber's incoming calls (voice or fax) from the network in accordance with the program the subscriber entered. Incomplete voice calls go to the subscriber's pager (if the subscriber has one) and then to voice mail.

List Associated Systems

The first activity is to list all the systems associated with the product that for various reasons must be tested independently. These are generally of three types:

- Base product and variations
- Supersystems
- Assurable acquired components

Variations are versions of the base product that are designed for different environments. For example, a product may be designed for Windows and Macintosh. *Supersystems* are combinations of the product or variations with other systems, where customers view the reliability or availability of the product or variation as that of the combination. An *assurable acquired component* is a component that the supplier does not develop for the product and that has some degree of risk associated with it, but where one can essentially remove the risk by early test, plus correction as needed.

Define "Just Right" Reliability

To define the "just right" level of reliability for a product, you first must define what "failure" means for the product, along with failure severity classes. In general terms, a *failure* is any departure of system behavior in execution from user needs. You need to interpret exactly what this means for your product. A failure is not the same thing as a fault; a *fault* is a defect in system implementation that causes the failure when executed. Beware, there are many situations where the two have been confused in the literature. A *failure severity class* is a set of failures that have the same per-failure impact on users. Table 2.1 shows the four failure severity classes used for Fone Follower, with a definition and an example for each class.

TABLE 2.1 FAILURE SEVERITY CLASSES USED FOR FONE FOLLOWER

Severity Class	Definition	Example
1	Key operation(s) unavailable	Calls not forwarded
2	Important operation(s) unavailable	Phone number entry inoperable
3	Operation(s) with workarounds unavailable	System administrators can't add subscribers from graphical user interface, but can use text interface.
4	Minor deficiencies in operations	System administrators' graphical interface screen doesn't display current date

The second step in defining the "just right" level of reliability is to choose a common measure for all failure intensities, either failures per some natural unit or failures per hour.

You then set the total system *failure intensity objective* (FIO) for each associated system. This involves first determining whether users need availability or reliability or both. To determine an objective, you should analyze the needs and expectations of users. If it is impossible to do this, you should use general guidelines, such as those shown in Tables 2.2 and 2.3.

TABLE 2.2 GENERAL RELIABILITY GUIDELINES

Failure Impact	Typical FIO (Failures/ Hr)	Time Between Failures
Hundreds of deaths, more than 10^9 cost	10^{-9}	114,000 years
One or two deaths, around 10^6 cost	10^{-6}	114 years
Around $1,000 cost	10^{-3}	6 weeks
Around $100 cost	10^{-2}	100 hr
Around $10 cost	10^{-1}	10 hr

TABLE 2.3 GENERAL AVAILABILITY GUIDELINES

Acceptable Down Time	Availability
5 min/yr	5 nines (0.99999)
5 min/mo or 1 hr/yr	4 nines (0.9999)
10 min/wk or 1 shift/yr	3 nines (0.999)

If one of the needs is for availability, convert that need to a failure intensity objective (FIO), using an objective for average down time per failure that you establish, based on operational considerations and costs.[3] Also convert any reliability objective to an FIO. If you now have two FIOs, take the smallest as the objective.

For each system you are developing, you need to compute a developed software total FIO. This involves subtracting the total of the expected failure intensities of all hardware and acquired software components from the system total FIOs. You need the developed software total FIOs so that you can track the reliability growth during system test of all the systems you are developing with the failure intensity to failure intensity objective (FI/FIO) ratios. You also need the developed software total FIOs so that you can select the best mix of strategies for cost-effectively meeting the objectives, based on previous experience. The mix is some combination of fault prevention, fault removal, and fault tolerant activities. Each of these activities breaks down into the application of various practices (for example, requirements review) and tools (for example, test case generators).

Your first attempts at engineering this mix of activities and specific practices and tools will necessarily be of a trial-and-error nature. We currently do not have much quantitative information on the effectiveness of various practices and tools in improving reliability. However, you should collect data on the FIOs, the mixes of activities, practices, and tools you use, and costs. Look for patterns that can become experiential rules.

It would be very helpful in performing this engineering if we had the capability of accurately predicting software reliability as a function of variables of the software product and process. I have proposed a structure for doing this prediction and identified many of the variables involved.[3] Accurate prediction capability awaits extensive data collection and analysis with respect to these variables.

Develop Operational Profiles

To fully understand this section, which deals with quantifying how software is used, we need to first consider what operations and operational profiles are. An *operation* is a major system logical task of short duration, which returns control to the system when complete, and whose processing is substantially different from other operations. Some illustrations from Fone Follower are phone number enter, process fax call, and audit a section of the phone number database.

An *operational profile* is a complete set of operations with its probabilities of occurrence. Table 2.4 shows an illustration of an operational profile from Fone Follower.

TABLE **2.4** FONE FOLLOWER OPERATIONAL PROFILE

Operation	Occurrence Probability
Process voice call, no pager, answer	0.18
Process voice call, no pager, no answer	0.17
Process voice call, pager, answer	0.17
Process fax call	0.15
Process voice call, pager, answer on page	0.12
Process voice call, pager, no answer on page	0.10
Phone number entry	0.10
Audit section—phone number data base	0.009
Add subscriber	0.0005
Delete subscriber	0.0005
Recover from hardware failure	0.000001
Total	1

There are four principal steps in developing an operational profile:

1. Identify the operation initiators.

2. List the operations invoked by each initiator.

3. Determine the occurrence rates.

4. Determine the occurrence probabilities by dividing the occurrence rates by the total occurrence rate.

There are three principal kinds of initiators: user types, which you can determine from customer types; external systems, and the system itself. For Fone Follower, one of the user types is subscribers and the principal external system is the telephone network. Among other operations, subscribers initiate phone number entry and the telephone network initiates process fax call. Fone Follower itself initiates audit a section of the phone number database. When implementing SRE for the first time, some software practitioners are concerned about possible difficulties in determining occurrence rates. Experience indicates that this is usually not a difficult problem.

Prepare for Test

The Prepare for Test activity uses the operational profiles you have developed to prepare test cases and test procedures. You allocate test cases in accordance with the operational profile, after preassigning some test cases to critical operations. For Fone Follower, for example, there were 496 test cases to allocate after preassignment. The process fax call operation had an occurrence probability of

0.15. Consequently, it was assigned 74 test cases. After you assign test cases to operations, you specify the test cases within the operations by selecting from all the possible intraoperation choices with equal probability. The selections are usually among different values of input variables associated with the operations, values that cause different processing to occur. For example, one input variable for the process fax call operation was destination (of the forwarded call) and one of the values of this input variable was local calling area.

Test procedures are the controllers that invoke test cases during execution. Preparation of test procedures primarily involves development of operational profiles for the various operational modes in which the software operates. Fone Follower had three operational modes: Peak hours, Prime hours, and Off hours. The test procedures also must take into account adjustments for critical operations and for reused operations from previous releases.

Execute Test

In the Execute Test activity, you will allocate test time, invoke test, identify failures, and determine when the failure occurred in natural or time units. You will also assign a severity class to each failure. Invoke tests at random times, choosing operations randomly in accord with the operational profile. Invoke feature tests first, followed by load tests. Invoke a regression test after each build involving significant change. Identify failures, along with when they occur. The "when" can be with respect to natural units or time. Finally, you assign a severity class to each failure.

Guide Test

The final activity involves guiding the product's software development process (particularly the system test phase) and release with reliability growth test. Reliability growth test couples tests with attempts to remove faults and hence cause reliability growth. The guide test activity also includes judging assurable acquired components and supersystems with certification test, which simply accepts or rejects the software in question. We also use certification test for any software that we expect customers will acceptance test.

Input failure data that you collect during reliability growth test to a reliability estimation program such as CASRE normalize the data by multiplying by the failure intensity objective in the same units.[2] Execute this program periodically and plot the FI/FIO ratio, as shown in Figure 2.2 for Fone Follower. If you observe a significant upward trend in this ratio, you should determine and correct the causes. The most common causes are system evolution, which may indicate poor change control, and changes in test selection probability, which may indicate a poor test process. When the FI/FIO ratio reaches 0.5, you should consider release as long as essential documentation is complete and outstanding high severity failures have been resolved (the faults causing them have been removed).

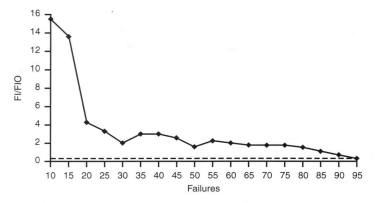

FIGURE 2.2 *Plot of FI/FIO ratio for Fone Follower.*

For the certification test, you also first normalize failure data by multiplying by the failure intensity objective. The unit "Mcalls" is millions of calls. Plot each new failure as it occurs on a reliability demonstration chart, as shown in Figure 2.3. Note that the first two failures fall in the Continue region, which signifies that there is not enough data to reach an accept or reject decision. The third failure falls in the Accept region, which means that you can accept the software, subject to the levels of risk associated with the chart you are using. If these levels of risk are unacceptable, you can simply construct another chart with the levels you desire.[3]

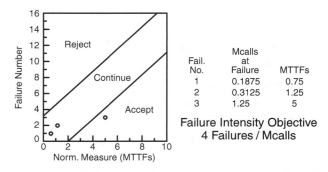

Fail. No.	Mcalls at Failure	MTTFs
1	0.1875	0.75
2	0.3125	1.25
3	1.25	5

**Failure Intensity Objective
4 Failures / Mcalls**

FIGURE 2.3 *Reliability demonstration chart applied to Fone Follower.*

Developers are sometimes concerned that systems with ultrareliable FIOs might require impractical long hours of test to verify the FIOs specified. But there are many ameliorating circumstances that make the problem more tractable than that for ultrareliable hardware.[3] First, in most cases only a few critical operations, not the entire system, must be ultrareliable. Second, software reliability relates to the execution time of the software, not the clock time for which the system is operating, and the execution time of the critical operations is often a small fraction of the clock time. Finally, because processing capacity is cheap and rapidly becoming cheaper, it is feasible to test at a rate that is hundreds of times real-time by using parallel processors. Hence, testing of ultrareliable software can be manageable.

Collect Field Data

The SRE process is not complete when a product is shipped. We collect certain field data to use in succeeding releases and in other products. In many cases, we can collect the data easily and inexpensively by building recording and reporting routines into the product. In this situation, we collect data from all field sites. For data that requires manual collection, take a small random sample of field sites.

We collect data on failure intensity and on customer satisfaction with the major quality characteristics of reliability, availability, delivery time, and life-cycle cost, and use this information in setting the failure intensity objective for the next release. We also measure operational profiles in the field and use this information to correct the operational profiles we estimated. Finally, we analyze the reliability strategies used and failure intensities achieved on different projects with different failure intensity objectives to develop and improve experiential rules for guiding future projects.

Summary

Users of SRE have noted that it is a unique practice; there are no alternatives that can provide the same results. They view it as powerful, thorough, methodical, and focused. It deals with the complete product, but it focuses on the software part. SRE takes a full-life-cycle, proactive view in which efficiency requires activities throughout the life cycle, for testing as well as development. It involves system engineers, system architects, developers, testers, users (or their representatives) and managers as collaborators. SRE is very customer-oriented. It involves direct interaction with customers, which generally enhances customers' images of the supplier and improves customer satisfaction, reducing the risk of angry users. SRE is highly correlated with and essential to attaining Levels 4 and 5 of the Software Engineering Institute Capability Maturity Model.

If you apply the principle "engineer the reliability" in all the software-based products you develop, you will find that you can be confident of the availability and reliability of the products. At the same time, you will deliver them in minimum time and cost. You will have maximized your efficiency in satisfying your customers' needs. This is a vital skill to have if you are to be competitive in today's marketplace.

To Explore Further

This section is provided to guide you in learning more about software reliability engineering. It recommends books, conferences, courses, Internet resources, journals, and professional organizations.

Books

Lyu, M. (Editor). 1996. *Handbook of Software Reliability Engineering* , ISBN 0-07-039400-8, McGraw-Hill, New York. Most valuable for its inclusion of a CD-ROM of the CASRE program, this book is a collection of many different contributions.

Musa, J.D., A. Iannino, and K. Okumoto. 1987. *Software Reliability: Measurement, Prediction, Application,* ISBN 0-07-044093-X, McGraw-Hill, New York. In addition to an overview of software reliability and a presentation of software reliability practice, this book has very thorough treatment of software reliability theory.

Musa, J. D. 1998a. *Software Reliability Engineering: More Reliable Software, Faster Development and Testing*, ISBN 0-07-913271-5, McGraw-Hill, New York. A very practitioner-oriented, systematic, thorough, up-to-date presentation of SRE practice. Includes more than 350 frequently asked questions.

Conference

International Symposium on Software Reliability Engineering (ISSRE)

Courses

John D. Musa conducts two-day public and onsite courses for practitioners. See website `http://members.aol.com/JohnDMusa/`.

The University of Maryland has a doctoral program. Contact Professor Carol Smidts.

Internet Resources

Software Reliability Engineering website. Overview, briefing for managers, bibliography of articles by software reliability engineering users, course information and announcements, useful references, and Question of the Month. `http://members.aol.com/JohnDMusa/`.

A mailing list (a good way to disseminate information or search for someone who may have experience with a particular problem). To join, send email to sw-rel@computer.org with only "subscribe" in the body of the message. To post a message after you have subscribed, send it to the preceding address.

Journals

IEEE Software

IEEE Transactions on Software Engineering

IEEE Transactions on Reliability

Professional Organization

The IEEE Computer Society Technical Committee on Software Reliability Engineering publishes a newsletter and sponsors the annual International Symposium on Software Reliability Engineering. You can obtain a membership application at http://www.tcse.org/tcseform.html.

References

1. Musa, J.D., A. Iannino, and K. Okumoto. 1987. *Software Reliability: Measurement, Prediction, Application,* ISBN 0-07-044093-X, McGraw-Hill, New York.

2. Lyu, M. (Editor). 1996. *Handbook of Software Reliability Engineering* , ISBN 0-07-039400-8, McGraw-Hill, New York (includes CD-ROM of CASRE program).

3. Musa, J. D. 1998. *Software Reliability Engineering: More Reliable Software, Faster Development and Testing,* ISBN 0-07-913271-5, McGraw-Hill, New York.

4. Tierney, J. 1997. *SRE at Microsoft.* Keynote speech at 8th International Symposium on Software Reliability Engineering, November 1997, Albuquerque, NM.

5. Musa, J. D. 1998 (updated regularly). *Software Reliability Engineering* Website: overview, briefing for managers, bibliography of articles by software reliability engineering users, course information, useful references, and Question of the Month. http://members.aol.com/JohnDMusa/.

CHAPTER **3**

User-Centered Design and Development

Scott Isensee and Karel Vredenburg,
BMC Software and IBM Corporation

What Is User-Centered Design?

We have all encountered products that are difficult to use. This impacts productivity and satisfaction. Today, it is widely recognized that ease of use is vital to the success of most products, but how can ease of use be designed into products? The answer is through *user-centered design* or *UCD*.

Figure 3.1 provides an example of a major corporation (IBM) making a public commitment to ease of use.

UCD is an approach to designing ease of use into the total experience for products and systems. UCD involves two fundamental elements: multi-disciplinary teamwork, and a set of specialized methods of acquiring user requirements and input, and then converting them into design.

Computing is about People, Not Machines

FIGURE 3.1   *An example of a major corporation advertising with emphasis on ease of use.*

Specialists from several disciplines, such as marketing, user interface design, visual/industrial design, user assistance design, technology architecture and engineering, service/support, and human factors engineering work together to design the product. A disciplined, integrated, user-based process is utilized throughout the design and development of offerings and solutions, which includes the following types of user activities:

- **Understanding users**. Provide an understanding of the users' characteristics, their environment, the tasks they currently perform, and the tasks they anticipate performing in the future.

- **Design**. Facilitate the high- and low-level design of the offering and evaluate the design iteratively with users.

- **Assessing competitiveness**. Assess the offering design relative to the prime competitor's offerings.

This chapter introduces the concept of usability and the cost-justification of it, articulates the differences between traditional and user-centered approaches to product design and development, describes the central principles of UCD, shows how UCD fits into the development process, and illustrates key UCD methods and techniques.

Usability

Usability is the attribute of products that is the prime target of user-centered design. Usability is typically defined as the extent to which a product can be used by specified users to achieve specified goals with effectiveness, efficiency, and satisfaction in a specified context of use.

Usability is determined by whether the users for whom the product is designed can achieve their goals. The extent to which a product has the characteristic of usability is determined by the *effectiveness* of the system in allowing the user to achieve his goals, the *efficiency* in carrying out his tasks, and the *satisfaction* the user experiences in interacting with the product. Usability often is further broken down into subcomponents, such as ease of acquisition, installation, learning, use, getting help, and so on. To the user, usability is simply the quality of interaction with a product or system.

Cost-Justifying Usability

Making products and interactive systems more user-centered has substantial business and personal benefits. More usable products and systems achieve the following goals:

- Are easier to understand and use, thus reducing training and support costs

- Reduce discomfort and stress and improve user satisfaction

- Improve the productivity of users and the operational efficiency of organizations

- Improve product quality, aesthetics, and impact, and provide a competitive advantage

The complete benefits of user-centered design come from calculating the total life-cycle costs of the product, including conception, design, implementation, support, use, and maintenance. Methods for calculating these benefits and have been developed and verified at several companies.[1] UCD techniques typically return several times their cost in savings to the company developing the software and more yet in benefits to companies or users purchasing the software.

A recent survey conducted by IBM shows that usability is one of the top three most critical characteristics that users expect of modern products. Usability is the most strongly related characteristic to overall product customer satisfaction.

Traditional Versus User-Centered Approach

Before delving into a description of user-centered design, we will differentiate it from more traditional approaches to software design and development. Table 3.1 lists the differences between traditional and user-centered approaches.

TABLE 3.1 COMPARISON OF TRADITIONAL AND USER-CENTERED DESIGN APPROACHES

Traditional Approach	User-Centered Design Approach
Technology driven	User driven
Limited multidisciplinary cooperation	Multidisciplinary teamwork
Component focus	Solution focus
Focus on internal architecture	Focus on external design
No specialization in user-experience design	Specialization in user-experience design
Some competitive focus	Focus on competition
Coding prior to user validation	Coding only user-validated designs
Code defect view of quality	User view of quality
Limited focus on user measurement	Prime focus on user measurement
Focus on current customers	Focus on current and future customers

User Involvement

The most obvious difference in the approaches concerns the involvement of users. Traditional approaches are fundamentally driven by technology. While they may collect customer requirements at the start of a project, little or no input from users is involved in the design and development process itself (see Figure 3.2). Design is often *inside out*; that is, the internal architecture is defined first and then a user interface is created in order for users to get access to the system functions. In contrast, UCD is fundamentally *user driven*. Users are involved in all stages of design and development. It is the user experience that is designed first and the product or system architecture is created to support this design. In other words, UCD involves design that is *outside in*. It is important to point out that this user focus is not simply design and development that takes the perspective of the user into account. Actual users that are representative of the end users of the product or system are involved during design and development.

FIGURE 3.2 *Be user driven, not technology driven.*

Multidisciplinary Teams

Traditional approaches involve some degree of multidisciplinary cooperation; however, this typically takes the form of independent work and then a hand-off of the work from one organization to another. In contrast, UCD requires all disciplines that contribute part of the total user experience work as a team to collaboratively define and design the aggregate product or system. For a commercial software product, for example, this includes the following:

- Marketing

- Development/engineering

- Visual design

- Human-computer interaction architecture

- User assistance architecture

- User research specialists

- Service and support specialists

Critical to the work of the team is trading off one aspect of the product or system against another. For example, the user assistance expert may believe that a multimedia tutorial best suits the needs of the users to address their ease of learning the product. This, of course, would require a multimedia computer. The marketing expert on the team, however, has examined the penetration of particular types of computers in the market and wants to target the largest possible market segment, one that does not typically own a multimedia computer. These two experts have to trade-off these product characteristics against one another to know how to proceed with the project. If they do this collaboratively at the beginning of the project as equal project team members, they will improve the design of the ultimate product. If both try to optimize their own respective elements without compromising based on user input, however, then the ultimate product will be worse as a result. The product will either be targeted at the widest definition of the market, or will be targeted unnecessarily at a narrower, high-end market with multimedia computers. In the former case, it will be frustrating for users wanting to run the multimedia tutorial but not able to with their systems not conforming to the tutorial's prerequisites, while in the latter case a multimedia tutorial will not be required or even desirable by users.

Scope

Traditionally, product design translates into component or subproduct design. In fact, even if usability engineering methods are involved, the scope often is still limited to the "on-the-glass" user interface. In contrast, the scope of user-centered design is the design of the total user experience in aggregate. This includes everything the user sees, touches, and experiences. In the broadest definition of the approach, this includes the advertising, packaging, installation, configuration, product usage, wizards, online help, manuals, as well as the service and support materials.

Focus

Most development organizations using traditional approaches focus primarily on the internal architecture and code development. Project design and status meetings focus on code implementation. On the other hand, organizations using a UCD approach focus, first and foremost, on the product from the user's perspective. Design meetings are characterized by creating a desirable user experience and ways of using technology to achieve this. Status meetings examine key UCD user metrics, together with code related ones to get a complete picture of the project.

Specialization

Key specialists in traditional organizations include architecture and engineering. Individuals with experience and training in these areas of specialization are, in fact, organizationally the most influential and powerful. In an organization practicing true user-centered design, however, architecture and engineering are equivalent to other key disciplines, such as visual design, human-computer interaction architecture, user assistance architecture, and so on. In fact, IBM has created a new role that has responsibility for the total user experience design and who leads these various disciplines in achieving it.

Competition

Most traditional approaches involve collecting requirements and translating them into product design. If any targets for such things as time to install are required, they often are arrived at by estimating or guessing. UCD, in contrast, includes the concept of beating the competition.

Competition in this context refers to the ways in which the majority of users currently accomplish the specified tasks. If a competitor's product has the majority market share, that is the competition. If, on the other hand, there is no current competitor and no computer-based solution exists, then the manual method is the competition. Whatever the prime way of doing the tasks is today, that forms the comparison and benchmark for the design and development effort. Specifying a target for time to install using UCD would involve examining the prime competitive solution to determine its installation time, and then specifying a target based on this information, together with the overall objective regarding how much better the product is attempting to be compared to the current competitive solution.

Validation

Traditional approaches often don't include any user validation. In fact, the initial delivery to customers is the *only* user validation. Using this approach, one version of the product is the prototype for the next version. Of course, if it takes 10 iterations or prototypes to get the design right, that means 10 versions of the product, which may mean 5 to 10 years of development effort, assuming that users will wait that long for a product to finally meet their needs. If user validation of designs is done using traditional approaches, it is carried out after code has been written and often when it is virtually complete. Of course, little or no change to the code can be made at this point in the development cycle without significant expense and time.

User input is central to user-centered design, and user validation of design occurs iteratively throughout the design and development cycle. The first versions of the design shown to users are created with pencil and paper and, therefore, are extremely inexpensive and quick to change. Subsequent, higher fidelity, prototypes that users evaluate also are comparatively inexpensive and quick to change. Final versions of the design are implemented in code and are as expensive and difficult to change as those developed using traditional methods; however, very few changes are typically required, given all of the user input gathered up to that point.

Quality

Quality in most traditional approaches to software development is understood to mean code quality; that is, the lack of coding defects that impact the reliability of the product. Some companies go to great lengths to drive down these types of defects at the expense of other aspects of quality. In addition, organizations that follow traditional approaches often discount problems encountered by users. If the code works "as designed," then the problem is not logged as a defect and instead is recorded as "user error." Little or nothing is ever done with items in the latter category. User-centered design focuses on quality as specified by the user. In fact, if users cannot proceed to complete a critical task using the product even though the product code is working perfectly, it is logged as a severity 1 problem and has to be fixed prior to product ship. The focus on the user view of quality ensures that products and systems work the way users expect them to and also at the level of reliability that is desired.

Measurement

Traditional approaches view usability as one of those ephemeral attributes of products that organizations can only hope to achieve but that no particular emphasis can be put on because it cannot be measured. This simply is not true. Core UCD measurements exist that can be taken at various points throughout a design and development cycle as input to design and as in-process indicators for project management. Figure 3.3 provides an example of the reports used to summarize UCD status for executive management at IBM.

UCD Report

Project Information

UCD Project Leader	User Audience	Prime Competitor	Fix Rate Model
?	?	?	?

User Problem Summary

Severity	Number	% Fixed	Target
1	?	?%	?%
2	?	?%	?%
3	?	?%	?%

Ease of Use Objectives

Objective	Validation	Status
?	?	?
?	?	?
?	?	?

Top 5 Open User Problems

Priority	Severity	Problem Description	Date Identified	Fix Date
1	?	?	?	?
2	?	?	?	?
3	?	?	?	?
4	?	?	?	?
5	?	?	?	?

User Satisfaction

Baseline	Current	Target	Competition
?	?	?	?

Enablement

Team	Schedule	Resource	Training	Budget
?	?	?	?	?

User Involvement (hours)

Understand	Evaluate	Test	Total
?	?	?	?

FIGURE 3.3 *Example of a report summarizing UCD status for executive management at IBM.*

Customers

The "voice of the customer" approaches championed by some traditional approaches focus on existing customers. Consider, for example, a product which only garnered 5 percent market share. While making current customers more satisfied is fine, in this example, 95 percent of the market were voting with their pocket books against the current design of the product. User-centered design focuses, instead, on users being targeted within the entire market segment, including those users currently using a competitor's product. In this way, the product is designed for the entire market and key characteristics of the design that current users of competitive products would like to see are included as well.

Following a UCD process can dramatically improve the usability of products and is readily noticed and appreciated by customers and evaluators. For example, Figure 3.4 shows what the press had to say about the ThinkPad 600 and 770 laptop computers after they were developed following UCD.

Gartner Report: "If winning in the notebook game is the result of attention to details, the 770 has it in spades, especially when it comes to usability."

PC Magazine: "The ThinkPad's [600] usability suffers no peer."

PC Computing: "...usability is where this machine truly shines."

Business Week: "IBM wins my vote for a huge display and excellent ergonomics...the keyboard is the best I have ever seen in a laptop."

PC Week: "The Trackpoint is the most useful pointing device we've seen to date on a notebook."

FIGURE 3.4   *Trade press reviews of IBM's ThinkPad notebook computers.*

The Five Principles of UCD

Making the transition from traditional approaches to full-scale user-centered design involves a major cultural transformation for an organization and a paradigm shift for practitioners. Several steps typically need to be taken to ensure that the key elements of this transition are carried out appropriately to ensure success. These key elements include identifying core principles, carrying out education, and integrating UCD into the company's business and development process. The five core UCD principles that communicate the essence of the approach and serve as the framework for individual methods and techniques are explained in the following sections.

Principle 1: Understand Users

The first principle of UCD concerns understanding users and says an understanding of the user is the driving force behind all design (see Figure 3.5).

UCD Principle #1

 **Understand Users**

An understanding of the user is the driving force behind all design

Tasks

Tools Problems

Environment

FIGURE 3.5 *Understand users.*

This principle is the basis for all other UCD work. Without an appropriate focus on the way users do things today and the way they want to do things differently in the future, design has no foundation.

To understand users, UCD project teams therefore must understand the current and future user tasks, the tools they use to carrying them out, what problems they're experiencing with them, and the key characteristics of the environment in which they carry out their tasks (for example, do they primarily work in groups, on the road, and so on).

Principle 2: Design the Total User Experience

The second principle focuses on the design of the total user experience and says everything a user sees and touches is designed together by a multi-disciplinary team.

The design effort must focus on the total solution and all aspects of the user experience with the offering; that is, it should be easy to buy, easy to set up, easy to learn, easy to use, intuitive, engaging, and of course, useful (see Figure 3.6).

UCD Principle #2

Design the Total User Experience

Everything a user sees and touches is designed together by a multidisciplinary team

Useful   Easy to Buy

Engaging   Easy to Set Up

Intuitive   Easy to Learn

Easy to Use

FIGURE 3.6 *Design the total user experience.*

You might be wondering why buying is considered part of the focus of UCD. Well, things such as advertising and packaging typically lead to the first user experience with an offering. As such, they set up expectations, establish the design signature, and yield the first positive or negative reaction to the offering. If they set an unrealistic expectation, establish a poor or inconsistent design signature, and/or yield a negative first impression for the offering, the success of the design of the actual product is compromised before anyone even touches it.

You also might be wondering about the attributes *intuitive* and *engaging*. There was a time when *usable* meant the absence of obvious user problems. The competitive bar, however, has been raised to point where products now have to be able to anticipate what users want to do and provide a visual/ industrial design that is pleasing and enjoyable.

All this reinforces the need to design the total user experience with specialists from various disciplines.

Principle 3: Evaluate Designs

This principle focuses on *evaluating designs* and says user feedback is gathered often with rigor and speed and drives product design.

Feedback has to be frequent to be useful. Most of the lead teams schedule a user feedback session once a week or once every two weeks. That way, when issues such as "I think users would want it this way or that," come up, the team can save time arguing and simply get user input on it at the next session that is scheduled.

Rigor also is important (see Figure 3.7). Simply asking a user or two what they think is not what is desired here. This type of approach can be more misleading, given lack of attention to bias, objectivity, and task coverage. Particular user feedback methods are specified in UCD that should provide the base.

FIGURE 3.7   *Evaluate designs.*

Lastly, the feedback collected from users must drive product design or else it makes no sense collecting the feedback at all.

There are broadly two approaches to collecting feedback on design. The first is typically referred to as *low fidelity* prototyping, which essentially is getting input using paper and pencil mockups of designs. This is most appropriate early in a design cycle and is preferable even when higher fidelity prototypes are available. We find that users give better input when it is clear that the prototype is not "finished."

The second type of feedback is *hands-on design validation testing* of a working prototype or actual early product. This allows tasks to be performed and data to be collected. It is a follow-on activity after the low fidelity prototypes.

Principle 4: Assess Competitiveness

The fourth UCD principle concerns *assessing competitiveness* and says competitive design requires a relentless focus on the competition and its customers.

What we mean by *competitor* here is whatever the majority of users are using today to carry out the tasks. That may be an actual competitor company's product, a combination of products, or even some analogue methods.

Scott Cook, the CEO of Intuit Corporation (makers of Quicken and TurboTax), talks about how he's had real difficulty unseating his main competitor. He goes on to talk about how tough this competitor is and how pervasive it is in the market. At this point, everyone thinks he is referring to Microsoft. However, he isn't. He points out that his main competitor is the "pen". It has incredible portability, ease of use, and a tough to beat price point. He feels that as long as he focuses his company on this competitor, in addition to Microsoft of course, then they'll be positioned for continued leadership.

The most common reaction we get from development organizations is that their product is unique and that it doesn't have any competitors. As this example shows, all products have some sort of competitor, some way people manage to do tasks without your product. This is the way we need to view competitors in terms of UCD.

We must examine our competitors by understanding the use of their offerings, evaluate our solutions relative to theirs, and carry out head-to-head, task based user tests to compare our solutions to theirs (see Figure 3.8).

UCD Principle #4

Assess Competitiveness

**Competitive design requires a relentless focus
on the competition and its customers**

**Understand
Use**

**Evaluate
Solutions**

**Test
Head-to-Head**

FIGURE 3.8   *Assess competitiveness.*

Principle 5: Manage for Users

The last, and perhaps most important, UCD principle concerns *managing for users* and says user feedback is integral to product plans, priorities, and decision making.

An organization can be completely in alignment with the first four principles, but if it is not in alignment with this principle, all is lost. There were projects in the past that had highly motivated design teams doing wonderful designs based on user input but the design never got into the product and, in turn, users didn't realize the benefits of the work (see Figure 3.9).

UCD Principle #5

 Manage for Users

User feedback is integral to product plans, priorities, and decision making

Investment

EOU Objectives   Resources

Skills   User Problems

Results

FIGURE 3.9   *Manage for users.*

Building ease of use into offerings using UCD involves a set of business decisions Ease of use needs to be managed into offerings:

- Making the appropriate investment decisions

- Setting ease of use objectives

- Building appropriate resources into the development/production plan

- Acquiring the requisite, key UCD skills

- Tracking user problems found through user feedback sessions as they are fixed in the product

- Keeping focused on the results from a user perspective by tracking user satisfaction

The UCD Process

The UCD process is a series of steps specifying the sequence of activities that should be performed.

How UCD Fits into the Software Development Process

UCD is a perspective for the software development process. It represents a recognition that meeting the needs of users is the central purpose of developing software. Specific activities are incorporated into the development process to ensure that user needs are understood and to verify they are being met.

Software Development Life Cycle

For many years, software development followed a sequential process called the "waterfall life cycle model." The number and names of the phases varied from one organization or project to the next, but they shared common characteristics of no overlap or iteration between phases. As each phase met its exit criteria, the output from that phase would pass on to the next phase and not be revisited. This model assumed that requirements do not change during the development cycle of the project (see Figure 3.10).

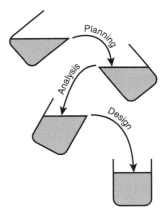

FIGURE 3.10 *The waterfall life cycle model of software development.*

Today, it generally is recognized that the waterfall model is flawed. Requirements do change during the development cycle, and the design should change in response to those requirements. Problems encountered in any phase of the development process may require changes to the products of earlier phases.

The software development life cycle approach has evolved from the waterfall model to a structured approach [2]. Barry Boehm [3] described a "spiral process," which addresses the deficiencies of the waterfall model. As problems are found, the process moves back to earlier phases and changes propagate through the process (see Figure 3.11).

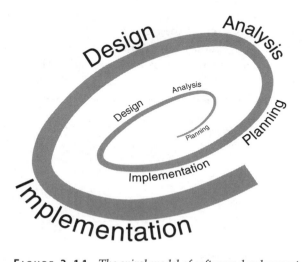

FIGURE 3.11 *The spiral model of software development.*

Iteration is very important in user interface design. It is extremely difficult to understand your users sufficiently and imagine a user interface so clearly that there won't be any surprises when users see it for the first time. Meeting your surprises throughout the design process is better than saving them for the end! By iterating design, implementation, and testing, you can fix user interface design problems along the way rather than doing expensive rework at the end of a project or shipping a product with user interface problems.

Do not view iteration as moving backward. Prototypes should be generated early in the process and updated as you go along. Prototypes provide a visible demonstration of progress throughout the project. Prototypes representing a stable implementation of portions of the planned program function can be delivered to users during development. This process is called *evolutionary development*.

Each phase of the spiral development process mirrors the activities of the entire project on a smaller scale.

Development Process Activities

The following is a typical list and sequence of methods for a UCD process. The techniques employed in each stage may vary, based on the nature of the project and the amount of resource available for UCD efforts.

Requirements Analysis

You need to understand the current and anticipated future tasks and task flows of a representative sample of users in the relevant market segment (see Figure 3.12). This understanding is not only important for the user interface, but is helpful in design of the entire system. Most software engineering methodologies advocate a form of customer requirements collection for code design. This information can be used for interface design as well.

FIGURE 3.12 *Great products are based on real user requirements.*

The umbrella term for the collection of information on user tasks is *task analysis*. In OO methodologies, task analysis also is known by terms such as *use cases* [4, 5], *scenarios* [6, 7], and *scripts* [8].

Requirements analysis may include a comparison of the tasks supported by competing products.

Modeling

Use task information from the requirements phase to develop designer's models.[9] These models identify the objects, interactions and relationships between the objects, and the views in which the user will see the objects. Such models are represented by class diagrams. These may be supplemented by other model representations, such as state diagrams and task flow diagrams.

Design

In the design phase, instantiate the models as user interfaces elements such as windows, icons, and interaction techniques. The design progresses from models to abstract visual design to concrete visuals. Design walkthroughs may be conducted. These can evaluate the total user experience by demonstrating concept prototypes, advertising, packaging, install and setup, user interface, user assistance, and service and support.

Design of the user interface and of the underlying code are modularized so that the user interface need not reflect all the complexities of the underlying code and so that changes to the user interface do not require extensive code redesign.

Prototyping

Prototype the user interface. Prototypes represent the interface design in forms that users and all members of the development team can understand. Prototypes range in fidelity from simple paper and pencil sketches to elaborate interactive programs. They serve as a common communication medium among all members of the team. They are vehicles for conducting user testing starting at early stages of the design cycle.

Evaluation

Conduct evaluations to verify that user requirements have been accurately understood and that the product being developed meets those requirements. The product is tested by users operating the prototype throughout the development cycle. This enables problems to be identified and appropriate design changes made as early in the design cycle as possible while these changes are most easily made. Measurements often include time on task, number of assists, number of errors, and user satisfaction ratings.

Implementation

Implement the product based on the prototypes and models developed in earlier stages. Throughout development, continue to conduct usability testing to verify that user needs are being met and to respond to any changes in those needs.

Development Team

The primary determinant of the success of a project is the quality of the people on the development team.[3] A project may seem to fail due to any number of external factors, but these often turn out to be secondary effects. Good people manage the forces outside the team, choose the right tools, and develop good software (see Figure 3.13).

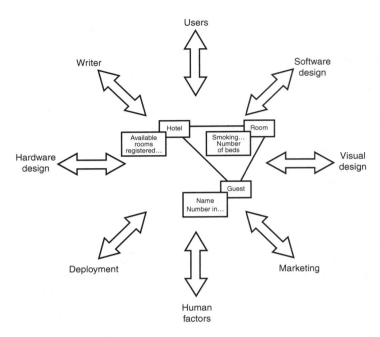

FIGURE 3.13 *Team development.*

Software is usually designed by teams, because the work involved exceeds the time and talents of a single individual.[10] We will describe some of the skills typically required on a successful software development team. Some members of the team may fill more than one role. Ideally, all members of the team know the other roles, because the work needs to be coordinated across people with different skills, and because some problems overlap multiple skill areas.

The size and makeup of the development team depends on your company and the needs of the project, but a few of the common skills are summarized here.

Application Domain Expertise

Knowledge of the domain for which a system or application is being developed is critical, if the system is to meet user needs successfully. This knowledge is most important in the early stages of development when the product is being defined, but also is useful on a continuing basis as the design evolves and is evaluated.

Members of the development team may capture domain knowledge through interviews, task analysis, observation, training courses, and by working temporarily in the application domain. The best process, however, is to involve an end user or a small group of end users in the design process. They can provide the other members of the team with information on user requirements and act as user advocates.

In designing a hotel application, for example, a desk clerk could describe current processes, define problems to be solved, answer questions, and evaluate proposed designs. These domain experts do not design the interface (that requires specialized skills), but they provide the information necessary for the team to design an interface that meets user needs.

User Interface Designer

The *user interface* (UI) designer balances customer needs and programming constraints to design an interface that meets the project goals. The UI designer constructs the models, identifies the objects and views, decides on the interaction techniques, and instantiates this with a concrete interface design. The UI designer receives much help and input from other team members, but generally is the focal point for all interface design activities.

Usability Specialist

The *usability specialist* (often called a *Human Factors Engineer*) is responsible for the efficiency and satisfaction characteristics of the user interface. The usability specialist is an expert in the interfaces between people and machines. The usability specialist has a knowledge of the extensive body of research in *human computer interaction* (HCI) and can use this information to provide advice on good design practice. He typically performs the task analysis and other user requirements collection. The usability specialist also is responsible for usability testing throughout the design process.

Visual Designer

The visual designer creates the interface visuals. The visuals should be easy for the user to understand, efficient to read and use, and esthetically appealing. This job is gradually changing to media designer as interfaces become richer in sound and other data types.

Software Engineer

The software engineer or programmer is responsible for implementing the design, but should be involved in the design team long before implementation begins. The programmer can make the team aware of implementation constraints so they can avoid expending effort on design paths that are not feasible. The programmer often develops prototypes so that team members and representative users can evaluate design alternatives or collect data from user testing.

Determining System Requirements

An interface should fit the needs, preferences, skills, and task requirements of the people who use it. You need to understand these requirements to build a system that meets the needs of your users.

User requirements are determined through a process called *task analysis*. This ensures that the software and particularly the user interface are designed to support the users' work activities. Output of the task analysis is analyzed to identify objects and their relationships.

Requirements gathering is the process of finding out what a customer requires from a software system. A variety of techniques can be used to determine these requirements. Some common techniques include interviews, observation, tests of prior versions of the system, and system analysis.

Requirements gathering is concerned with not only determining needs, but understanding them. This gives the designer the knowledge to set requirements for the system and also provides information to perform analysis as decisions come up during the development process. The result of requirements gathering is a representation of the problems with the current system and the requirements for a new system.

There are two categories of system requirements. *Functional requirements* specify what the system must do. *User requirements* specify the acceptable level of user performance and satisfaction with the system.

Functional Requirements

Developers should concern themselves with the entire human-computer system. Functional requirements refer to both what the system does and what the user does. *Task allocation* is the decision process through which activities are allocated to the computer and to the user. This step is deferred until after a task analysis has been done.

Functional requirements may be documented in a *functional specification*. The degree of formality for the functional specification varies greatly. Larger projects typically produce more formal and detailed specifications. The specification often is written in multiple levels starting with abstract requirements (for example, "the hotel management system should provide the capability to manage the allocation of rooms") down to very detailed requirements (for example, "a confirmation dialog must be provided to verify requests to delete a reservation").

Functional requirements are often constrained. For example, the client for the hotel reservation system may specify that the existing hardware and operating system be used for running the new software placing limits on the type of interface we can design.

Functional requirements may be documented as a text document or as a dataflow diagram (see Figure 3.14).

FIGURE 3.14 *Dataflow diagram for a hotel registration function.*

User Requirements

The objectives of the user requirements process are to identify who the users of the systems will be, to understand the characteristics of these users, and to determine the usability requirements for the system.

Identifying the end users and their characteristics makes designers aware of whom they are designing for. This sounds obvious, but is all too often over-looked. In the absence of knowledge about end users, designers often design for people like themselves. This is seldom desirable because users typically differ from designers in their skills, task requirements, mental models, and preferences.

Usability requirements specify design objectives. The design can be evaluated against these objectives throughout the development process. Without explic-itly specifying usability objectives, it is very unlikely these performance levels will be met. Through iterative design, usability measurements are compared against the goals and the design refined. Explicit requirements help designers to concentrate their efforts in areas where usability is most critical.

User Classes

Many software systems are used by more than one class of user. A user class is a subset of the user population, which is similar in system usage and relevant personal characteristics. The members of a user class should be similar in their pattern of usage and usability requirements.

A given task may be performed by more than one class of users. For example, booking a room in a hotel reservation system may be performed by a desk clerk, a supervisor, or a trainee. User requirements should be developed for each distinct user class.

User class descriptions include information such as experience level of user, computer skills, other systems operated by the user, education, motivation, and tasks performed.

The user classes should include not only direct users of the system, but also indirect users and remote users. *Direct users* are those who actually operate the system. A desk clerk is a direct user of a hotel management system. He will have operational requirements for the system. *Indirect users* are those who ask others to operate the system for them and make use of the output. The hotel manager may be an indirect user of the hotel management system. The manager may require that the system provide particular information, but not care how the information is generated. *Remote users* are those who depend on the input or output of the system. A guest is an indirect user of the hotel management system. They do not use the system directly, but may require that statements are correct and complete, for example.

Usability Requirements

A well-known researcher of usability, Ben Schneiderman [11] recommends the following five types of usability requirements:

- Time to learn

- Speed of performance

- Rate of errors by users

- Retention over time

- Subjective satisfaction

There frequently are tradeoffs between usability requirements. The relative priority of each requirement should be stated at the beginning of a project to aid in making these tradeoffs.

Each usability requirement should have a reason documented. For example, we may require that training time for hotel management system be less than 2 hours because there is 50 percent annual turnover at the hotel and a system that requires more extensive training would not be cost effective.

Specific criteria and methods of measurement should be specified for each usability requirement. These may be specified as targets, minimum acceptable levels, and/or acceptable ranges. The measures are referred to as *usability metrics* and are detailed in a *usability specification*. Examples of usability metrics include completion time for specified tasks, number of errors per task, and time to complete each task.

TABLE 3.2 SAMPLE ROWS FROM A USABILITY SPECIFICATION

Attribute	Measuring method	Worst case	Planned level	Best case	Current level
Installability	Time to install	1 hour	30 minutes	10 minutes	Many can't install
Configuration	Success rate	0%	90%	100%	80%
Editing	Satisfaction	1	6	7	5

Adapted from Whiteside et al. 1988

Usability requirements are established through interviews with existing or prospective users, business needs, and system analysis. Economic analyses are frequently done to determine whether development of a system meeting specifications will result in a net cost savings through increased efficiency, sales, better decision making, and so on.

A number of techniques have been developed for collecting and documenting user requirements. Preece et. al. [12] provides a good overview.

User Interface Design

We all go around with a model of the world in our heads. This model describes the objects and situations we confront and the relationships between them. When users see information onscreen, they subconsciously refer to this *mental model*. If the information is already part of their model, they know how to interact with it. If the information is new, their model is of no direct help and they must try to match the information with known objects or tasks.

Consider, for example, the telephone. At one time, most telephones had rotary dials, but today most have been replaced by pushbutton models. Most users guessed how to use the pushbutton model by relying on their existing knowledge of how telephones work. They noted the differences, and updated their mental model. When differences are small, as in this case, the new situation is easy to manage or *intuitive*. If the differences are large, the situation becomes more difficult (see Figure 3.15).

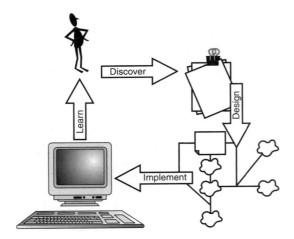

FIGURE 3.15 *The development of models.*

In user interface design, we call the model in users' head the *user's model*. We try to take advantage of how users employ this model in our designs. We also use two other models in product design: the designer's model and the implementer's model. The *designer's model* (see Figure 3.16) is what the users are supposed to see when the use the product (the specification). The *implementation model* is what the programmers really build (the code). We can sum up the design process in terms of these three models.

In the discovery phase, the designers come to understand the users' mental models. In the design phase, the designers develop a designer's model to complement the user models and thus be easier to learn. During implementation, programmers try to develop a product which matches the designer's model. Finally, in the learning phase, users launch the application, try to understand the designer's model, and adapt their own model to accommodate it.

The designer's model is represented by an object model. This is similar to the implementation object models from traditional software engineering approaches, with the difference being that the objects are those the user will interact with, not code objects. Other software engineering models, such as task flow diagrams and Harel diagrams, are useful in user interface design as well. These models are then mapped to user interface controls such as windows, menus, and so on.

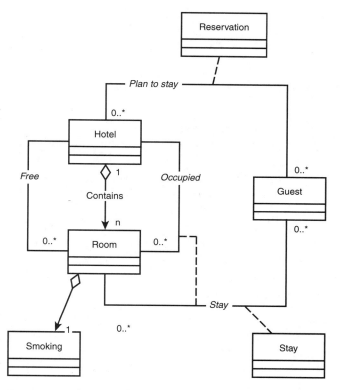

FIGURE 3.16   *Example of a designer's model.*

Prototyping

A *prototype* is a model of an application. It simulates the user interface and important functions of the program being modeled.

Isensee and Rudd [12] identify the major advantages of prototyping as the following:

- Better collection of customer requirements
- Cost saving
- Increased quality
- Evaluation of new interface techniques and functions
- Demonstration of feasibility
- Sales tool
- Defines a clear specification

- Allows early testing

- Demonstration of early progress

- Increases user satisfaction

- Results in a better design

The use of prototypes as an aid in customer requirements collection is particularly important in an iterative development methodology. Waterfall design methodologies required that the clients or end users have a clear idea of what they want a program to do and how they want it implemented, but users rarely have this level of understanding and vision. They just know that they have a problem and seek an expert to design a solution. Boar[13] reported that 20 to 40 percent of all system problems can be traced to problems in the design process while 60 to 80 percent can be traced to inaccurate requirements definitions. The cost to correct an error in a program increases dramatically as the life cycle progresses, so it is critical to catch errors in requirements and design before coding starts.

Prototypes can be used throughout the development cycle to continually verify customer requirements and test that the interface under development is meeting those requirements. User interface prototypes are very valuable are long as they are conducted in a disciplined requirements management process so that closure is assured.

Low Fidelity Prototypes

Low fidelity prototypes are limited function and limited interaction prototypes. They are constructed to depict concepts, design alternatives, and screen layouts rather than to model the user interaction with a system. Low fidelity prototypes are constructed quickly and provide limited or no functionality.

Users do not exercise a low fidelity prototype to get a first hand idea how it operates; rather, low fidelity prototypes are demonstrated by someone skilled at operating or explaining the prototype. Low fidelity prototypes are used early in the design cycle to show general conceptual approaches without much investment in development.

There are two forms of low fidelity prototype: abstract and concrete. *Abstract prototypes* serve as a communication vehicle between the interface designer and visual designer (see Figure 3.17). The designer's model is translated into views that are represented in an abstract form. For example, the following abstract prototype for the IBM RealPhone represents the controls in block diagram form. The interface designer can use this prototype to communicate the design to the rest of the team.

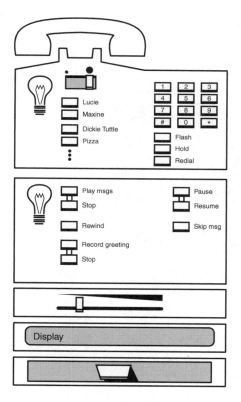

FIGURE 3.17   *Example of an abstract low fidelity prototype.*

The visual designer works from the abstract prototype and produces drawings of the interface as a concrete low fidelity prototype (see Figure 3.18). This level of prototype is more easily understood by end users than the abstract version.

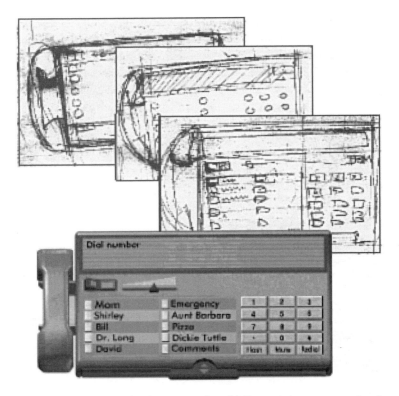

FIGURE 3.18 *Example of a concrete low fidelity prototype, progressing from sketches to a 3D model.*

High Fidelity Prototypes

High fidelity prototypes are fully interactive (see Figure 3.19). Users can enter data, respond to messages, open windows and, in general, interact with the prototype just as they would a real application.

High fidelity prototypes trade off speed for accuracy. They are not as quick and easy to create as low fidelity prototypes, but they faithfully represent the interface to be implemented in the product. They can be made so realistic that the user cannot distinguish them from the actual product.

High fidelity prototypes are invaluable for usability testing. While low fidelity prototypes address the layout and visuals of an interface (surface presentation), high fidelity prototypes address the issues of navigation and flow. The user can operate the prototype as they would the real product. Windows can be opened and data entered. Messages are delivered at appropriate times. Data can be displayed in realtime and the user can take action in response to the data. Errors and deviations from the expected path can be flagged and identified to the user as if using a real product. The user can get a sense of how the product will operate and can make informed recommendations about how to improve the user interface.

Usability testing can be conducted early in the design process with the prototype as a test vehicle.

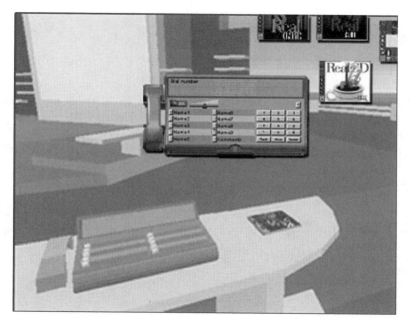

FIGURE 3.19   *Example of a high fidelity prototype that is fully interactive.*

Comparison

High and low fidelity prototypes each have their place in the development process. The following Table 3.3 compares the advantages and disadvantages of each to help in choosing which is most appropriate for a given situation on your interface design project.

TABLE 3.3   ADVANTAGES OF LOW AND HIGH FIDELITY PROTOTYPES

Low Fidelity Prototype

Advantages	Disadvantages
Lower development cost	Limited error checking
Evaluate multiple design concepts	Poorly detailed specification for coding
Useful communication vehicle	Facilitator driven
Address screen layout issues	Limited utility after requirements established
Useful for identifying market	Limitations in usability testing requirements
Proof of concept	Navigational and flow limitations

High Fidelity Prototype

Advantages	Disadvantages
High degree of functionality	More expensive to develop
Fully interactive	Time-consuming to create
User driven	Inefficient for proof of concept designs
Clearly defines navigational scheme	Not effective for requirements gathering
Useful for exploration and testing	
Look and feel of final product	
A living specification	
Marketing and sales tool	

Usability Evaluation

Usability evaluations are formal procedures for problem determination.

Reasons for Conducting User Evaluations

Conduct evaluations to identify problems users will have with software in all facets of its use: installing, learning, operating, customizing, and so on. Without user testing, products would reach the market untried and could fail due to problems that could have been identified and fixed during development.

Evaluations that are conducted during design of a product as referred to as *formative* evaluations. Formative evaluations guide a development team in producing products which are usable and useful.

Evaluations that take place after a product has been developed are referred to as *summative* because they are concerned with making judgments about a completed product. These typically are run to ensure that a product meets certain criteria before it ships.

Leading researchers on user evaluation techniques, Preece et. al. [14] identified the following reasons for doing evaluations:

- **Understanding the real world**. Determines whether a design can be improved to fit the work environment better. This kind of activity is particularly important during requirements gathering and then later for checking that prototypes of the system do fulfill users' needs.

- **Comparing designs**. Which is best? There are various occasions when designers want to compare two or more designs or design ideas. Early in the design process, for example, there may be debate about which way to implement a particular function. An evaluation may be conducted to empirically determine which one works best.

- **Engineering towards a target**. Is it good enough? The design process can be viewed as a form of engineering. The designers have a target, which often is expressed as some form of metric, and their goal is to make sure their design produces a product which meets the criteria. For example, the product may need to be better than competing products for it to be viable.

Types of User Evaluations

Different types of evaluations are conducted at different points in the development cycle, depending on the type of information most needed at each point. In general, evaluations in the early stages of the development cycle are quick, informal, and frequent. Evaluations later in the cycle tend to be longer and more formal.

During requirements gathering, evaluations are conducted to determine the needs of the users for which the system will be designed. As design of the interface starts, design alternatives are tested to make sure they work adequately or to find out which of multiple alternatives works best. As design of the interface is completed, evaluations determine whether design criteria have been met. Different kinds of evaluations may be carried out at different stages of design for different reasons, but the role of the evaluation is always to verify and improve the design.

Field Evaluation

Field evaluations are common at both the beginning and the end of the development cycle (see Figure 3.20). At the beginning of the cycle, they are used to collect customer requirements. Users are observed performing the tasks the system will automate or replace. User requirements are elicited through interviews or questionnaires.

Late in the development cycle, field tests are performed to validate the earlier lab testing. This verifies that the lab results were representative of actual field performance.

FIGURE 3.20   *An example of a field evaluation.*

Walkthrough/Inspection

A walkthrough is an informal verification of the interface (see Figure 3.21). The evaluator(s) step through a set of tasks to exercise the interface. They make sure the interface works as designed and look for any obvious usability problems.

FIGURE 3.21 *An example of a walkthrough/inspection.*

Formal Lab Test

Formal lab testing is the most rigorous form of evaluation (see Figure 3.22). It typically employs experimental design methodology to measure user performance with an interface in a manner that allows statistical comparisons to be made and conclusions to be drawn.

A prominent researcher on usability test techniques, Jakob Nielsen [14] provides a good overview of the elements of a usability lab and test techniques. Consult his book for a more in-depth treatment.

FIGURE 3.22   *An example of a formal lab test.*

Summary

UCD is an approach that designs ease of use into the total user experience for a product or service. It now has been employed by a large number of companies of varying sizes and industries and has shown great success. It has been found to be applicable to all types of user interfaces, such as hardware, software, GUI, Web, speech, and so on.

UCD takes user needs and input into account throughout the development process. It involves a multidisciplinary team that designs all aspects of the product into a coherent whole, which provides a pleasing and effective total user experience. It integrates well into modern software engineering methodologies.

The effectiveness of UCD and the techniques for practicing it are becoming well-accepted. The next stage of evolution for the UCD process will be the development of tools that allow interface design and user analysis to be conducted more quickly and efficiently to match the ever shrinking timelines of product development.

References

1. Bias, R. and Mayhew, D. (1994) *Cost-Justifying Usability*. Boston: Academic Press.

2. Yourdon, E. *(1989)* Modern Structured Analysis. *Englewood Cliffs, NJ: Yourdon Press.*

3. Boehm, B. (1988) A Spiral Model of Software Development and Enhancement. *IEEE Computer*, May.

4. Jacobson, I. (1992) *Object-Oriented Software Engineering: A Use Case Driven Approach.* Reading, MA: Addison-Wesley.

5. Booch, G. (1994) *Object-Oriented Analysis and Design*. Redwood City, CA: Benjamin/Cummings.

6. Wirfs-Brock, R, Wilkerson, B. and Wiener, L. (1990) *Designing Object-Oriented Software*. Englewood Cliffs, NJ: Prentice-Hall.

7. Rumbaugh, J. (1991) *Object-Oriented Modeling and Design*. Englewood Cliffs, NJ: Prentice-Hall.

8. Rubin, K. and Goldberg, A. (1992) Object Behavior Analysis. *Communications of the ACM*, September.

9. Roberts, D., Berry, R., Isensee, S. and Mullaly, J. (1998) *Designing for the User with OVID: Bridging User Interface Design and Software Engineering*. Indianapolis: Macmillan Technical Publishing.

10. Collins, D. (1995) *Designing Object-Oriented User Interfaces*. Redwood City, CA: Benjamin/Cummings.

11. Schneiderman, B. (1998) *Designing the User Interface: Strategies for Effective Human-Computer Interaction*. Addison-Wesley.

12. Isensee, S. and Rudd, J. (1996) *The Art of Rapid Prototyping*. Boston: International Thomson Computer Press.

13. Boar, B. (1984) *Application Prototyping: A Requirement's Definition Strategy for the '80s*, New York: John Wiley

14. Preece, J., Rogers, Y., Sharp, H., Benyon, D., Holland, S. and Carey, T. (1994) *Human-Computer Interaction*. Reading, MA: Addison-Wesley.

15. Nielsen, J. (1993) *Usability Engineering*. Chestnut Hill, MA: AP Professional.

PART II

Quality Designs

CHAPTER 4

Software Architecture and Quality

Rick Kazman and Len Bass, Software Engineering Institute, Carnegie Mellon University (This work is supported by the U.S. Department of Defense.)

In this chapter, we discuss software architecture and its relationship to software quality attributes. Once that relationship is established, we then discuss how it can be exploited during the design of large systems and during the evaluation of that design. Finally, many existing systems do not have properly documented architectures and so we discuss techniques for reconstructing the architecture from the code of a system.

What Is Software Architecture and Why Is it Important?

Software architecture has been a subject of increasing industrial and academic attention over the past 5 to 10 years. Its roots reach back more than 30 years to the work of Parnas, Brooks, Dijkstra, and Blaauw, but the intense attention of the last 5 to 10 years is new. Why is this? Quite simply, this field is of interest because it fills a gaping hole that existed in the development practices for large software-intensive systems The hole existed between the requirements gathering and analysis and the detailed design stages of development.

> **Note**
>
> *Throughout this document we will typically talk about software architecture, but this clearly includes a consideration of non-software aspects of a complex system. We are primarily interested in software intensive systems however, and so the software architecture is our primary concern.*

This is why. Once the requirements for a project are understood well enough to proceed to design, there is a temptation to proceed directly to detailed design and coding. In small to medium sized projects, this technique can work well, particularly if the staff is clever and familiar with the domain. And for many years, this was all that was needed for most system development. In large development efforts or in unprecedented development, however, this technique does not work. The kind of human ingenuity and attention to detail that enables us to create reasonable small- and medium-sized systems does not scale up to large systems. What is needed is an intermediate level of design, and this is the level of architectural design. In projects where architectural design was not explicitly identified as an area of study and design, the software architecture of a complex system typically evolves in an *ad hoc* manner.

Now that the need for some intermediate design step has been identified, we must turn to defining more precisely what we mean by software architecture. First, let's look at a common representation of a software architecture, as shown in Figure 4.1. This example was taken from a software architecture description of an acoustic modeling system, as reported in a technical journal.

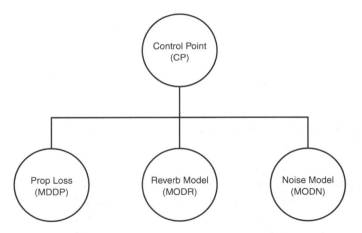

FIGURE 4.1 *A typical representation of a software architecture.*

While representations of software architecture such as this are extremely common, and may be useful for marketing, they are of little use for any software engineering. Why is this?

It is because there is too much ambiguity in the diagram. For example, what is the nature of the components? What is the significance of their separation in the diagram? Do the components run on separate processors? Do they run at distinct times? Do the components consist of processes, threads, programs, or something else? Do the components represent ways in which the project labor will be divided, or do they convey the system's runtime separation?

Similarly, we can inquire as to the nature of the connections between the components. Do the links mean that the components communicate with each other, control each other, send data to each other, use each other, invoke each other, synchronize with each other, or some combination of these relations? We need to understand the mechanisms for both communication and control.

And finally, we can ask questions about the topology or configuration of the components and connectors in Figure 4.1. What is the significance of the layout? Why is the Control Process depicted on a separate level? Does it call the other three components? Are the others not allowed to call it, or was there simply not room enough to put all four components on the same row in the diagram? In addition, we would like to use the layout to understand how the architecture operates at runtime. For example, how do data and control *flow* through the system?

We *must* raise these questions if the software architecture is to give us any intellectual control! Thus, the diagram in Figure 4.1, as given, is useless.

So, now you know, at least intuitively, what software architecture is not. It is not just bubble-and-line diagrams. These are unsatisfactory because they do not provide enough information to the software engineer to make engineering decisions. The following is a better definition:

> The software architecture of a program or computing system is the structure or structures of the system, which comprise software components, the externally visible properties of those components, and the relationships among them.[1]

This definition has several interesting implications. First, architecture is an abstraction of information about components and connectors. To be specific, we need to know about the following:

- Component functionality and specifications

- APIs

- Data connections

- Control connections

- Coordination strategies

- Properties of components and connectors

Second, systems can have more than one architectural structure or view. "The" architecture doesn't exist. The important structures (adapted from Kruchten [2]) are: functional, concurrency, physical, and code. Following are brief descriptions of each:

- **Functional**. Consists of key system functions or domain elements, functional dependencies or usage relations, and data flow.

- **Concurrency**. Contains processes and threads, interprocess communications, and synchronization events.

- **Physical**. Contains processors, memory, storage, networks and other communication devices, and sensors.

- **Code**. Contains files, directories, functions, objects, classes, modules, and abstractions such as layers or subsystems.

Each of these structures is important for engineering some aspect of the system. For example, a software engineer considers the concurrency and physical view when doing performance engineering. A software engineer considers the code and functional views when planning for modifiability, portability, and reusability. Each view contains separate information that is germane to some portion of the design and development life cycle. This information must be managed, cross-linked, and maintained throughout the system's life cycle.

Engineering a system to meet specific functional and quality goals from early in its design is one of the reasons that software architecture is important. However, it brings other benefits to a development project as well, such as:

- **Mutual communication**. A software architecture represents a common high-level abstraction of the system that the system's stakeholders can use as a basis for creating a mutual understanding and for coming to consensus on important system issues.

- **Managing change**. It is widely held that 80 percent of a system's cost occurs *after* initial deployment. Assessing the consequences of proposed changes requires insight into the relationships, dependencies, and behavioral aspects of system components. Reasoning at the level of software architecture can provide the insight *at the appropriate level of abstraction* necessary to plan for change early in the architectural design process. Any software architecture partitions possible change into three categories: local, non-local, and architectural. We want to design a system in which the majority of expected changes are local ones (those that affect only a single component).

- **Transferable abstraction of a system**. A software architecture is a relatively small and intellectually graspable model of how a system is statically structured and how it operates at runtime. This model can be applied to other systems exhibiting similar requirements, and can promote large scale reuse. Related to this is the notion of a *software product line*.

- **Early design decisions**. A software architecture is the record and manifestation of the earliest set of design decisions about a system. These early bindings are the hardest to change. They include constraints on both the architectural design and therefore on the organizational structure of the organization that implements the architecture.

- **Training**. The architectural structure, plus a high-level description of how components interact, can serve as the first introduction to the system for new project members.

- **Evolutionary prototyping**. After an architecture has been defined, it can be analyzed and then prototyped as an executable model. This has two positive benefits for the development process. The first is that the system can be executable early in the product's life cycle, with its fidelity increasing as prototyped or stubbed portions are replaced by completed software components. The second benefit is that potential performance problems can be identified, and addressed, early in the product's life.

- **Organizational structure**. After the software architecture has been established, it becomes almost impossible, for managerial reasons, to modify it. The architecture dictates units of planning, scheduling, and budget; configuration control and file system organization; integration and test plans and procedures; naming conventions; personnel training; and so on. Hence, a group whose responsibility is one of the subsystems will resist having their responsibilities distributed across other groups. Additionally, if these responsibilities are embodied in a contractual relationship, then changing them could be expensive.

Finally, software architecture provides a means by which quality attributes can be designed into a system from the start, and even predicted. In this way, the overall risk of a large development project can be substantially reduced.

Qualities and Their Relationship to Software Architecture

Quality is the fitness of a system for its intended uses. In this definition, there are two elements we will explore to understand the relationship between quality and software architecture. One element is that there are multiple users for a system and the second element is that there are multiple different facets of use.

The multiple users of a system are called the *stakeholders* and they all have different perspectives on the system. The stakeholders include the following:

- End users
- Developers
- Testers
- Customers
- System administrators
- Representatives of interacting systems

We will not address the details of the various types of stakeholders and their perspectives here, but we will return to stakeholders in the "Evaluation" section. For the purposes of this section, the concept of stakeholders motivates the different aspects of quality: the quality attributes.

Some quality attributes are relevant to both runtime (performance, reliability, usability, and achievement of function) and to development time (modifiability, integrability, and reusability). For each such attribute, we can identify external stimuli that activate the system relevant to that attribute, and we can identify responses that measure how the system responds to those particular stimuli. To use performance as an example, periodic or aperiodic events "arrive" at the system during its execution. Thus, the performance stimuli are events. The response to these events is measured in terms of latency or throughput. Modifiability stimuli, on the other hand, are changes to the system and the response of modifiability is measured in terms of the cost of the changes (caused by changes to component internals, interfaces, and connectors).

In addition, architectural choices are used by an architect to achieve the desired responses for particular attributes. An architectural choice is a decision on some aspect of the architectural design where the decision affects a particular attribute. Interposing of a virtual layer to achieve a particular type of independence to modifications, using a cyclic executive scheduler to meet realtime performance deadlines, having a number of redundant servers serving a particular class of requests to increase reliability, or using encryption to attempt to prevent theft of data are examples of architectural choices. These choices are frequently embodied in design patterns [3] or architectural styles [4] but, in any case, architectural choices are used to achieve the quality attributes. Using the two examples of performance and modifiability again, to achieve a particular measurable performance response, we would change the resource usage of various components, change the assignment of components to threads, to processes and to processors, or change the scheduling or queuing or synchronization strategy being used. To achieve modifiability, we would choose variations on either information hiding or decoupling the producers and consumers of data.

Notice that the collection of architectural choices and their relationship to qualities are independent of the functionality or purpose of any particular system. The *selection* of a particular choice and how it is applied in a particular context will, of course, depend on the goals to be achieved and the purpose of the system, but the list of choices, themselves, and their relationship to the qualities is independent of a particular context or system. For example, separation is a choice we use to achieve modifiability. This choice does not depend on a context other than a desire to achieve modifiability. On the other hand, choosing *what* to separate does depend on the context of a particular system. We will return to this point during our discussion of design.

Now let us return to the question of the relationship of quality attributes and software architectures. Some attributes, in particular functionality and usability, are not achieved through architectural means. We can achieve specific functionality, for example, through many different architectures and the functionality largely independent of the architectural choices we make. This has been known at least since the seminal work of Parnas in the early 1970s [5]. We make architectural choices through the desire to achieve other quality attributes, such as performance or reliability, not functionality. Also, usability is determined by the particular metaphors or widgets used within the user interface of the system and this is not influenced by the structure of the system. We also usually have a desire to make the metaphor or widgets easy to modify so that we can improve the user interface, but this is really just another way of saying that the attribute of modifiability is also important to user interface development and not that usability is architecturally determined.

Other attributes, such as modifiability and reusability, *are* primarily determined by architectural choices. For example, object-oriented design methods are predicated partially on the assumption that correct encapsulation of function will simplify modifications and enable reuse. As previously stated, the two important choices used for modifiability are information hiding and decoupling producers and consumers of data. There are a number of variants in the ways in which we realize these choices, such as layering or abstract data types or facades as techniques for information hiding, and blackboard or publish/ subscribe as techniques for decoupling the producer and consumer.

A third class of attributes, such as performance or security, are determined both by architectural choices and by coding techniques. To achieve performance goals, for example, we use architectural choices such as a scheduling discipline; however, performance is also impacted by the choice of algorithms used within a particular component. To achieve security goals, we may use architectural choices, such as a firewall, to deflect unauthorized use. How the firewall is coded, however, is as important as its existence to the achievement of security.

One test as to whether the achievement of a particular attribute is based primarily on architectural choices is to ask yourself "When a particular system does not achieve its goals for a specific quality attribute, can I improve its rating for that attribute by making structural changes?" In subsequent sections, we discuss exploiting the relationship between quality attributes and architectural choices during both design and evaluation and it is important to understand what and how much of each quality attribute is affected by architectural choices.

Quality attributes, by themselves, are too abstract for either design or evaluation. For example, if for a particular system, the color of the background screen can be changed by changing a value in a resource file but hundreds of modules must be changed to implement a new data format, is that system modifiable? The answer is, of course, "it depends." Attributes must be given a context to be useful.

Quality scenarios are the context that we use for some discussions of attributes. A quality scenario is a short description of some quality attribute stimuli to the system under discussion. "Change background color of screen," "Eavesdrop on network traffic," and "Respond to a screen refresh request within 10 milliseconds" are examples of such quality scenarios.

The study of quality attributes is a well-established part of software engineering and there are specialized communities devoted to modeling particular quality attributes. Performance, for example, has a community that develops and applies queuing models as well as other types of models. The reliability community focuses on Markov models as a tool for analyzing systems. It is important for system designers and evaluators to realize that many models exist for predicting quality attributes and to be aware of how these models can be used for the analysis of particular system architectures.

A software architecture that was explicitly designed to address quality attributes is that of the original architecture for the World Wide Web. This software architecture was realized in a library that was called libWWW. The most important requirements for the World Wide Web software were extensibility of data, extensibility of software (particularly protocols and data types), scalability in terms of the number of Web sites, and interoperability (people using different hardware and software platforms had to be able to interoperate seamlessly with each other). The software architecture of libWWW was designed, from the start, with these quality goals in mind. It was designed, from the coder's perspective, as a layered system, as shown in Figure 4.2.

| Application Modules |
| Access Modules |
| Stream Modules |
| Core |
| Generic Utilities |

F I G U R E 4.2 *The code view of libWWW expressed as layers.*

This layering served the following several purposes:

- It provided a separation of concerns, so that different layers could be focused on achieving different quality goals.

- It allowed systems built upon libWWW to be *portable* and *interoperable*, because the Generic Utilities layer provided a common abstraction of the underlying implementation platform.

- It supported *extensibility*, because the Core and Access Modules are actually skeletons. The Core provides network access, data management, parsing, and logging; functions that virtually any WWW application needs; however, the Core does not do any of these functions directly. They are all achieved via *plug-ins* and *call-outs*, external functions that are registered with the WWW application at runtime. The Access Modules are similarly structured. They provide a number of network-aware protocol modules (such as HTTP, WAIS, Gopher, Telnet, and FTP) and make it easy to add new modules.

From a deployment perspective, the WWW was designed as a client server system, and libWWW had to support this. A typical client-server software architecture is shown in Figure 4.3. The client-server structure helped to achieve the other quality goal of *scalability*. It did this by separating producers and consumers of data, and having no explicit links between them and no central control or agent through which all requests needed to be routed.

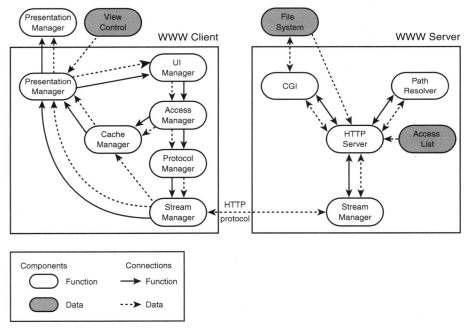

FIGURE 4.3 *A typical WWW client-server runtime architecture.*

Understanding Quality Attributes

Following are the main points from this discussion of quality that you should carry forward to the design and evaluation processes:

- Quality is multifaceted and these facets are represented by the quality attributes

- Most of the quality attributes are primarily determined by architectural mechanisms (usability and function being the prime exceptions)

- Quality attributes can be discussed in terms of stimulus/response and the choices that are used to achieve them

- Quality attributes, by themselves, are too vague for design and analysis and are given a context by the use of quality scenarios

- Some quality attributes have well-established models and modeling techniques

We now turn to the explicit incorporation of quality related aspects into a design process.

A Quality-Based Design Process

Design is a process of making decisions: of choosing some avenues for investigation and rejecting others. This is true, whether you are designing a computer system, a house, or a musical composition. You can view the design process as an enumeration of the possibilities for a particular aspect of the artifact being designed within the constraints of decisions already made, and then the choice of one of those possibilities. Every decision potentially provides a constraint for all of the subsequent decisions. At the least, there is a dependency of design decisions so that any particular decision is dependent on some of the prior decisions that have been made. You could, conceptually, construct a dependency graph of decisions that reflects which decisions depend on which other decisions.

Of course, most designers do not design through this process but create a design through intuition, prior experiences, and insight. Viewing design as a sequence of decisions, however, enables us to discuss the ordering of development and to develop a process that enables a designer to capture design rationale and to verify design decisions. Even if the decisions are made on the basis of intuition and insight, capturing that in a rationale provides a basis for reconsidering decisions, if necessary.

The design process that is presented here has the following major elements:

- Identify architectural drivers—the key requirements that shape the possible form of any solution—and then elaborate these drivers into a set of architectural requirements. These requirements are then translated into architectural choices that achieve those drivers.

- Identify major cohesive functional portions of the solution. This is an iteration of the functional structure.

- Decide which architectural choices will be used in the particular system, based on a consideration of the concurrency and functional structures of the cohesive functional portions.

- Decide on the distribution characteristics of the functional portions identified. This is an iteration of the concurrency structure.

- Verify decisions based on use cases [6] and quality scenarios.

- Refine the functional and concurrency structures and iterate.

- Every major decision made during this process is recorded together with its rationale and the consequences of the decision.

These steps, within the dependency graph of decisions, allow a variety of ordering of decisions. The particular sequence chosen depends on the business context within which a development is proceeding, as well as the experience and intuition of the architect. Experienced architects, typically, do not explicitly articulate particular decisions but proceed on the basis of the decisions they have made on previous similar systems.

Architects inexperienced in a particular domain or designing unprecedented systems need to proceed more carefully and thoroughly. Even within a thorough design process, however, there is a variety of different ordering of decisions that might be made. We advocate a process that results first, in an end-to-end thread; second, in a "skeletal system"; and third, in a system that realizes some subset of the functionality.

Figure 4.4 shows, at a high level of abstraction, how the design for a system proceeds. There are decisions relevant to the concurrency structure, those relevant to the functional structure, and intermediate points where a check is made that a satisfactory system could be constructed within the constraints of the decisions made thus far. As more decisions are made with respect to each structure, they depend more on decisions made with respect to both structures. Hence, we show the refinements coming closer together.

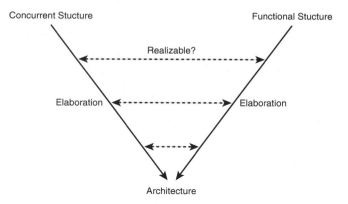

FIGURE 4.4   *Overview of the design process.*

In this brief description, we have introduced a variety of new concepts. We will now elaborate on these concepts.

Architectural Drivers, Requirements, and Choices

Systems typically have a small number of quality requirements that drive the architecture. These requirements may be requirements for reliability, for modifiability, or for particular performance. The architect must often elaborate these drivers to make them concrete. For example, a driving architectural requirement may be the requirement that the architecture be suitable for a collection of systems (a product line), some members of which are as yet unknown. This leads to an elaboration of the driving requirement into a list of architectural requirements that enumerate the types of variations that might be expected with the collection of systems, such as variation in the user interface, variation in the physical structure, and so on. An *architectural requirement* is a requirement that is concrete enough to be tested. Architectural requirements can be realized by the architectural choices that were discussed in the previous section of this chapter.

Now consider the WWW discussion of the previous section in light of the design problem. Architectural drivers for the WWW are the scalability and extensibility. When the architect elaborated these drivers into requirements, scalability became the requirements to add new users, new data without central control. Extensibility became the requirement to add new data types, new protocols, and new functions. In addition, portability and interoperability, although not drivers, are architectural requirements.

Following our design process, the architect would not, for each of these requirements, enumerate at least one architectural choice that would allow the achievement of these requirements. These choices are manifested in our architectural diagram of the WWW.

Refining the Functional Structure

The architect refines the functional structure as the architecture definition process proceeds. The refinements identify the following:

- Domains (large chunks of related functionality)

- Subsystems

- Aggregated components

- Components

- Interfaces

Domains are identified through a process called *domain analysis* [7] which is out of the scope of this chapter. Subsystems are identified from the domains and from the architectural choices by a consideration of how the potential subsystems are affected by the concurrency decisions. Further refinement proceeds by considering concurrency decisions already made, and decomposing the functions of the particular iteration into smaller units.

Refining the Concurrency Structure

The concurrency structure also is, simultaneously, refined as the process proceeds. The architect begins by considering how a particular subsystem could be distributed across the physical structure. This leads to identification of portions of subsystems that might be executed in parallel, typically for performance reasons. The architect also considers the threads that exist within the subsystems. That is, which sequences of execution must be sequential (belong to the same thread) and which threads can be concurrent. Initially, the architect identifies *virtual threads*——threads that exist if the system exists on a single processor. The architect next identifies *physical threads*—threads that exist in a single processor and are sequenced by the passage of a message from one processor to another. This consideration of threads and messages identifies additional components for the functional structure. A message manager, for example, may be identified as a result of consideration of messages.

In subsequent stages, the architect refines the concurrency structure. The refinements identify the following:

- Units of distribution and parallelism

- Patterns for common solutions that are applied across different processes

- Objects

- Threads

- Interfaces

Within these refinements, there will be performance budgets (time, CPU, and memory, for example) allocated to the highest level concurrent units. These budgets then will be allocated within each high level unit to subunits. Prototyping and modeling may be necessary to determine how to best do this allocation. Consideration of network and processor characteristics affect these decisions, as well as potentials for security threats based on different designs.

Use Cases and Quality Scenarios

A *use case* is a short description of a use of the system by an end user. A *quality scenario* is a short description of a stimulus that affects a quality attribute. Both are concrete interactions between a stakeholder and the system being designed. As such, they are specific enough so that one can reflect on the decisions made thus far, and determine the reaction of the system to the use case or the quality scenario. In some cases, quality-attribute specific models of the system can be built to formally characterize the system's response to some set of use cases or scenarios, and to experiment with different architectural design choices as they affect the responses of the model. Again, consideration of the quality scenarios results in additions to the functional structure and these additions must be considered by the architect in terms of concurrency.

This whole process of the architect placing function in the functional structure, considering it from the concurrency structure, revising the functional structure, and considering the quality scenarios, iterates until the architect is satisfied that all quality scenarios can be achieved within the existing proposed structure. At that point, the architect can move on to the next refinement.

End-to-End Thread and Skeletal Systems

An *end-to-end thread execution* of a system is a control path from a stimulus to its response. What we mean by implementing an end-to-end thread is that the system being designed gives the proper response to a chosen stimuli. The components do not, necessarily, exist in their full generality; however, much of each of them may be stubbed. Sufficient functionality should be implemented, however, so that interfaces are tested and the control and data paths are tested.

A skeletal system is a system for which the full architectural infrastructure has been implemented—the ways in which components initialize, communicate, report failures, recover from failures, terminate, get data, and so on—but no end user functionality has been implemented. This provides a basis for incremental prototyping and development, and for the implementation of the most important functionality prior to less important functions. In an end-to-end thread, for example, a data management subsystem may be stubbed and the stub returns a fixed or small set of data in response to each call. In the skeletal system implementation, the data management routine actually looks into its repository to respond to queries.

Elements of an Architectural Design Process

Although there is not the space here to detail a complete architectural design process, we have enumerated the key elements of such a process, as follows:

- **Functional requirements**. Those requirements that detail functions or features of the desired system. These functions or features are visible to a user.

- **Quality attribute requirements**. These requirements detail the quality attributes of the desired system. They are refined, as described previously, into architectural drivers and requirements.

- **Constraints on the solution**. Portions of the solution are typically prespecified for various business reasons, such as compatibility with legacy software, interoperation with other systems, conformance to standards, cost constraints, or time-to-market constraints. It is possible that any portion of the design may be constrained for business reasons.

- **Architectural choices to achieve quality attributes**. These currently come from the architect's background and experience. In time, there will be handbooks that enumerate architectural choices and how they relate to quality attributes.

All requirements must be sufficiently explicit so that they can be tested. As discussed in the previous section, for quality attribute requirements, this means providing use cases and scenarios with enough specificity in terms of the expected stimuli and responses.

During the process of selecting an architectural choice, the architect should examine the choice from the point of view of *all* of the quality requirements and quality scenarios. The examination consists of both qualitative and quantitative reasoning. The types of models used for the examination are those that encompass the type of information available at that level. At the first iteration, for example, the only decisions the architect makes on the concurrency structure are those of allocation to the physical structure. Performance can be evaluated from the point of view of network traffic and the necessary speed of the processors based on assumptions of resource usage. These assumptions are necessarily crude because processes have not yet been defined, but an initial judgement can be formed as to whether the physical structure is adequate.

The type of reasoning that is used varies from quality to quality. Because there is no system to measure, however, the architect's understanding of how a particular architectural proposal will behave, with respect to the different stimuli for the quality in question, is always the basis for the reasoning.

Evaluation

After a software architecture has been designed, it must be *evaluated* for fitness, with respect to its intended quality goals. Architectural walkthroughs and analysis methods are a means of doing just that. The architectures of large, complex systems, however, typically cannot be easily grasped. Even at the level of abstraction that we call architecture, they are still tremendously complex. Thus, methods are needed to aid in the orderly evaluation of such systems to control the complexity of the process. We will present one such method, although others are described in Bass, Clements, and Kazman.[8]

The problem with evaluating an architecture is the reverse of the design problem. The evaluators must understand and/or be able to accomplish the following:

- Architecture

- Recognize the architectural choices that were used

- Know the implications of these architectural choices, with respect to quality attributes

- Compare these implications to the requirements for the system

A further problem is that the documentation for both of the requirements and the architecture often are incomplete, with respect to the needs of an evaluation.

Because an architectural evaluation is intended to be performed on an architecture and not on an existing system, the output is, inherently, imprecise. The results of an architecture evaluation, then, are used as an indication to the architect of problem areas in the architecture and as a risk reduction mechanism by management. The problem areas identified, in ATAM, are called *sensitivity points* and *trade-off points*. A sensitivity point is a collection of components in the architecture that are critical for the achievement of a particular quality attribute. A trade-off point is a sensitivity point that is critical for the achievement of multiple attributes.

Given the problems enumerated, ATAM utilizes these elements to determine the following the sensitivity and trade-off points:

- Quality scenarios (both expected and unexpected) are used as a manifestation of the quality attribute requirements.

- Stakeholders are used as the generators of the quality scenarios.

- Quality scenarios and use cases are used as an elicitation technique for the architecture.

- The architect is used as the interpreter of the quality scenarios and the use cases.

- The quality attribute taxonomies are used to provide the evaluators with a catalog of architectural choices and the appropriate stimuli.

An ATAM typically is planned to take three full days, where each day consists, in some measure, of the following:

- Scenario elicitation

- Architecture elicitation

- Mapping of scenarios onto the architecture representation

- Analysis

In Days 1 and 2, more emphasis is on the early steps of the method (scenario elicitation, architecture elicitation, and scenario mapping), and in Days 2 and 3, more emphasis is on the later steps of the method (model building and analysis, sensitivity point identification, and tradeoff point identification). Graphically, we see the relationship of the three activities with respect to time, as shown in Figure 4.5.

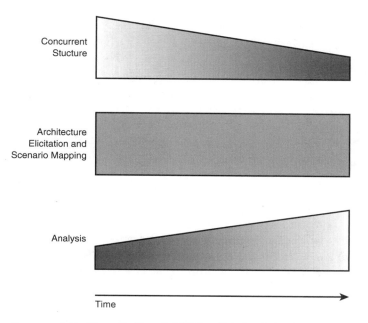

FIGURE 4.5 *The activities of ATAM and their relative importance over time.*

The width of the polygon at each activity shows the amount of anticipated activity within that activity at that time (on Day 0, for example, we expect relatively little analysis to take place, and on Day 3, we expect most of the activity to be taken up with scenario mapping, and analysis).

A detailed explanation of the ATAM is beyond the scope of this chapter; however, you can find it, along with an extended example, in Kazman, et al.[9]

Architecture Reconstruction

We have now discussed why it is important to have a software architecture, how to design and analyze one, and its relationship to quality attributes. Just having a software architecture, however, is not the same as having an architecture that is well-documented, well-disseminated, or well-maintained. If any of these are not done, however, then the architecture will inevitably drift from its original precepts. This is a risk. If the architecture drifts in multiple ways (because of changes by multiple developers) that are not mutually consistent, or who do not follow the original rationale for design decisions, then the achievement of quality attributes that had been so carefully designed and analyzed in the original system will be compromised. So, how can you ensure that the architecture of the as-designed system and the architecture of the as-built and as-maintained system remain congruent?

Assessing the conformance of an architecture to its design manually is a dreary and error-prone task. So, one technique that has been gaining popularity over the past five years is to use tools to extract the architecture of the as-built system and check it for *conformance* to the as-designed system.

This technique, however, even with tool support, is not straightforward for the following several reasons:

- Software architectures are seldom documented in practice

- When they are documented, they are often not maintained

- When they are documented, the documentation often is ambiguous

This final point is worth some attention. Many architectural constructs have no realization in the development artifacts that programmers actually create and maintain. Nowhere in the code and header files of a typical source repository will we find a layer or a subsystem or a functional grouping or a class category. These concepts typically only exist within the minds of the architect and a select group of programmers, and their mapping to development artifacts is unclear. Hence, architectural reconstruction typically has an *interpretive* aspect, where the architect associates certain naming conventions, file or directory structures, or structural constraints with an architectural construct. For example, a layer might be realized as any function that directly accesses the database. A subsystem might be defined by all of the files in the IO directory, or by all subclasses of the PrimitiveOp class. Yet these abstractions are useful and we want to be able to support their existence and enforce their continued existence throughout a system's lifetime.

There are other reasons for wanting to extract the software architecture of an existing system than simply for redocumentation, as follows:

- An organization may want to reengineer an existing system and so needs to know which assets with which it is currently working to plan the re-engineering effort, or to decide that the existing assets are not worth reusing.

- An organization may want to mine its existing assets to form a reuse library or the core of a product line, and so it needs to know what dependencies on those assets exist in the system.

- An organization may want to analyze its existing system with respect to its future prospects, growth potential, suitability for integration with other systems, or scalability. For each of these analyses, an accurate representation of the architecture is a crucial prerequisite.

Tools, such as the Dali workbench, have been developed to aid an analyst in extracting information from an existing system. The extracted information can be wide ranging in scope: its code, build files, execution traces, results of instrumentation, file structure, and so on. The analyst then needs to work with the architect defining the patterns that describe such mappings. Typically, this is an iterative, interpretive process. The patterns are defined, applied to the extracted artifacts, and viewed by the architect, potentially resulting in a redefinition of the patterns. Once such patterns have been defined and suitably refined, they become the set of rules that *define* the architecture and against which the as-built architecture can be assessed for conformance.

These rules typically then are applied to the extracted artifacts, and any remaining anomalies can be manually or automatically noted.[10] Based upon the results of this extraction and conformance activity, the following three possible outcomes may result:

- The documentation might be updated to reflect the reality of the existing code base.

- The code base may be brought into conformance with the architectural rules that have been explicitly defined (perhaps for the first time).

- The anomalies might simply be recorded as anomalies with no further action for the time being.

Whichever of these options is chosen, the result is increased understanding and, hence, intellectual control over the system and its future uses. This activity, thus, is a crucial step in a complete view of the architectural life cycle. The architecture must be documented and maintained just as any other system asset is maintained.

Conclusions

This chapter has presented the notion of a software architecture, and has argued that it is integral to the achievement of quality attributes such as modifiability, performance, security, and reliability. We have discussed techniques for designing a software architecture, achieving quality attribute goals via architecture, analyzing an architecture, and assessing the conformance of an as-designed architecture with its as-built realization.

Although a software architecture does not guarantee the achievement of any quality attribute goal, it is our experience that, as systems grow in size and complexity, the achievement of these goals is simply not possible without paying strict attention to how they are aided or hindered by the software architecture. The individual heroic efforts of programmers do not scale up to address the ever increasing size and complexity of modern development efforts. We need to increase the level of abstraction of design, and we need to understand how to manage this higher level of abstraction, if we are to meet the challenges of designing the ever larger software systems that we continue to field.

References

1. L. Bass, P. Clements, R. Kazman, *Software Architecture in Practice*, Addison-Wesley, 1998.

2. P. Kruchten, "The 4+1 View Model of Software Architecture," *IEEE Software*, November. 1995, 42-50.

3. I. Jacobson, M. Christerson, P. Jonsson and G. Overgaard, *Object-Oriented Software Engineering: A Use Case Driving Approach*, Addison-Wesley, 1992.

4. M. Shaw and D. Garlan, *Software Architectures: Perspectives on an Emerging Discipline*, Prentice-Hall, 1996.

5. D. Parnas, "On the criteria for decomposing systems into modules," Communications of the ACM, 15:12, 1053-1058, December 1972.

6. I. Jacobson, M. Christerson, P. Jonsson and G. Overgaard, *Object-Oriented Software Engineering: A Use Case Driving Approach*, Addison-Wesley, 1992.

7. K. Kang, et al. "Feature-Oriented Domain Analysis (FODA). CMU/SEI-90-TR-021, Pittsburgh, Pa. Software Engineering Institute, 1990.

8. L. Bass, P. Clements, R. Kazman, *Software Architecture in Practice*, Addison-Wesley, 1998.

9. R. Kazman, S. J. Carriere, "Playing Detective: Reconstructing Software Architecture from Available Evidence," *Automated Software Engineering*, 6:2, April 1999.

10. G. Murphy, D. Notkin, K. Sullivan, "Software Reflexion Models: Bridging the Gap between Source and High-Level Models", *Proceedings of the Third ACM SIGSOFT Symposium on the Foundations of Software Engineering*.

CHAPTER 5

Rationalize Your Design

Paul C. Clements, Software Engineering Institute,
Carnegie Mellon University

Introduction

This chapter revisits a subject that David Parnas and I first wrote about in a software engineering paper entitled "A Rational Design Process: How and Why to Fake It." [1] This essentially simple paper turned out to be amazingly popular, rising to the top of lists of papers cited. I've always suspected that the catchy title had something to do with that, although the paper's message clearly resonated with a large number of people. That message was this: even though we cannot develop software in a completely rational step-by-step fashion, it still pays to document your project as though that was exactly how it happened. The analogy that it used was that of mathematical proofs: mathematicians published polished proofs, not the ones that led to the discovery of their theorems. The published proofs are the results of possibly years of improvement, and contrast starkly to the "working" proofs that may have been scratched on the backs of dinner napkins. The mathematician publishes a proof so that we can better understand the theorem; not so that we can better understand the unrepeatable thought processes that may have led to it.

And so it is with software. The documentation that a project should produce, and leave behind as its legacy for others, is documentation that best helps others understand the software and not the likely chaotic development history that produced it.

Let us clarify what we mean by *rational* and *rationalize*. A perfectly rational person is one who always has a good reason for each step taken. Each step can be shown to be the best way to get to a well-defined goal. When we rationalize our actions, we assign a rational explanation to them that others can understand, empathize with, and appreciate. *Rationalize* has recently fallen into some disrepute, coming to suggest assigning a plausible (but bogus) explanation to questionable actions in order to excuse them. This is not what we mean by "rationalize." By rationalizing, we mean that another rational person would likely view your actions as rational in light of your explanation.

Most of us like to think of ourselves as rational professionals. In the context of software development, an ideally rational process is one in which we derive our programs from a statement of requirements in the same sense that theorems are derived from axioms in a published proof. All design methodologies, especially those that can be considered "top down," are the result of our desire to have a rational, systematic way of designing software.

Why Can't We Achieve a Rational Design Process?

Have you ever completed a nontrivial software project in a completely rational fashion? No? You're not alone. There are many reasons that software development can never really proceed in a completely rational fashion, beginning with a clear and complete statement of requirements and proceeding directly through design and implementation. Some of the reasons include the following:

- Requirements often are not known (or not known completely) before it is time to begin building the system. The user may not know what exactly is wanted, or may not be able to communicate all that is known about the domain to us. Sometimes what the user wants is a function of what you are able to build, or build economically. Worse, often "the user" is really a community of thousands or even millions of vastly different individuals, each of which "requires" something a little different. Users change as their experience grows, and what they want and require changes as well. Requirements change as our expertise in the domain grows, and we learn more about the feasibility of our project. In addition, requirements also change in the face of schedule slippage and budgetary pressures. What was once a "requirement" may easily be demoted to a "fond wish." In short, requirements evolve as we build the system.

- Even if the requirements were fixed—known from beginning to end— the requirements specifications do not contain all the properties that the system must exhibit to be considered successful. The model of design we were all taught in software engineering class—essentially that a full and complete requirements specification is tossed through the transom window and lands with a thud on the designer's desk, from which he or she can begin designing—is a lie. It is a naive designer who does not understand that the developing organization itself exerts considerable pressure on the design of a system. It should be buildable with the tool environment in which the company has just invested millions of dollars; it should make good use the database group that is currently idle or under-employed; it should be an object-oriented design because the company just sponsored OO training for everyone, and so on. Perhaps the company has ambitions for this system that go beyond its current customer base, such as using it to launch a product line in its domain. The design will have to support that capability, which transcends the requirements for any one system that may be developed from the design.

- Even if the requirements were fixed and all required properties of the system were known, it is not possible to "derive" a design from them. There are many design solutions that solve a given problem. Which one is chosen may depend as much on the architect's background and experience as much as the intrinsic properties of any single design.

- We often are encouraged, for economic reasons, to use software that was developed for some other project or that is available as a commercial or publicly available product. In other situations, we may be encouraged to share our software with another ongoing project. The resulting software may not be the ideal software for either project, that is, not the software that we would develop based on its requirements alone, but it is good enough and will save effort.

- Finally, even if all the preceding problems were somehow rendered irrelevant, human error is unavoidable in any endeavor in which humans are involved. Mistakes happen.

These and other reasons all contribute to the unhappy reality that projects are not going to proceed in a rational fashion, as we have defined it. As we learn more, as conditions change, as mistakes are made, previous design decisions are invalidated and we must backtrack. Because we try to minimize lost work, the resulting design may be one that would not result from a rational design process.

Why Is a Rationalized Design Useful Nevertheless?

So, our software is not developed in a rational (derived) fashion. The point of this chapter, however, is to argue that you should leave in your wake a picture of a project that appears rational to the observers who come afterward. We know now that the bulk of the cost of a software product occurs after its initial deployment or release to its customers. This cost takes the form of making changes to the software. So it is clearly in our interest to make changing the product as simple and inexpensive as we can.

Most of the people who work on a product over its lifetime were not there at its inception. It is useful to think of the rationalized design that we leave behind as being for those people. But the goal is also useful to the developers working on the project in the first place. Why is this so?

- Designers need guidance. When we undertake a large project, we can easily be overwhelmed by the enormity of the task. We will be unsure about what to do first. A good understanding of the ideal process will help us to know how to proceed.

- We will come closer to a rational design, if we try to follow the process rather than proceed on an ad hoc basis. Even if we cannot know all the facts necessary to design an ideal system, for example, the effort to find those facts before we start to code will help us to design better and backtrack less.

- When an organization undertakes many software projects, there are advantages to having a standard procedure. It makes it easier to have good design reviews, to transfer people, ideas, and software from one project to another. If we are going to specify a standard process, it seems reasonable that it should be a rational one.

- If we have agreed on an ideal process, it becomes much easier to measure the progress that a project is making. We can compare the project's achievements with those that the ideal process calls for. We can identify areas in which we are behind (or ahead).

- Regular review of the project's progress by outsiders is essential to good management. If the project is attempting to follow a standard process, it will be easier to review.

In short, maintainers will thank you for a rationalized design. But equally (if not more) importantly, so will developers.

How Do We Produce a Rationalized Design?

If it is a good idea to work to a rational design process, and to leave in our wake a description of our software as though it were the result of a rational design process, how do we produce this rationalized legacy? The answer is simple: documentation.

Now, this is not going to be an eat-your-vegetables lecture about documenting your software because it's good for you. Many people regard documentation as a necessary evil; many more seem to regard it as an *unnecessary* evil. In fact, it should be neither. Documentation should be written if it is useful, but only if it is useful. Regarding it as other than an integral part of the finished product will be a self-fulfilling prophecy. People will not invest time and effort in writing documentation that they don't believe will be used, and documentation written under those assumptions certainly won't be.

What Documentation Do We Produce?

The exact set of development documentation that your project should produce will vary, but at a minimum it should include documentation for the software requirements, the software architecture (what some people refer to by the unhelpful name "high-level design"), and the internal structure of the architectural components. All this documentation should include rationale, or explanations of why decisions were made the way they were.

Documenting the Requirements

If we are to be rational designers, we must begin knowing what we must do to succeed. That information should be recorded in a work product known as a *requirements document*. Completion of this document before we start would allow us to design with all the requirements in front of us. Completion of this document after we start (as the requirements change, or more are discovered) will show which constraints were in place when the system was fielded. Along the way, however, a requirements document serves the following purposes:

- We need a place to record the desired behavior of the system as described to us by the user; we need a document that the user, or his representative, can review.

- We want to avoid making requirements decisions accidentally while designing the program. Programmers working on a system often are not familiar with the application. Having a complete reference on externally visible behavior relieves them of any need to decide what is best for the user.

- We want to avoid duplication and inconsistency. Without a requirements document, many of the questions it answered would be asked repeatedly throughout the development by designers, programmers and reviewers. This would be expensive and would often result in inconsistent answers.

- A complete requirements document is necessary (but not sufficient) for making good estimates of the amount of work and other resources that it will take to build the system.

- A requirements document is valuable insurance against the costs of personnel turnover. The knowledge that we gain about the requirements will not be lost when someone leaves the project.

- A requirements document provides a good basis for test plan development. Without it, we do not know what to test for.

- A requirements document can be used, long after the system is in use, to define the constraints for future changes.

Determining the detailed requirements may well be the most difficult part of the software design process because there usually are no well-organized sources of information. The definition of the ideal requirements document is simple. It should contain everything you need to know to write software that is acceptable to the customer, and no more. Of course, we may use references to existing information, if that information is accurate and well organized. Acceptance criteria for an ideal requirements document include the following:

- Every statement should be valid for all acceptable products; none should depend on implementation decisions.

- The document should be complete in the sense that if a product satisfies every statement, it should be acceptable.

- Where information is not available before development must begin, the areas of incompleteness should be explicitly indicated. Never just leave an entry blank or omit information without noting that the information is missing.

- The product should be organized as a reference document rather than an introductory narrative about the system.

Although it takes considerable effort to produce such a document, and a reference work is more difficult to browse than an introduction, it saves labor in the long run. The information that is obtained in this stage is recorded in a form that allows easy reference throughout the project.

Ideally, the requirements document would be written by the users or their representatives. In fact, users are rarely equipped to write such a document. Instead, the software developers must produce a draft document and get it reviewed and, eventually, approved by the user representatives.

Consistency and completeness in the requirements document is obtained by using separation of concerns. One scheme that has worked particularly well with realtime embedded systems prescribes the following sections:

(1) **Computer Specification:** A specification of the machines on which the software must run. If the implementers will be working directly with the machine, a programmers' reference manual often serves in this role. The machine need not be hardware—for some software, this section might simply be a pointer to a language reference manual;

(2) **Input/Output Interfaces:** A specification of the interfaces that the software must use to communicate with the outside world. This information might be given by naming the input or output items and describing each in a template such as the following:

> Name of item: BAROALT
>
> Meaning: The altitude above sea level, as measured by the barometric altimeter mounted on the aircraft.
>
> Unit of measure: Feet
>
> Range: −1024 to 50,000
>
> Accuracy: +/− MAX(40 feet, .3% of reading) at −54 degrees C. to +/− MAX(25 feet, .25% of reading) at +50 degrees C.
>
> Resolution: 1 foot
>
> Maximum rate of change: +/− 1000 feet per minute
>
> Data representation: Bits 1–12 of Discrete Input Word 6; 12-bit positive number with scale 4096/61020 and offset 1020
>
> Timing characteristics: Analog to digital conversion requiring 135 to 300 microseconds

(3) **Specification of Output Values:** For each output, a specification of its value in terms of the system's current state and values of inputs from the system's environment. A table [2] often is the best way to give this information. Each row of the table identifies a set of overriding conditions (such as what mode the system is currently in). The columns of the table specify distinguishing conditions that determine the value to be computed. Here is an example:

Mode	Condition	
Navigation mode	Never	Always
Weapon delivery mode	Target in range and Master Arm switch on	Target not in range or Master Arm switch off
OUTPUT	Release enable := TRUE	Release enable := FALSE

(4) **Timing Constraints:** For each output, how often, or how quickly, the software is required to recompute it;.

(5) **Accuracy Constraints:** For each output, how accurate it is required to be.

(6) **Likely Changes:** If the system is required to be easy to change, the requirements should contain a definition of the areas that are considered likely to change. You cannot design a system so that everything is equally easy to change. Programmers should not have to decide which changes are most likely.

(7) **Undesired Event Handling:** The requirements also should contain a discussion of what the system should do when, because of undesired events, it cannot fulfil its full requirements. Most requirements documents ignore those situations; they leave the decision about what to do in the event of partial failures to the programmer.

It is clear that good software cannot be written unless the above information is available. An example of a complete document produced in this way is given and discussed in Henniger.[3, 4]

Documenting the Architecture

By *architecture*, we mean the structure of structures of the system, which comprise software components, the externally visible properties of those components, and the relationships among them.[5] The architecture is one of the earliest products of the design process. Whether a large system will be able to exhibit its desired (or required) quality attributes is substantially determined by the time the architecture is chosen. A small system can achieve its quality attributes through methods such as coding and testing. These techniques become increasingly inadequate as systems grow, however, because quality attributes are increasingly satisfied in a large software system's structure and division of functionality rather than in its algorithms and data structures. Modifiability, for example, depends extensively on the system's modularization, which reflects the system's encapsulation strategies. Reusability of components depends on how strongly coupled they are with other components in the system. Performance depends on the volume and complexity of intercomponent communication and coordination, especially if the components are physically distributed processes. It should be easy to see how architecture can strongly affect many kinds of quality attributes.

The structures of software are the result of explicit design decisions. Large projects, for example, usually are partitioned into components that are used as work assignments for programming teams. Let's call those components *modules*. A module comprises programs and data that software in other modules can call or access, and programs and data that are private. Modules may be subdivided for assignment to subteams. This is one kind of structure often used to describe a system. Suppose that the system is to be built as a set of parallel processes. The set of processes that will exist at runtime, the programs in the various modules that are strung together sequentially to form each process, and the synchronization relations among the processes form another kind of structure often used to describe a system.

The architecture consists of these structures and possibly others. Because architecture can comprise more than one kind of structure, there is more than one kind of component (for example, modules and processes), more than one kind of interaction among components (such as subdivision and synchronization), and even more than one context (such as development time versus runtime).

Documenting the architecture, then, means documenting those software structures that were designed to carry quality properties for the system. Following are some of the most common and useful software structures:

- **Module structure**. The units are work assignments and have products (such as interface specifications, code, test plans, and so on) associated with them. They are linked by the "is a submodule of" relation. Module structure is used to allocate a project's labor and other resources during maintenance as well as development.

- **Conceptual, or logical, structure**. The units are abstractions of the system's functional requirements. These abstractions are related by the or "shares data with" relation. A reference model, defined earlier, is an example. This view is useful for understanding the interactions between entities in the problem space, and their variation.

- **Process structure, or coordination, structure**. This view is orthogonal to the module and conceptual views and deals with the dynamic aspects of a running system. The units are processes or threads. Relations represented by the links include "synchronizes with," "can't run without," "can't run with," "preempts," or any of several other relations dealing with process synchronization and concurrency.

- **Physical structure**. This view shows the mapping of software onto hardware. It is particularly of interest in distributed or parallel systems. The components are hardware entities (processors) and the links are communication pathways. Relations between the processors are "communicates with." This view allows an engineer to reason about performance, availability, and security.

- **Uses structure**. The units are procedures or modules; they are linked by the "assumes the correct presence of" relation. Uses structure is used to engineer systems that can be easily subsetted or extended such as using an incremental build approach to integration.

- **Calls structure**. The units usually are (sub)procedures; they are related by the "calls" or "invokes" relation. The calls structure is used to trace flow of execution in a program.

- **Data flow**. Units are programs or modules; the relation is "may send data to." The links are labeled with the name of the data transmitted. The data flow view is most useful for requirements traceability.

- **Control flow**. Units are programs, modules, or system states; the relation is "becomes active after." This view is useful for verifying the functional behavior of the system as well as timing properties. If the only mechanism for transferring control is the program call, then this is identical to the calls structure.

- **Class structure**. Units are objects; the relation is "inherits from" or "is an instance of." This view supports reasoning about collections of similar behavior (such as the classes that other classes inherit from), and parameterized differences from the core, which are captured by sub-classing.

Table 5.1 summarizes these structures. The table lists the meaning of the nodes and arcs in each structure and tells what each structure might be used for.

TABLE **5.1** ARCHITECTURAL STRUCTURES OF A SYSTEM

	Units	Relation represented by the links	Useful for
Module	Work assignments	Is a submodule of; shares secret with	Resource allocation and project structuring and planning; information hiding, encapsulation; configuration control; avoid gaps and duplication in work
Conceptual	Functions	Shares data with	Understanding the problem space
Process	Programs	Runs concurrently with; may run concurrently with; excludes; precedes; and so on.	Scheduling analysis; performance analysis
Physical	Hardware	Communicates with	Performance, availability, security analysis
Uses	Programs	Requires the correct presence of	Engineering subsets; engineering extensions
Calls	Programs	Invokes with parameters	Performance profiling; bottleneck elimination
Data flow	Functional tasks	May send data to	Traceability of functional requirements
Control flow	System states or modes	Transitions to, subject to the events and conditions labeling the link	With timing information, can be basis for automatic simulation and verification of timing and functional behavior
Class	Objects	Is an instance of; Shares access methods of	In object-oriented design systems, producing rapid almost-alike implementations from a common template

The behavior of each component is part of the architecture, insofar as that behavior can be observed or discerned from the point of view of another component. This behavior is what allows components to interact with each other, which is clearly part of the architecture.

While there are many useful architectural structures, the module structure is first among equals. Efficient and rapid production of software requires that the programmers are able to work independently and the module structure is the structure that enables this, since its components are work assignments. The module structure also usually dictates the structure of the project, since work assignments are reflected by the division of the project into teams, and the team structure is the basis for resource allocation, schedules and budgets, documentation libraries, test and integration plans, and project measurements.

The module structure also carries information about the other architectural structures in it. For example, each module may consist of one or more processes. The process structure of the system is distributed among the individual modules. Similarly, the data flow structure is recorded as a set of paths among modules that data follows. The module documentation will refer to these other architectural views of the system.

A *module interface specification* must be written for each module. It must be formal and provide a black box picture of each module. Written by a senior designer, it is reviewed by both the future implementers and the programmers who will use the module. An interface specification for a module contains just enough information for the programmer of another module to use its facilities, and no more. The same information is needed by the implementer. The specifications include the following:

- A list of programs that can be invoked by the programs of other modules. These often are called "access programs," or if the modules are objects, "methods."

- The parameters for those programs and their data types.

- The externally visible effects of each program, including changes in the module's state or future behavior as a result of calling the program, and shared resources consumed by the program. By *externally visible*, we mean discernible by software in other modules in our system, or in the external world (such as an external system inter-operating with ours, or a human user).

- Timing constraints and accuracy constraints, where necessary.

- Definition of errors (sometimes called "undesired events" or "exceptions") that the program will detect and report, and the behavior that it exhibits when doing so.

In many ways, this module specification is analogous to the requirements document. However, the notation and organization used is more appropriate for the software-to-software interfaces that is the format that we use for the requirements. Published examples and explanations include Parker and Britton.[6, 7]

This does not mean that the exact behavior and performance of every component must be documented in all circumstances. It is, after all, counter to the principle of information-hiding to reveal everything about a component, but to the extent that a component's behavior influences how another component must be written to interact with it, or influences the acceptability of the system as a whole, this behavior should be part of an interface specification for that component.

All systems do not warrant multiple architectural structures. Experience has shown that the larger the system, the more dramatic the difference between these structures. For small systems, however, the conceptual and module structures may be so similar that they can be described together. If there is only one process or program, there is clearly no need for the process structure. If there is to be no distribution (that is, if there is just one processor), there is no need for the physical structure. In the case of most systems of significant size and complexity, however, if we were to attempt to combine these structures into one, we would add detail that would cripple the usefulness of the architecture as an artifact. This separation of concerns afforded by multiple structures proves beneficial in managing the complexity of large systems.

One of the most useful but under-utilized architectural structures is the *uses structure*. This structure can be completed after we know all of the modules and their access programs. It is conveniently documented as a binary matrix, where the entry in position (A,B) is true if and only if the correctness of program A is allowed to depend on the presence in the system of a correct program B. In practice, it is often documented as a list that is part of the documentation for each program. The list tells the implementer what other programs his program is allowed to use. Part of a programmer's implementation task is choosing from among the programs they are allowed to use. After implementation, the "allowed to use" structure (which is a prescriptive artifact) is converted into an "actually uses" structure (which is descriptive). Both are maintained, as both are important for future development.

The uses structure defines the set of subsets that can be obtained from the whole system without rewriting any program. If program "A" is to be included in a subset, then all programs under the transitive closure of the "A actually uses" relation must also be included. By prescribing the "allowed to use" structure to prevent undisciplined usage of programs, small and useful subsets can be quickly built. It is important for incremental development, for staged deliveries, for fail soft systems, and the development of program families [8]or product lines. Also, when schedules slip and deadlines are missed, being able to deliver a substantial subset on the due date is much preferable to being able to deliver nothing at all; only by engineering the "uses" structure in the architecture is this possible.

Documenting the Components' Internal Structures

After a module interface has been specified, its implementation can be carried out as an independent task except for reviews. Before coding the major design, however, decisions are recorded in a document called the module design document.[9] This document is designed to allow an efficient review of the design before the coding begins and to explain the intent behind the code to a future maintenance programmer. In some cases, the module is divided into submodules and the design document is another module guide, in which case the design process for that module resumes at the architectural step above. Otherwise, the internal data structures are described; in some cases, these data structures are implemented (and hidden) by submodules. For each of the access programs, a function or relation describes its effect on the data structures. For each value returned by the module to its caller, another mathematical is provided that maps the values of the data structure into the values that are returned. For each of the undesired events, we describe how we check for it. Finally, there is a *verification*, an argument that programs with these properties would satisfy the module specification. The decomposition into and design of submodules is continued until each work assignment is small enough that we could afford to discard it and begin again if the programmer assigned to do it left the project.

If you can, appeal to previously packaged design decisions to guide you and refer to those packages in your documentation. Design patterns [10] offer a particularly rich set of documented internal designs with known quality attributes and areas of applicability associated with them.

Documenting the Rationale

The documentation we prescribe differs from the ideal documentation in one important way. We make a policy of recording all the design alternatives that were considered and rejected. For each, we explain why it was considered and why it was finally rejected. Months, weeks, or even hours later, when we wonder why we did what we did, we can find out. Years from now, the maintainer will have many of the same questions and will find his answers in these documents.

Documenting the rationale is easy to do once you get into the habit. It usually is recorded as a simple prose paragraph under a special section of each document. Engineers like to explain why they made a particular decision, but generally aren't used to being asked to do so. Rationale often surfaces at design reviews, and a good manager will develop an ear for rejected alternatives that should be recorded.

In the requirements specification, record the following:

- Why you structured the information the way you did.

- The source of each of the requirements: who said it and when and why, and what the rejected alternatives were.

- What you know about the future of this application, or trends in this domain, that may have influenced the statement of the requirements.

In the architecture documentation, record the following:

- Why you chose the structures to design and document that you did, and why you didn't think other structures were worthwhile.

- What your partitioning principles were, and how you used those principles to adjudicate gray areas in the design.

- What module interface facilities and designs you considered and rejected, and why.

- How you decided on the repertoire of data types in your software design.

In the module internal documentation, write down the following:

- Data structures that you considered but decided against.

- Algorithms that were considered and rejected, and why.

All the documentation products need to carry rationale with them. This is how the design is rationalized. Recall that a rational design is one that carries with it an explanation, a justification for its existence. The rationale is this explanation.

Documentation Principles

Much of today's software documentation is incomplete and inaccurate, but those are not the main problems. If those were the main problems, the documents could be corrected by adding or correcting information. In fact, there are underlying organizational problems that lead to incompleteness and incorrectness and those problems that follow are not easily repaired:

- **Poor organization**. Most documentation today can be characterized as *stream of consciousness*, and *stream of execution*. Stream of consciousness writing puts information at the point in the text that the author was writing when the thought occurred to him. Stream of execution writing describes the system in the order that things will happen when it runs. The problem with both of these documentation styles is subsequent readers cannot find the information that they seek. It, therefore, will not be easy to determine that facts are missing, or to correct them when they are wrong. It will not be easy to find all the parts of the document that should be changed when the software is changed. The documentation will be expensive to maintain and, in most cases, will not be maintained.

- **Boring prose**. Many words are used to say what could be said by a single programming language statement, a formula, or a diagram. Certain facts are repeated in many different sections, and usually in slightly different ways. This increases the cost of the documentation and its maintenance. More importantly, it leads to inattentive reading and undiscovered errors.

- **Confusing and inconsistent terminology**. Any complex system requires the invention and definition of new terminology. Without it, the documentation would be far too long. The writers of software documentation, however, often fail to provide precise definitions for the terms that they use. As a result, there are many terms used for the same concept and many similar but distinct concepts described by the same term.

- **Myopia**. Documentation that is written when the project is nearing completion is written by people who have lived with the system for so long that they take the major decisions for granted. They document the small details that they think they will forget. Unfortunately, the result is a document useful to people who know the system well but impenetrable for newcomers.

- **Imprecise target audience**. A document written for nobody in particular will be useful to nobody in particular.

Documentation in the ideal design process meets the needs of the initial developers as well as the needs of the programmers who come later. Each of the documents mentioned previously records requirements or design decisions and is used as a reference document for the rest of the design. However, they also provide the information that the maintainers will need. Because the documents are used as reference manuals throughout the building of the software, they will be mature and ready for use in the later work. The documentation in this design process is not an afterthought; it is viewed as one of the primary products of the project. Some systematic checks can be applied to increase completeness and consistency. One of the major advantages of this approach to documentation is the amelioration of the Mythical Man-Month effect.[11] When new programmers join the project, they do not have to depend completely on the old staff for their information. They will have an up-to-date and rational set of documents available.

Try to employ the following principles for documentation:

- Avoid "stream of consciousness" and "stream of execution" documentation by designing the structure of each document. Design each document by stating the questions that it must answer and refining the questions until each defines the content of an individual section.

- Aim for a precise audience by identifying the information that members of that audience need, and do not need. Use that information to help you state the preceding questions.

- Make sure that there is one, and only one, place for every fact that will be in a document. The questions are answered, such as the document is written, only after the structure of a document has been defined Design every document in accordance with the same principle that guides good software design: separation of concerns. Each aspect of the system should be described in exactly one section and nothing else is described in that section.

- Optimize a document's organization for its readers, not its writers. A software development document is nominally written only once and read cover to cover seldom, if ever. A good document, however, is used to find information hundreds or thousands of times. Organize your documents for the rapid look-up of facts, not to be read like a novel.

- When there are several documents of a certain kind (module interface specifications are a good example), write a standard organization for those documents. When documents are reviewed, have them reviewed for adherence to the documentation rules as well as for accuracy of contents.

- Be precise! If anything you write can be interpreted in more than one way, you can be certain it will be. In this regard, follow Brooks' edict that "it is better to be wrong than vague." [12] If you are vague, everyone will silently apply their own interpretation and the ambiguity will go underground until late in the project when it will be much more expensive to correct. If you are precise but wrong, however, someone will tell in short order.

The resulting documentation is not easy or relaxing reading, but it is not boring. It makes use of tables, formulae, and other formal notation to increase the density of information. The organizational rules prevent the duplication of information. The result is documentation that must be read very attentively but rewards its reader with detailed and precise information.

Rationalizing the Design

The preceding describes the ideal process that we would like to follow and the documentation that would be produced during that process. The process is "faked" by producing the documents that we would have produced if we had done things the ideal way. One attempts to produce the documents in the order that we have described. If a piece of information is unavailable, that fact is noted in the part of the document where the information should go and the design proceeds as if that information were expected to change. If errors are found, they must be corrected and the consequent changes in subsequent documents must be made. The documentation is our medium of design and no design decisions are considered to be made until their incorporation into the documents. No matter how often we stumble on our way, the final documentation will be rational and accurate.

Those who read the software documentation want to understand the programs, not to relive their discovery. By presenting rationalized documentation, we provide what they need. The clear message is that, if documentation is produced with care, it will be useful for a long time. Conversely, if it is going to be extensively used, it is worth doing right.

It is very hard to be a rational designer; even faking that process is quite difficult. However, the result is a product that can be understood, maintained, and reused. If the project is worth doing, the methods described here are worth using.

The following summarizes the advice:

- Insist on producing documentation that defines the requirements, architecture, and component designs.

- Product a documentation plan that defines the audience, questions to answer, and organization for each document.

- Organize your documents to help someone looking something up, more so than for cover-to-cover readers and more so than for the writers. Avoid stream of consciousness and stream of execution.

- If information is not yet known, never leave the space blank in the documentation. Mark it as to be filled in later.

- Review documents for adherence to structural form as well as accuracy of content.

- Listen for rejected requirements or design alternatives and practice writing them down (and compelling others to write them down).

- Include rationale in all of your documents.

References

1. Parnas, D.L., and Clements, P. *A Rational Design Process: How and Why To Fake It*, IEEE Transactions on Software Engineering, Vol. SE-12, Number 2, pp. 251-257, Feb. 1986.

2. Parnas, D.L. *Tabular Representation of Relations*, CRL Report #260, Software Engineering Research Group, CRL, McMaster University, Hamilton, Ontario, Canada L8S 4K1.

3. Heninger, K., Kallander, J., Parnas, D.L. and Shore, J. *Software Requirements for the A-7E Aircraft*, NRL Memorandum Report 3876, 27 November, 1978.

4. Heninger, K.L. "Specifying Software Requirements for Complex Systems: New Techniques and their Application," *IEEE Transactions on Software Engineering*, vol. SE-6, pp. 2-13, Jan. 1980.

5. Bass, Clements, Kazman: *Software Architecture in Practice*, Addison-Wesley Longman, 1998.

6. Parker, A., Heninger, K., Parnas, D. and Shore, J. *Abstract Interface Specifications for the A-7E Device Interface Module*, NRL Memorandum Report 4385, 20 November, 1980.

7. Britton, K.H., Parker, R.A. and Parnas, D.L. "A Procedure for Designing Abstract Interfaces for Device Interface Modules," *Proceedings of the Fifth International Conference on Software Engineering*, 1981.

8. Parnas, D.L. "On the Design and Development of Program Families," *IEEE Transactions on Software Engineering*, Vol. SE-2, No. 1, March, 1976.

9. Parnas, D.L., and Clements, P. "A Rational Design Process: How And Why To Fake It," *IEEE Transactions on Software Engineering*, Vol. SE-12, Number 2, pp. 251-257, Feb. 1986.

10. Erich Gamma, Richard Helm, Ralph Johnson, John Vlissides *Design Patterns: Elements of Reusable Object-Oriented Software* Addison-Wesley Professional Computing, 1995.

11. Brooks, F.P. Jr. *The Mythical Man-Month: Essays on Software Engineering (20th anniversary edition)*. Addison-Wesley Publishing Company, 1995.

12. Ibid.

CHAPTER **6**

Building Systems from Pieces with Component-Based Software Engineering

Alan W. Brown, Sterling Software

Background

Software projects rarely develop all of an application from scratch. Typically, an application is constructed from newly developed pieces, together with a collection of existing fragments produced during previous projects, acquired from third parties, or recovered from legacy systems. This form of reuse culture is essential to almost every organization developing software today. However, for the majority of organizations, most forms of reuse are ill-coordinated and poorly managed efforts. They succeed more as a result of individual heroics on the part of developers, than as a result of well-defined processes and tools supporting reuse as the accepted way of working.

Despite the current state of affairs, efforts toward institutionalizing software reuse have taken place for more than a decade. The dream of software engineering managers has been the move toward "software factories," where standard pieces of an application are selected from a catalog, assembled with some value-added local pieces or customizations, and rapidly deployed to the field to address a key business need.

In the 1980s, this vision was pursued by considering relatively broad application domains, gathering application pieces (or more generally "assets"), and waiting for the flood of customers to make use of them. It didn't work. The majority of "reuse initiatives" did not succeed, and in hindsight, it was for all of the obvious reasons: the technical infrastructure supporting reuse was immature, cataloging assets was hard, the assets were diverse and of varying quality, the interfaces and behavior of assets were poorly defined, and the culture of reuse undervalued and insufficiently rewarded by the sponsoring organizations.

The late-1990s is witnessing a massive revival of reuse initiatives under the banner of *component-based software engineering* (CBSE).[4, 9, 12, 13] Indeed, it difficult to attend any software development conference, or open the current issue of any software-focused journal or magazine without hearing a great deal about how components and component-based development will be central to the future of software engineering. Why is CBSE now being accepted across a wide portion of the software engineering community? The answer appears to lie in the fact that CBSE builds on many of the lessons of reuse from the past, while allowing organizations to take advantage of some recent technical and marketplace advances.

This chapter provides an introduction to the principles and practice of CBSE. It considers the questions that must be addressed by anyone interested in following a component-based approach to the development of large-scale mission-critical systems in any business domain. The chapter is organized around the following five broad steps to adopting a CBSE approach:

1. **Understand the context for CBSE.** Gain an appreciation for why components and component-based solutions can be valuable to your organization. In particular, you must begin by considering the strengths and weaknesses of a component approach in comparison with existing approaches and your own existing software practices.

2. **Decide what you mean by a component.** Currently, there is much confusion and misunderstanding about components. You must recognize the different perspectives on components and choose the one most appropriate to your needs.

3. **Take a component-oriented perspective on application design.** To be successful, a new design approach is needed using a component-oriented approach. You must understand this approach and begin to practice it.

4. **Select an appropriate component infrastructure.** There is a number of competing component infrastructure technologies to choose from. You must recognize their differences and select one of these infrastructures as the basis for your solution.

5. **Learn from others who are practicing a component-based approach.** Get help and advice from others providing or applying a component approach. Learn from their mistakes.

Each of these steps is addressed in subsequent sections of this chapter. A short summary and a list of references where many more details of component approaches can be found concludes the chapter.

The Context for CBSE

The past few years have seen a number of interesting changes in the needs, tactics, and expectations of application developers. This, in turn, has resulted in important new requirements for the methods, tools, and technologies required to support them. Consequently, a number of distinct advances spur today's interest in CBSE.

The first is the economic push moving many organizations toward greater use of available commercial solutions. In the commercial IT market, this has been through the outsourcing of many IT department functions, and the apparent economic advantages of the use of commercial packaged applications over homegrown solutions. The rapid growth of package application companies, such as SAP, BAAN, and Peoplesoft, are clear examples of this trend. Similarly, in the federal government, and, in particular, in the U.S. Department of Defense and its contractors, there have been recent mandates concerning the use of *Commercial Off-The-Shelf* (COTS) applications as a way to reduce costs, speed up technology refreshment, and improve interoperability.[14]

As a result, many application systems consist of a combination of commercial packages (typically with local adaptations and customizations), legacy data, homegrown solutions, and integration code. The only way to design, assemble, and maintain these application systems is to consider them to be collections of pieces modeled as interacting components.

Second, the style and architecture of the applications being developed has significantly changed. Over the past decade, there has been a major shift from centralized mainframe-based applications accessed via terminals over proprietary networks toward distributed, multitiered applications remotely accessible from a variety of client machines over intranets and the Internet. Building such applications requires an understanding of the strengths and limitations of Web-based network computing, and the use of methods and techniques designed to support software development in such an environment. Where organizations used to be involved in a small number of large projects, they now are typically involved in a larger number of smaller projects whose results must be shared.

Finally, there are a number of specific technological reasons why CBSE may be more effective in the late 1990s than a number of other reuse efforts were in the 1980s. These reasons include

- Object-oriented languages have a better structure for facilitating CBSE than traditional 3GLs. Smalltalk, C++, and Eiffel have had the most impact in this regard. As these OO languages have gained a foothold in the mainstream software development community, libraries of available classes have increased.

- We must also factor Java into this. Its OO structure makes it ideal for creating Java component libraries, and building Java applets and applications from them. An added advantage is that Java byte code is portable, and contains sufficient information that interface and inheritance details can be determined from a Java component, even when you don't have the component's source. A standard concerning the structure of Java applets, such as JavaBeans, further increases the ease with which Java components can be interchanged and assembled.

- Domain-specific libraries and frameworks are starting to appear. Concentrating on domain-specific component libraries means that a number of assumptions can be made about the likely architectures of applications in the domain, and the ways in which components usually interact. This makes the cataloguing and composition of components much easier to manage. It may also mean that the integration code can be predefined to some extent to include some intelligence about its tasks.

- The current CBSE initiatives are being vendor-led and supported. Inevitably, this means some of what is produced is hype and market positioning. However, it also means that robust technology support, an established market and distribution channels, and near-term orientation will provide usable tools in a reasonable timeframe. These will underwhelm the research community, but are likely to provide some measure of simple, effective tools and techniques for developers writing applications. Companies such as Microsoft, IBM, Sun, Sterling Software, Rational, Select, PowerSoft, Centura, and NeuronData have already announced detailed CBSE strategies and have released a number of tools.

- The Web infrastructure is maturing. While there is a great deal of chaos and competing technology, there is also some basic shape to the infrastructure that allows collections of independently developed software applications to be searched, remotely invoked, communicate, and share data. There is at least a hope that the technologies will converge, or at least interoperate sufficiently well that selecting among them will be based on price and performance rather than which integration strategy you want to be tied to.

Understanding Component Concepts

It is easy to provide a general, broad understanding of what is meant by a component: a component is a useful fragment of a software system that can be assembled with other fragments to form larger pieces or complete applications. Such a definition highlights the emphasis placed by CBSE on the partitioning of an application into pieces, and on assembly as a primary means of application construction.

However, to be able to compare and contrast specific component technologies and approaches, a much more precise analysis of component characteristics is required. For this discussion, we develop a detailed conceptual model of component concepts capturing many important aspects of a component. To do this, we consider three particular perspectives that reveal many of the most interesting characteristics of components:

- **Packaging perspective.** A component as the unit of packaging, distribution, or delivery

- **Service perspective**. A component as the provider of services

- **Integrity perspective**. A component as a data integrity or encapsulation boundary

These perspectives are abstracted from a number of concrete uses of components in a range of component technologies. In each of these technologies, it is possible to consider their approach as primarily rooted in one of these perspectives.

Packaging Perspective

The packaging perspective considers a component to be an organizational concept, focusing on identifying a set of elements that can be reused as a unit. The emphasis here is on *reuse*. This is a broad definition and covers any reusable application development artifact including documents, source code files, object modules, link libraries, databases, and so on.

This is the perspective assumed by UML 1.0 and 1.1, defining a component as follows:

> "A component is a reusable part that provides the physical packaging of model elements."

It is useful to distinguish a number of different kinds of artifacts that could be considered a component. UML, for example, identifies a number of specializations (or stereotypes) of component such as executable, document, file, library, and table. From this perspective, each of these can be considered a particular kind of component.

Some people also find it useful to consider a special kind of packaging component focused on the physical packaging of an executable component. This is valuable, for example, when a component is an executable file or a Dynamic Link Library (DLL). In these cases, there is often specific information needed about the physical characteristics of the component required for determining where and how that component executes. This is a specialization of a packaging component referred to as a component server, as illustrated in Figure 6.1. This shows *Component Server* as a specialization of *Packaging Component*.

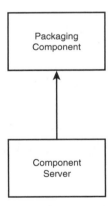

Figure 6.1 *Packaging component and component server.*

The packaging of a component (executable) into servers generally will be based on the deployment or distribution requirements of that component. For example, a large enterprise-level component that manages one or more disparate databases may be partitioned into a number of DLLs, which can be allocated to specific nodes in an enterprise network. At the opposite end of the spectrum, simple desktop-based components can be bundled into a single library or executable to simplify delivery.

Service Perspective

The service perspective considers a component to be a software entity that offers services (operations or functions) to its consumers. The emphasis here is on components as *service providers*. Designing and implementing an application involves understanding how a collection of components collaborates by making calls to each others' services.

This perspective highlights the importance of a contract between the provider and the consumer of a set of services. Services are grouped into coherent, contractual units called *interfaces*. An interface is a set of operations that a consuming component can call on to access the services of another component. The interface can be compared to a contract because it describes everything that a potential consumer of that component's services can rely on, and is the only way for a potential customer of those services to gain access to them.

This is the perspective taken in the *Component Description Model* (Cde), part of the *Open Information Model* (OIM) supplied with the Microsoft Repository.[5] The Cde offers a services-oriented component definition:

> "A component is a software package, which offers services through interfaces."

The service perspective of a component is a "logical" notion of a component because how a developer decides to partition the functionality required into meaningful service components is essentially a design decision. With respect to the earlier description of the "physical" packaging perspective of a component, a many-to-many relationship may exist between a service component and a component server. For example, we may decide that a set of services for managing the maintenance of a list of customers forms the "logical" service component we will call "Customer Management." In a particular implementation, this may be realized as many "physical" component servers via a set of related DLLs. This is illustrated in Figure 6.2. Both *Service Component* and *Component Server* are specializations of *Packaging Component*.

By focusing on the notion of a contract, the service perspective introduces an important distinction between the specification of a component (*what* it does) and its implementation and executable forms (*how* it does it). This distinction is fundamental to the management of dependencies between components and begins to address the important requirement to be able to *replace* a component with minimal impact on the consumer, often referred to as "plug-and-play."

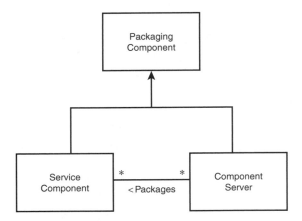

FIGURE 6.2 *The packaging and service perspectives.*

This distinction between specification and implementation is important. Consumers of a component should only be dependent on the specification of that component. Any dependency on its implementation (whether through direct knowledge or due to unspecified assumptions which happen to be supported) will mean that the application is likely to fail when the component is upgraded or replaced.

Integrity Perspective

Although the service perspective allows dependencies between components to be managed, it does not identify the component replacement boundary. This is a further perspective on components emphasizing that a component can provide an independent, replaceable unit of behavior. We can refer to this as an *independent* component.

The *integrity perspective* defines a component as an implementation encapsulation boundary, that set of software that collectively maintains the integrity of the data it manages, and, therefore, is independent of the implementation of other components. This criterion is a necessary condition for *component replacement.*

An integrity perspective is the approach supported by a number of different reuse-oriented technologies. Sterling Software's CBSE96 standard, for example, supports the reuse of business functionality across applications built using the COOL:Gen tool.[15] It defines a component as follows:

> "A component is an independently deliverable package of software operations that can be used to build applications or larger components."

This emphasis on independence is important because service components do not necessarily have implementation independence. Typically, they share data or have some other dependency on another component. As a result, collections of service components may be part of one independent, replaceable component. An independent component and all its subcomponents form a single implementation encapsulation boundary and therefore can be replaced as a single unit. Subcomponents are still components in that they offer services through interfaces, but they do not designate an encapsulation boundary. This is illustrated in Figure 6.3.

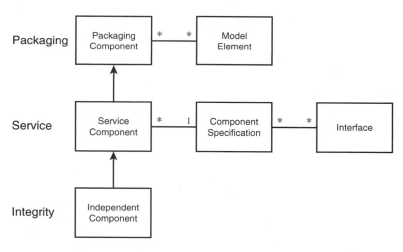

FIGURE 6.3 *Three component perspectives.*

In Figure 6.3, we illustrate the relationships between the three perspectives on components and enrich the conceptual model by introducing interfaces, component specifications, and model elements. Each of these perspectives builds on the other. The service perspective, for example, is a specialization of the packaging perspective.

An Illustrative Example: Microsoft Excel

To illustrate these different perspectives, consider a familiar component-based application, Microsoft Excel. The packaged item is *excel.exe*. This is a single "physical" component server and contains a number of "logical" service components such as *Application*, *Chart*, and *Sheet*. Each of these is an independent component providing an encapsulation boundary. As a result, each of them could potentially be individually replaced. An alternative implementation of the *Sheet* component, for example, could be implemented which could interoperate correctly with the *Application* component, without having any implementation knowledge of the *Application* component.

Within each component, there are a number of subcomponents. The *Sheet* component contains the *Range* and *Cell* components, for example. But *Sheet*, *Range* and *Cell* share implementation and data knowledge and so are not independently replaceable; they can only be replaced as a unit.

Table 6.1 provides an illustrative categorization of a variety of existing software development artifacts into one of the preceding perspectives. The categorization given for a particular item relies on assumptions about that particular item. Class libraries, for example, have been placed in the packaging column because they do not separate specification from implementation, and reuse (through implementation inheritance) usually makes use of implementation knowledge. Frameworks have been placed in the integrity column on the assumption that they are binary modules that make calls to application-specific extension code, and their implementation logic is not exposed.

TABLE 6.1 EXAMPLE COMPONENT CATEGORIZATION

Packaging	Service	Integrity
Files, documents, directories	Database services	Databases
	Operating system services	Operating systems
Source code files		Frameworks
Class libraries	Function libraries	ActiveX controls
Templates, tables	System utilities	Some COM classes
Executables, dll's	Individual API functions	Java Applets
		Applications
	COM classes	Complete APIs

Designing Component-Based Solutions

Earlier sections of this chapter highlighted the differences that exist between component-oriented design and traditional application design. To take advantage of CBSE requires developers to begin to think differently about how they design and assemble applications. The goal of application development shifts from building single applications, to one of building a portfolio of reusable components from which a family of applications can be assembled. Taking this approach raises some important questions, including the following:

- What is an appropriate size and scope for a component?

- How do I describe dependencies that may exist among components in an assembled application?

- How do I document components to allow others to find them, and to assess their value within a given context?

- How does the maintenance and evolution of my application change when I make use of components? How do I manage this evolution?

Traditional software engineering methods provide little help with these questions. To answer them requires fundamental changes in the way in which an organization carries out its software development and maintenance. These CBSE-oriented methods must allow applications to be developed by focusing on interfaces and interface-based design, and by supporting the selection, evaluation, and assembly of components to create new applications. Specifically, the requirements for tools supporting CBSE-oriented methods include the need to perform the following tasks:

- Model interfaces and component specifications as first class elements in the design process

- Provide improved modeling for inter- and intracomponent dependencies, and hence allow greater visualization of the logical application architecture

- Enable component specifications to be developed independently of a specific implementation technology, facilitating application assembly from components implemented in multiple technologies

- Support new component-oriented development approaches based on object-oriented analysis and design techniques

Fortunately, a number of recent advances in modeling techniques and tools have taken place. These advances include the standardization on a common notation for behavior-based design of systems, and the emergence of methods for component design targeting this notation.

The Basic Steps of Component Modeling

How do we describe the behavior expected from each component, and arrive at an appropriate component architecture for our application? The answer lies in following the steps of a component-based modeling approach. Broadly speaking, this consists of describing the behavior within the domain of interest, and packaging that behavior into meaningful pieces that together form the application of interest. As shown in Figure 6.4, translating the business need to a business solution requires three key steps: understanding the context, defining the architecture, and provisioning the solution. These may occur in any order.

In fact, it is typical that as a new development project starts many aspects of the provisioned solution are already fixed (that is, use of legacy code, a technical infrastructure, and various existing practices).

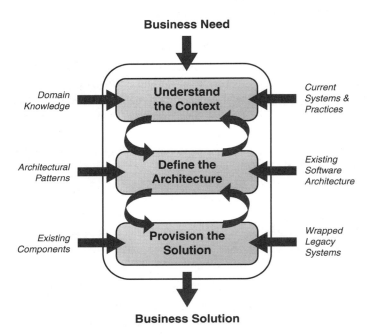

FIGURE 6.4 *Elements of a component-based development approach.*

Understand the Context

Two aspects of the domain of interest must be described: the *static* and *dynamic* behavior. These may be in the form of a high level description of some of the primary business types in a domain, or a may be a more detailed domain model. Much of this could be modeled via a combination of class modeling, use-case modeling, and sequence/collaboration modeling.

For each type in a domain, the user continues by describing its features (attributes and operations) in detail. Particularly important are the pre and post conditions that define the semantics of each operation by describing the state that must exist before the operation can take place, and the state that will result having executed the operation. Informal definitions of the pre and post conditions can be given. However, more valuable are pre and post conditions in some formal, verifiable notation supported by the component modeling tool.

Define the Architecture

Having modeled the static and dynamic aspects of a domain, the user must decide how that behavior should be packaged in terms of implementable units, which may be developed independently, shared across projects, and executed on different machines.

In particular, it is likely that a number of the interfaces will be realized by implementations that come from existing legacy systems, packages, or third-party components. Hence, to a large extent, this packaging decision may have already been carried out, or may require writing of wrappers to present that functionality via the specified interfaces. In any case, the specification provides the understanding of how that functionality can be accessed from other components.

In general, component packaging takes place by defining which interfaces will be packaged within a single component specification. Each behavior-bearing type is an interface offering a set of operations. The user selectively decides on the grouping of those interfaces into component specifications. Hence, each component specification is an identification of the interfaces it supports.

Now we are able to view the defined functionality in terms of a set of components. These components have dependencies based on the previously modeled interactions among their constituent interfaces. The collection of components and their dependencies can be viewed as a component specification architecture for the application.

Note that modeling the component specification architecture is most often an ongoing parallel activity to behavior specification. An initial, first cut component architecture can be produced based on a high-level domain model and knowledge of existing components or legacy code to be used as part of the implementation. This then can be successively refined as the individual interfaces and component specifications are identified in more detail.

Provision the Solution

The final system will be implemented through detailed design and implementation of each of the constituent components, together with their assembly into an overall system as dictated by the component specification architecture. There are many potential choices for implementation technologies. Sometimes, the choice of implementation technology has already been made (for example, when reusing existing components or wrapping legacy code). Other times, the implementers are free to choose an implementation technology that matches their domain needs and skills.

Additionally, the implementation choice is governed by the particular component technology infrastructure to be used. For example, if Microsoft's COM+ has been chosen, then the implementation languages and tools will be those supported by Microsoft: Visual Basic, Java, or C++ via the Microsoft Visual Studio tools. In most cases, the choice of component infrastructure technology is made at a corporate or departmental level. In any case, the components to be implemented must all be designed and coded using techniques appropriate to the technology.

Having created detailed, well-defined interfaces, the implemented components can be developed independently. Dependencies among components are well-known, and the sharing among components defined by the specified interfaces. From the component models and component specification architecture it is possible to generate the interface description language code used by the component infrastructure technology (for example, the OMG's Interface Definition Language (IDL)). A number of products such as Rational's Rose and Sterling Software's COOL:Jex are already able to generate IDL from appropriate design models. The component implementers then would be responsible for making the design decisions and implementing the described functionality.

As implementation proceeds, much more is learned about the application being developed, the needs of the users, and the architecture of the required system. Frequently, while developing the component implementations and assembling the final application, it will be required to change the component specifications or component dependencies accordingly. To be effective, these changes must be documented within the component specifications and component architecture diagrams, maintaining this tight relationship between understanding the context, defining the architecture, and provisioning the solution. Unfortunately, to achieve this with current tools and technologies is far from automatic, and requires a great deal of discipline on behalf of the developers.

The Unified Modeling Language (UML)

One of the most frustrating problems facing many application developers is the lack of consistency of modeling notations used across the software engineering community. A great deal of effort is spent in understanding unfamiliar notations, converting models from one notation to another, and retraining staff on new notations as they arise. To address this problem, a consortium of tool vendors led by Grady Booch, Jim Rumbaugh, and Ivar Jacobsen at Rational Corp. is involved in an effort to create a single, unified notation that can be used for describing software systems. This notation is called the *Unified Modeling Language* (UML).[10] The latest version of the UML was submitted and has been approved as a standard by the consortium of organizations that form the Object Management Group (OMG). Already, there are over 20 tools supporting some parts of the UML standard.

Although initiated by Rational Corp., a number of organizations have been contributing members of the UML consortium from its earliest days. Each of the different consortium members comes to the table with very different perspectives. Organizations such as Sterling Software and ICON Computing have ensured that the UML is a suitable basis for modeling components and component-oriented applications. Specifically, UML includes broad, general notions of components, component dependency, and collaborations.

As illustrated in Figure 6.5, the diagram shows a component, *Component A*, that realizes interfaces *Ione* and *Itwo*. Realization of an interface by a component means that the component offers the operations defined by the interface. A component may realize any number of interfaces. *Component A* is also dependent on the interface *Ithree*, as shown by the dashed arrow. Dependency of a component on an interface means that the component requires the services of other components, which realize the interface. A component may be dependent on any number of interfaces.

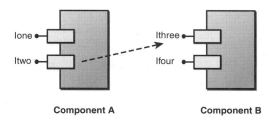

FIGURE 6.5   *An example of components and component dependencies in UML.*

Additional semantics can be applied to the UML to allow it to be used to model a stronger notion of component behavior through formally defined interfaces. The ubiquity of UML enables components to be defined using one tool, independently from its implementation via another tools. The component specifications can be stored in a component catalog, and capture sufficient semantics to enable meaningful analysis by subsequent third-party component implementation tools.

Component Modeling Using the UML

The UML provides a basic notation for capturing many aspects of components and component-based applications. However, taking full advantage of CBSE requires new analysis and design methods that are much more closely aligned with CBSE principles. The characteristics of such a method would include at least the following:

- Systems can be modeled as collections of interacting components.

- System behavior can be analyzed in terms of a set of component interfaces.

- Component specifications can be described independently of the components' implementations.

- A precise, formal notation is available for describing component specifications, sufficient for rigorous analysis of those specification against a user's needs.

- Patterns of component interactions can be explicitly modeled, and subsequently reused across system designs.

- A rigorous, repeatable refinement process is followed to relate an abstract description of a system's behavior to a more detailed one.

- Modeling concepts are mapped directly to concrete representations in UML.

- Familiar, best-practice modeling concepts from current object-oriented and structured methods are incorporated wherever possible.

These characteristics provide the basis of a number of CBSE-oriented methods currently being developed. Four categories of such methods are worthy of note.

First, the work by Bertrand Meyer on "design-by-contract" has had a great deal of influence on component modeling approaches.[16] In support of his Eiffel language, Meyer proposed an approach to component-based development in which he compared the formal description of how components interact to a legal contract between two parties. He then describes an approach to the creation and management of these contracts as a primary design artifact. The Eiffel language enables these contracts to be directly encoded in the language. The experiences gained by this approach are documented in his very well-referenced book on object-oriented design.

Second, coming from the object-oriented analysis community is a component-oriented approach authored by Desmond D'Souza and Alan Cameron Wills called *Catalysis*.[6] It is described as a "next generation methodology for modeling and constructing open systems from components and frameworks."

While the details of Catalysis are somewhat complex, the approach itself is based on a small number of underlying concepts. The four main concepts it depends upon are types, conformance, collaborations, and frameworks. From a very high-level perspective, Catalysis supports the modeling of a system by using type models to capture the external visible behavior of sets of objects. Refinements from abstract to more detailed descriptions of a system are recorded by capturing conformance between types. The interactions among types are modeled as collaborations. This captures a set of actions involving multiple, typed objects playing defined roles with respect to each other. Recurring patterns of structure or behavior are captured using frameworks. Placeholders can be used in a framework to make it more generic, and to widen its applicability.

Third, a number of approaches to component-based development are being developed in support of the Java programming language. Java explicitly supports the notion of interface (separate from class) as part of the programming language. In helping people to design applications targeting Java, authors such as Peter Coad have developed techniques for interface-based design.[7] These techniques share many of the characteristics of component-based applications, sharing pieces of Java programs as components through libraries.

Fourth, vendors of enterprise application development tools have developed a number of proprietary component-oriented design methods. As these vendors began to encourage the creation of large-scale applications from available assets (such as legacy code, packages, third-party solutions), they required methods advice for their customers on how to achieve the assembly of those pieces within their own tool environments. This resulted in a variety of component-oriented methods and techniques. The best known of these includes CBD96 from Sterling Software,[15] Select's Perspective method,[17] and Rational's Unified Process.[18]

The first wave of tools supporting these CBSE-oriented methods is beginning to appear. In some cases, such as Rational Corp.'s Rose 98 and ICON Computing's Xtend:Specs, this is through additions to existing products. In other cases, such as Select's Component Manager, Sterling Software's COOL:Spex, and Object International's Together/J, they have been purpose-built to support component specification and component architecture visualization. Such tools can be used to describe the interfaces offered by the components and the collaborations that occur among them when constructing an application from components.

A key aspect of these new tools is that they support a strong notion of interface-based design as a key approach to the development of component-based applications. For example, Rose 98 is building on the previous work of the "three amigos" at Rational, the UML, and the Objectory approach. In contrast, COOL:Spex draws many of its ideas from the Catalysis approach to component development. Catalysis is a method and set of techniques successfully applied to a number of large software development projects. It is the basis for the COOL:Spex product in the sense that Catalysis provides the conceptual approach to component specification and design that flavors many aspects of the development process when using COOL:Spex. As a result, the diagramming notations and techniques supported by COOL:Spex are those that have been tried and tested in Catalysis and lead developers to produce accurate and complete component specifications captured as type models, interface models, and collaboration models. This is illustrated in the Catalysis-style collaboration diagram shown in Figure 6.6.

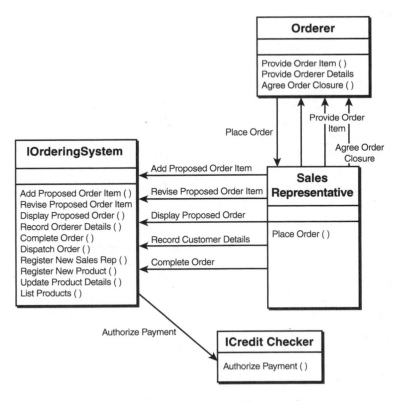

FIGURE 6.6 *An example catalysis-style collaboration diagram.*

In Figure 6.6, the double border boxes represent potential interfaces, with services offered by each interface listed inside the box. Interactions among interfaces to carry out a task are shown as arrows labeled with the service being requested. These requests form a partially ordered set of actions required to achieve a high-level task (in this case the task of handling an order for a product).

Choosing a Component Infrastructure

To support a component-based approach, it is common to use some form of component infrastructure (sometimes also called "component-oriented middleware") to handle all of the complex details of component coordination.[11] Essentially, the component infrastructure provides a common set of component management services made available to all components interested in using that infrastructure. The component infrastructure imposes constraints on the design and implementation of the components. In return for abiding by these constraints, however, the component developer and application assembler are relieved from the burden of developing many complex services within their application.

To understand component infrastructures, it is necessary to understand the kinds of services the infrastructure can make available, and the different competing infrastructure implementations currently available.

Component Infrastructure Services

The use of a component infrastructure arises as a result of a simple premise: the services common to many components should be extracted and provided once in a consistent way to all components. This provides greater control and flexibility over those common services, and allows component developers to concentrate on the specification and implementation of business aspects of the component.

There are many kinds of services that the component infrastructure may offer. However, as described by Roger Sessions,[11] the component infrastructure is typically responsible for at least the following categories of services:

- **Packaging**. When developing a component, it is necessary to provide some description of that component in a form that is understandable to the component infrastructure. At a minimum, the component infra-structure needs to know what services the component makes available, and the signatures of the methods which invoke those services. Requests for external component services also must be made in some standard form so that they can be recognized by the component infrastructure.

- **Distribution**. The distribution services are responsible for activating and deactivating component instances, and for managing the allocation of component instances to remote host processes on which they execute. After a client of a component service makes a request, the component infrastructure is responsible for routing that request to the appropriate component instance, which may involve activating a component instance to service the request. This provides location transparency between clients and servers of requests; the client does not need to know where the component instance servicing the request resides, and the component instance does not need to have knowledge of the origin of possible requests.

- **Security**. In distributed systems, there must be services for authenticating the source of requests and responses to requests, and for privacy of connections when information is transmitted. The component infrastructure may provide various levels of privacy to ensure secure, trusted connections between components can take place.

- **Transaction Management**. As each component may manage its own persistent data, a single high-level function may require many interactions among components, affecting many individually managed pieces of data. As a result, partially completed functions have the potential for leaving this collection of data in an inconsistent state. Distributed transaction management is provided by the component infrastructure to manage and coordinate these complex component interactions.

- **Asynchronous communication**. It is not always necessary or possible to communicate synchronously between components. Because components may be distributed across multiple host processes, there is always the possibility that some components will be unavailable to respond to requests. The component infrastructure supports asynchronous communication among components, typically through some form of queuing system for requests.

Component Infrastructure Implementations

In the world of component infrastructure technologies, the battle lines have already been drawn. Currently, there are three dominant component infrastructure choices possible: The Object Management Group's (OMG's) Object Management Architecture, Microsoft's distributed computing architecture, and Sun's Java-based distributed component technology. In each of these, there is a vision for building enterprise-scale component-based applications supported by a set of standards and products. Here, we briefly review the main elements of these approaches.

OMG's Object Management Architecture

The need for a widely agreed component infrastructure led to the formation of the *Object Management Group* (OMG), a large consortium of over 800 companies attempting to come to agreement on an appropriate component model and services for building component-based distributed systems. The OMG is a large and complex organization, with many special interest groups, focus areas, and task forces. It attempts to provide standards for building component-oriented applications, and encourages those standards to be followed by vendors of component infrastructure products and developers of component-oriented applications. While there are many OMG standards under development, a much smaller number is currently being actively supported by products.

OMG's vision for component-oriented applications is defined in its *Object Management Architecture* (OMA).[1] This consists of a specification of the underlying distributed architecture for component communication providing the packaging services and some of the distribution services. The remaining component infrastructure services are developed to make use of those services.

The main component infrastructure standard provided by OMG is the *Common Object Request Broker Architecture* (CORBA).[2] This defines the basic distribution architecture for component-oriented applications. There are three major aspects of CORBA:

- The OMG's Interface Definition Language (IDL), which describes how business functionality is packaged for external access through interfaces.

- The CORBA component model describing how components can make requests of each others' services.

- The Internet Interoperability Protocol (IIOP), which allows different CORBA implementations to interoperate.

Together with the CORBA standard, a set of additional capabilities is defined in the CORBA Services standards. A wide range of services has been defined, or is currently under investigation. However, the following services are those that are most often found in currently available implementations:

- Life cycle services, which control the creation and release of component instances.

- Naming services, which allow identification and sharing of component instances.

- Security services, which provide privacy of connection between a client and provider of services.

- Transaction service, which allows a user to control the start and completion of distributed transactions across components.

A number of implementations conforming to the OMG standards are now available on a variety of platforms. For distributed applications executing across heterogeneous platforms, the OMG approach to component infrastructure has been shown to be a viable way to build component-based applications. There are a number of examples of successful component-based implementations in applications domains such as banking, telecommunications, and retail.

Microsoft's Distributed Computing Architecture

As can be expected, Microsoft has had a major influence in how people think about components and CBSE. As Microsoft shifts its focus from desktop applications to enterprise-scale commercial applications, it has described its vision for the future of application development as a component-oriented approach building on Microsoft's existing dominant desktop technologies.

To enable sharing of functionality across desktop application, Microsoft developed the Component Object Model (COM) as the basis for interapplication communication.[8] Realizing the value of COM as a generic approach to component interoperation, Microsoft has defined its strategy of component-based applications to consist of two parts. The first is its packaging and distribution services, Distributed COM (DCOM), providing intercomponent communication.[3] The second is currently referred to as Microsoft's Distributed interNet Applications (DNA) architecture, providing the additional categories of component infrastructure services making use of DCOM.

The packaging and distribution services implemented in DCOM, consist of the following three major aspects:

- The Microsoft Interface Definition Language (MIDL), which describes how business functionality is packaged for external access through interfaces.

- The COM component model describing how components can make requests of each others' services.

- The DCOM additions to COM providing support for location transparency of component access across a network.

The following additional component infrastructure services are provided by Microsoft via two products, both making extensive use of the underlying packaging and distribution services:

- The Microsoft Transaction Service (MTS), which provides security and transaction management services.

- The Microsoft Message Queue (MSMQ), which provide support for asynchronous communication between components via message queues.

The Microsoft component infrastructure services offer significant functionality to builders of component-based applications for Windows platforms. For anyone building a distributed WindowsNT solution, these services provide essential capabilities to greatly reduce the cost of assembling and maintaining component-based applications.

Sun's Java-Based Distributed Component Environment
One of the most astonishing successes of the past five years has been the rapid adoption of Java as the language for developing client-side applications for the Web. However, the impact of Java is likely to be much more than a programming language for animating Web pages. Java is in an advantageous position to become the backbone of a set of technologies for developing component-based, distributed systems. Part of this is a result of a number of properties of Java as a language for writing programs, including the following:

- Java was designed specifically to build network-based applications. The language includes support for distributed, multithreaded control of applications.

- Java's runtime environment allows pieces of Java applications to be changed while a Java-based application is executing. This supports various kinds of incremental evolution of applications.

- Java is an easier language to learn and use for component-based applications. Many of the more complex aspects of memory management have been simplified in Java.

- Java includes constructs within the language supporting key component-based concepts such as separating component specification and implementation via the interface and class constructs.

However, Java is much more than a programming language. There are a number of Java technologies supporting the development of component-based, distributed systems. This is what allows us to consider Java as a component infrastructure technology. More specifically, there are a number of Java technologies providing packaging and distribution services. These include the following:

- JavaBeans is the client-focused component model for Java. It is a set of standards for packaging Java-implemented services as components. By following this standard, tools can be built to inspect and control various properties of the component.

- Remote Method Invocation (RMI), which allows Java classes on one machine to access the services of classes on another machine.

- Java Naming and Directory Interface (JNDI), which manages the unique identification of Java classes in a distributed environment.

An additional set of technologies support the remaining component infrastructure services. These are necessary to allow Java to be used for the development of enterprise-scale distributed systems. These technologies are defined within the Enterprise JavaBeans standard. Enterprise JavaBeans (EJB) is a standard for server-side portability of Java applications. It provides the definition of a minimum set services that must be available on any server conforming to the specification. The services include the following:

- Process and thread dispatching, and scheduling

- Resource management

- Naming and directory services

- Network transport services

- Security services

- Transaction management services

The EJB specification has only recently been announced; however, a number of vendors have already begun to provide EJB-compliant containers. These implement the component infrastructure services that any application developer can rely on when designing a component-based application in Java. The strong support for EJB from both Sun and IBM provides significant impetus to the case for EJB as an important player in the future of component infrastructure services.

Current Practice in CBSE

A number of organizations are practicing CBSE today using a variety of technologies. While many component approaches are limited to client desktop applications (via ActiveX controls, visual JavaBeans, and so on), there are others that are beginning to address larger scale applications with significant business functionality. There are a number of very valuable lessons being learned by these pioneers of component approaches. Originally, many of these lessons were related to the vagaries and incompatibilities of specific component technologies. More recently, a number of published accounts discuss a much broader range of critical success factors for component approaches in areas such as organizational readiness, costs of component development, and management of deployed component-based applications.

Much can be learned from these existing users of components. There are four main ways that a great deal of useful information can be obtained; special interest groups, vendor-led user groups, specialist component service providers, and published experience reports and advice.

Special Interest Groups

As component-based approaches begin to gain in popularity, a number of special interest groups have been formed which concentrate in this area. These groups tend to offer broad-based advice and experience covering a range of technologies. While a number of these groups exist, one particular group worthy of attention is the Butler Group CBD forum (see `http://www.butlerforums.com/cbdindex.htm` for more details).

The CBD Forum provides a source of information and best practice on management issues surrounding delivery of enterprise-level business software applications. The CBD Forum provides vendor independent information which is based on practical user experience. The resources of the Forum are organized to allow users of component technology to learn from independent, unbiased sources, and to avoid costly mistakes.

A particular initiative of interest is the CBD Forums attempts to define a set of *Universal Component Concepts* (UCC). The UCC initiative aims to deliver a set of generally applicable concepts covering the basics of component-based development. It is envisaged that the set of concepts will provide clarity and lead to better general understanding in the area of components and component-based approaches. The initiative, for example, will aim to clear up common misunderstanding between objects and components. In addition, the initiative aims to identify the generic process framework needed for component-based development.

As a result, the CBD Forum tries to provide insight on architecture, process and technology issues. Forum members include development managers, architects, strategists, project managers, analysts, and developers covering all types of technology and business environments.

Vendor-Led User Groups

With the availability of a range of tools supporting component-based approaches, many vendors are organizing user groups to share best practices in the use of those technologies. In many cases, these user groups offer the opportunity for those organizations new to component-based approaches to learn from the practical experience of others based on previous knowledge of the use of a specific technology solution.

All major component technology providers offer user groups of one sort or another. To illustrate the most advanced groups in this area, we briefly consider the Sterling Software Component-based Development Advisory Board (CAB) (see `http://www.cool.sterling.com/cbd` for more details).

The Sterling Software CAB was formed in 1994 and today consists of over 80 member companies and is growing rapidly. The CAB is a voluntary, self-run group whose primary objective is to facilitate the sharing of information regarding component-based development. The CAB provides a forum to network, to ask others for their opinions, to learn about different approaches to CBD, and to influence Sterling Software's direction in regards to its component technologies. Information is exchanged via monthly teleconference calls, worldwide biannual meetings, and a dedicated Web site which delivers meeting notes, best practices, and a library of research materials.

Specialist Component Service Providers

As component approaches have become more popular, a number of specialist component service providers have emerged to support those interested in taking this approach. These services are an invaluable "jump-start" for organizations using a CBSE approach. There appear to be four major roles assumed by these organizations:

- **Component developers**. A number of organizations specialize in developing components for a particular component infrastructure technology. Their primary business is the sale, distribution, and support of these components. Examine the Web sites and literature of the major component infrastructure vendors and supporters to obtain lists of component providers for a specific technology. For example, the OMG maintains a product and services guide for buyers of CORBA-based products at its Web site (`http://www.omg.org`).

- **Component brokers**. The growth and variety of component providers has led to some organizations specializing as component brokers. Essentially, they offer a single point of contact for a variety of components from many vendors targeting many domains and multiple component infrastructure technologies. One of the best known of these component brokers is Component Source. Third-party component providers become members of Component Source and make their products available on the Component Source Web site (http://www.componentsource.com).

- **Component educators**. Interest in component technologies and component-oriented design practices have also stimulated the education market to offer a number of appropriate courses, tutorials, and certification examinations. Most often, these are focused on a particular component technology or development approach, and are associated with a vendor in support of that technology. However, a number of independent organizations are now offering courses in general component concepts and their application. A Web search will result in many organizations specializing in different kinds of customers.

- **Component-based consulting**. One of the best ways of getting started with component-based approaches is with the help and guidance of experienced consultants who have developed similar projects in the past. Their mentoring and advice can be essential to the success of the first component-based projects that an organization attempts. Mentoring services are very diverse in nature and frequently span broad technical and business areas. The most common use of a mentor is in situations where a client is moving from one technology to another. The mentor typically advises the client's strategist, planners, designers and developers on matters requiring architecture, costing, estimating, business judgements, case histories, human resources, access to technical information and actual hands on instruction, and on occasion, production of the actual results. Again, these consulting services are usually tied to a specific component technology and can be found by accessing the technology vendor's Web site.

Experience Reports and Advice

The amount of available literature on components and component-oriented approaches is continuing to grow. There are now books describing the details of every kind of component technology, and frequent technical articles in software-focused magazines and journals.

However, perhaps the best source of advice on the practical application of component technology appears in a number of specialist magazines and conference targeting component-based approaches to software engineering. Two of the most influential are the monthly magazines *Component Strategies* and *Distributed Computing*. Both of these magazines specifically target the development of large-scale distributed systems using component technologies. Every edition contains success stories, experience reports, and practical advice on the application of component technologies.

Equally important are a number of conference series aimed at educating organization on component-based approaches. While many conferences target specific technologies or approaches, the most significant conference series aimed at a broad set of component technologies is the SIGS-sponsored Component Development conference series (see `http://www.componentdevelopment.com` for more details). At these conferences specific examples of the application of a range of component-oriented approaches is presented.

Summary

Component-based development of software is an important development approach for software systems that must be rapidly assembled, take advantage of the latest Web-based technologies, and be amenable to change as both the technology and application needs evolve. One of the key challenges facing software engineers is to make CBSE an efficient and effective practice that does not succumb to the shortcomings of previous reuse-based efforts of the 1970s and 1980s.

Fortunately, the past few years has seen a number of major advances in both our understanding of the issues to be addressed to make reuse successful and the technology support available to realize those advances. These are embodied in the rapidly growing field of component-based software engineering. This approach encourages a new way of application development that focuses on the following:

- Separation of component specification from component implementation to enable technology-independent application design

- Use of more rigorous descriptions of component behaviors via methods that encourage interface-level design

- Flexible tool architectures for CBSE leveraging existing tool technologies and standards

This chapter has identified a set of steps that must be taken by anyone wanting to adopt a component-based approach to software engineering, and discussed each if these steps in detail. These have been explored in the context of improving our understanding of CBSE, assessing the current state of CBSE technology, and improving an organization's software practices to enhance the effectiveness and viability of large-scale software development through the reuse of components. This will help to lead organizations toward an interface-based approach to application development and design that encourages the creation of systems that are more easily distributed, repartitioned, and reused. These attributes are essential to improve the future effectiveness of organizations in their development and use of large-scale software systems.

Acknowledgments

The ideas described in this chapter have been developed cooperatively with a number of colleagues and former colleagues at Sterling Software. In particular, I recognize the important contributions made by Balbir Barn, John Cheesman, John Daniels, and John Dodd. Additionally, Doug McCammish and Kurt Wallnau provided many useful comments on earlier drafts of this chapter.

References

1. R. Ofali, D. Harkey, J. Edwards, "The Essential Distributed Object Survival Guide," John Wiley Press, 1996.

2. OMG, "The Common Object Request Broker Architecture (CORBA)," Object Management Group, Framingham, MA, 1995, `http://www.omg.org`.

3. Microsoft, "Distributed Component Object Model Protocol DCOM/1.0 Specification," May 1996, `http://www.microsoft.com/oledev/olecom/dcomsepc.txt`.

4. D. Kara, "Components Defined," Application Development Trends, June 1996. Available also at `http://spgnet.com/ADT/june96/fe603too.html`.

5. Microsoft; "Component Description Information Model"; July 1997. See `http://www.microsoft.com/repository`.

6. D.F. D'Souza and A.C. Wills, "Objects, Components, and Frameworks with UML – the Catalysis Approach"; Addison-Wesley, 1998.

7. P. Coad and M. Mayfield, "Java Design: Building Better Apps and Applets," Prentice-Hall, 1997.

8. R. Sessions, "COM and DCOM," John Wiley Press, 1998.

9. C. Szyperski, "Component Software: Beyond Object-Oriented Programming," Addison-Wesley, 1998.

10. M. Fowler and K. Scott, "UML Distilled," Addison-Wesley, 1998.

11. R. Sessions, "Component-Oriented Middleware," Component Strategies, October 1998.

12. A.W. Brown and K.C. Wallnau, "The Current State of CBSE," IEEE Software September/October 1998.

13. A.W. Brown (ed.), "Component-Based Software Engineering," IEEE Computer Society Press, 1997.

14. "Monograph Series: Commercial Software in Government Systems," Software Engineering Institute, Carnegie Mellon University, available at http://www.sei.cmu.edu/cbs/monographs.html.

15. Sterling Software, "The CBSE96 Standard," Version 2.1, http://www.cool.sterling.com/CBSE/CBSE96.htm, 1998

16. B. Meyer, "Object-Oriented Software Construction," 2nd Edition, Prentice-Hall, 1997.

17. P. Allen and S. Frost, "Component-Based Development for Enterprise Systems: Applying the Select Perspective," Cambridge University Press, 1997.

PART III

Quality Projects

CHAPTER 7

Teamwork Considerations for Superior Software Development

by Herb Krasner

Introduction

Software development is like a football team that is in need of player development, a good play book, practice sessions, more effective teamwork, and good coaching.

When software engineers are asked about problems they have encountered when working in software teams they often cite:

- Management treating people as cogs in machines

- Unwarranted organizational boundaries

- Performance evaluations based on criteria that didn't match the objectives of the team

- Personal agendas that effect the team's agenda

- Not being able to agree on goals and procedures

- Unclear project objectives

- Unclear understanding of roles and relationships

- Changing team membership

- Prolonged floundering deciding what the scope of the project should be

- Problems and breakdowns in communication

When experienced software managers are asked about problems that they have encountered when working with software teams, they cite the usual litany of project management problems:

- Unqualified leaders and team members

- Understaffed team

- Schedules dictated without input or "buy-in" from team members who are responsible for the work

- Deadlines established before the scope of work to be done is known

- Lack of a good change-management process

- Lack of mentoring, and/or on-the-job training (for the team and individuals)

The potential damage caused by these problems is significant because, in team-based software development projects, most of an individual's time is spent in communication and coordination tasks—according to some studies roughly between 50–75 percent.

We want high performance teams producing superior software on mission critical system projects. This is what we must try to achieve on every software development project. This way we can turn dismal success rates into a winning record for the new millennium. While there are many books and articles on the social dimension of teams, few focus on the technical aspects of effective software teams. This chapter gives you a better framework for looking at your own software teams.

Teams in Organizational Context

Our discussions of teamwork and team processes assume a project context. A software development project is a scoped and planned undertaking that is guided by a documented technical and management approach. The plan typically describes the project charter, development objectives, work to be done, resources required, methods used, process to be followed, schedules to be met, risks to be managed and the way that the project is to be organized. The project presumably follows the plan until (or unless) either the plan or the work needs to be changed in light of revised objectives or new information. Other principles related to the proper organizational context in which effective software development projects occur may be found in such sources as the CMM for Software [1] and the MBNQA criteria.[2] A view of the overall software process is as a collection of layered behavioral processes as shown in Figure 7.1.

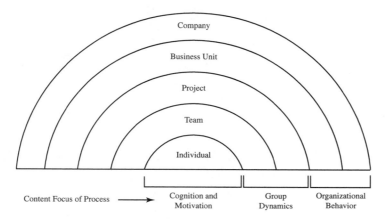

FIGURE 7.1   *The layered behavioral model of software processes.*

This model focuses on the processes of those creating the work products, rather than on the work products or artifacts produced. At the individual level, software development is viewed as an intellectual task subject to the effects of skills, learning, cognitive, and motivational processes. When the development task exceeds the capacity of a single software engineer, a team is convened and social processes interact with individual processes in performing technical work. In large projects, many individuals and perhaps several sub-teams must integrate their work on different parts of the system, and *interteam* group dynamics are added on top of *intrateam* group dynamics. The process of software development as practiced by a team is more than just a collection of individual processes. It is also a process of coordination, skill and knowledge blending, information pooling, idea exchange, knowledge discovery, group problem solving, checks and balances, and team resources management. Projects that produce products/systems must be aligned with business unit and product goals and are affected by corporate politics, culture, and procedures. Business strategy, product objectives, and incentive/reward systems establish a context in which a software project operates. Interaction with other corporations either as partners, suppliers, or as customers, introduces external influences from the broader business marketplace.

Consistent with the layered behavioral model and the focus on projects, the issues that determine whether a software project will be a success or a failure are summarized in Table 7.1.

TABLE **7.1** ISSUES IN DETERMINING SUCCESS AND FAILURE

Issues	Success	Failure
Managerial context and processes	Well-formed business objectives and strategy, experienced and effective project management, historical data, formal planning and progress tracking	None of these things
Engineering discipline	Good processes, methods and support tools, good SQA, stable requirements, significant reuse	Poor SQA, unprecedented application, fuzzy/unstable requirements, lack of a good process
Collaborative work	Good communications and team coordination, effective use of specialists	Use of generalists, poor communications, lack of role integration
Cognitive issues	In-depth knowledge in all areas required for success; relevant experience on similar systems; superstars in key positions	Gaps in crucial knowledge areas; underqualified staff

Success here includes development success, delivery success, and ultimately, product and business success.

- **Development success.** A project that is completed on time, on budget, and with all features and functions originally specified.

- **Delivery success.** Producing and delivering a system of reasonable quality that satisfies the customer's needs.

- **Ultimate success.** Satisfied or delighted customers using the product, who feel that they got reasonable value for their money, and want more features or products in the future.

The scope and structure of any specific project determines how much influence each issue will have on the outcome. Individual cognitive and talent issues dominate smaller projects. The larger the project, the more that teamwork, engineering discipline, and project and executive management issues dominate the outcome. Effective teamwork is a crucial ingredient for success in any project with more than one person involved.

Avoiding the Chaos Trap

Effective teamwork is also crucial to avoiding the chaos trap. To paraphrase Watts Humphrey,[3] in the chaotic organization, software professionals are driven, like a herd, from crisis to crisis by unplanned priorities and unmanaged change. These projects generally do not meet their delivery commitments. While their managers present an impressive "trust me" story and they may even meet their interim checkpoints, there is often a last-minute crisis that blows the schedule out of the water. An on-time delivery is the exception and is generally due to Herculean individual efforts rather than the intrinsic capability of the organization. Such projects may be staffed with well-intentioned people who seem to be both busy and over-committed.

However, the lack of effective management and planning, means flawed schedules, ineffective staffing, inadequate resources, poor coordination, and vague status reports. This results in frequent disasters and almost constant surprises. Unfortunately, the surprises are rarely pleasant. Plans are ad hoc, schedules are arbitrary, design control is nonexistent, and resources are inadequate. In some cases, schedule is the only the priority, but when the team does deliver, nobody likes the result.

Many first-class professionals leave as soon as they can. Software project managers are frequently replaced, but when the new managers learn the problems, they sound like their predecessors, and they too are soon discredited. In a frantic search for a Lone Ranger to clear up the problems, senior management often makes things worse. When the time comes to ship a new program, nobody will remember what test cases were run, or some module update will inadvertently be left out of the new build version. Old problems that were seemingly fixed continually recur. Even after shipment, the "official" copy is sometimes lost and somebody has to scurry around to reconstruct a new master. Few people learn from past mistakes, and those who do end up having little influence.

From the customers' perspective, chaotic projects are tolerated only as long as there is no alternative or they still have some patience left to try. Many of these projects have to be canceled, and some end up in litigation and/or cause corporate demise.

Combating Chaos with Effective Teamwork

Chaos often comes from a team not knowing how to deal with the non-normal (that is, unplanned or unknown) aspects of the project. Some of the important non-normal aspects of a project involve the following:

- Dealing with risks, uncertainties, unknowns, and variation
- Dealing with a changing world around the project and business
- Renegotiating objectives and requirements
- Multitask switching
- Wasting time pursuing nonfruitful development paths
- Fixing nonconformances, problems, and other related rework
- Injecting defects, defect management, and prevention
- Unplanned learning needs (for example, training)
- Various unplanned communications (for example, meetings)
- Spurious product and process evaluations, appraisals, and audits
- Canceled projects and/or being involved in litigation

Clearly the effectiveness of any team process depends on the skills, experience, and capability of the people performing the various roles within the process. For example, we might assume that a software development project is being led by a professional software engineer, and being managed by a certified software project manager. Unfortunately too few of these professionals are currently available to satisfy this assumption.

Our notions of teamwork will change over the next decade as reshaped by the emergence of software job specialties, as well as, the new technologies available to support them individually and collectively. We have already seen the emergence of specialists in:

- Software project management
- Software testing
- Software quality engineering
- "illity" specialists
- Application domain experts (for example, banking, aerospace, and so on)

An "illity" specialist refers to a person responsible for one of the defined quality characteristics of a system. For example, in the FURPS [4] model, we find the need for Software Usability Engineers, Software Reliability Engineers, and so on. In the near future, we will likely see the emergence of other kinds of specialists in software and systems engineering.

The Team and Its Lifecycle

Several models are needed to guide a successful project. These include: a business model (objectives), a functional scope model (target), teamwork and development process models, project planning models with the schedule of milestones and key events, a system architecture model, and the technical design/development approach. Figure 7.2 shows a conceptual model that identifies where the team fits within the project and individual levels of the layered behavioral model.

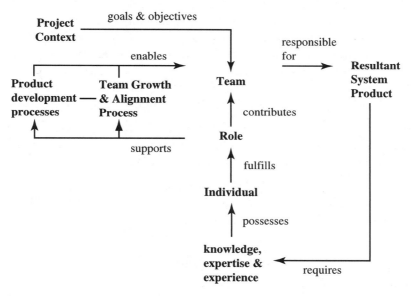

FIGURE 7.2   *Team conceptual model.*

In this conceptual team model, the expected result establishes the team purpose and focus. This result must be clearly defined. The expected result also defines the required expertise needed by the project. The team is built from those requirements rather than from the set of available people. The team growth process enables the team's effective performance by integrating the roles over time, tasks, responsibilities, expertise areas, and so on. Individuals contribute to the team based on their role within the team instead of just being participants. The team roles define the expectations of each individual within the team. Individuals must possess the necessary knowledge, expertise, and experience to fulfill the role(s) they assume.

With this view of teams, an organization can have teams that can flexibly re-form and respond to rapidly changing demands using different role combinations rather than organizing around standing organizational units. Team structures will better fit the creative talents of software professionals. Organizations can better recruit and grow talent with a role-based approach, and can become proficiency- and competency-based. This allows gaps to be more easily identifiable.

Individuals within teams benefit by having clearer expectations of their responsibilities and expected performance—both for themselves and as to how they should interact with others. They share a common understanding of each other's roles and responsibilities, which leads to mutual respect for the value of those roles. Career progression and performance levels can be defined within those roles. When a team model and team process are defined and in place, members of the team don't have to reinvent their roles and relationships, thus allowing them more time to focus on creative and technical issues.

In many observed situations, the key software team roles have been miscast and misplayed. Wrong-headed thinking has led to situations in which the individual roles and relationships are not defined. For example:

- A project manager thinks his job is to enforce upper-management edicts (for example, delivery dates) on the team, to never say no to additional requests, and then shield the team from outside influences as they perform the *death march*.[5]

- A software engineer on the team thinks his job is to write code.

- A software quality engineer thinks his job is to test code.

- An application specialist thinks his job is to write requirements specifications.

- There is no chief system architect on the project.

Lack of effective teamwork drags the team into chaos.

The following can be viewed as team success factors, team process requirements, and also as indicator areas to look at when evaluating team effectiveness. The software team should have:

- Clear team purpose, mission, and/or goals

- A plan to guide schedules and progress indicators, and also to identify resources needed

- Clearly defined roles and relationships

- Clear communication

- Reasonably balanced participation of the team members

- Established ground rules for individual and team behavior—a written code of conduct

- Effective interactions and meetings using the different skill sets of members

- A well-defined decision making process

- An awareness of and buy-in to the teamwork and development processes by all members

- Understanding of how to use the scientific approach (that is, using data, tools, and causal analysis to enable problem solving and decision making).

The Team Growth Model

Software teams are born, grow, mature, perform, and eventually disband in a definable pattern.

There are four issues that differentiate organizations that use software teams effectively from those that do not. These are

- How teams are formed

- How teams are focused/directed/led

- How teams perform their essential development tasks

- How teams adapt to situation changes, including disbanding

A team growth model describes the evolution, change dynamics, collaborative patterns and later shrinkage patterns of an effective, holistic software team. This describes a team maturity process in the interpersonal and social dimension. Teams evolve from a collection of individuals, to a cohesive, high-performance unit of mutually supportive members in which the use of conflict and diversity has been turned from a negative to a positive success factor. Teams go through the distinct stages of: formation, alignment, performance, and transition to closure.

Formation

Formation establishes the core team members. The team has not yet jelled, but should be made up of competent individuals that cover the crucial knowledge areas needed.

During this stage, such questions as the following need to be answered by each team member as he/she comes onto the team:

- What is the work that needs to be done?

- What am I responsible for?

- What are the criteria for success?

- How do I feel if I am being held responsible for work when I don't know what results I will be expected to deliver?

- Who can I talk to and what can I ask without looking stupid?

There is nothing worse than a team member feeling that he really shouldn't be here, don't a clue what is going on, or that he is out of his league. The result can be disorientation, uncertainty, fear, resistance, and lack of trust—all of which will later interfere with team performance.

Alignment

Alignment establishes a shared vision of a successful result, which is committed to by the entire team. This involves the establishment of mutually understood expectations for team success—aligning personal and team objectives—that embraces individual roles and adopts the team's ground rules for behavior and process. Goals and expected outcomes, and roles and relationships, are defined and clarified by team members. Goals and roles should take team members' personal agendas into account. There is nothing wrong with satisfying people's desires as long as the work gets done. There may be skepticism at this stage, such as whether the project is doable, or whether the necessary talent to complete the project exists on the team. Attention must be paid to skepticism because it may be warranted. If not addressed it can lead to failure in performance.

Performance

Performance produces the software system that achieves the project's objectives and the customer's needs. At this stage, processes are established, task assignments are made, and the tasks are executed in a disciplined manner.

Within that:

- The big task is divided up based on the work to be done and team member's abilities to do it.

- Team synchronization is needed to make sure everyone is on the same page. Frequency depends on how long and complicated the development task is.

- The results of the team member's subtasks must be integrated into the whole system.

- Team realignment and related problems due to the emerging dynamics of the development situation need to be dealt with.

- Adaptation to changes in the team is an iterative process that must be revisited as the team's makeup evolves over time.

High performance requires flexibility and communication, to support a high degree of synergy between team members. This is no easy feat. Disharmony and overload prevent a high level of performance from occurring. Conflict and confusion can lead to misalignment and result in missed deadlines. Observable resistance patterns include team members dragging their feet, working on other less unpleasant things and/or being engaged in passive-aggressive conflicts with others. Unresolved resistance may result in undesirable dependencies between team members, and ultimately project failure.

Dissolvement and/or Transition

An effective team produces a high-energy experience that cannot continue forever. If the work continues for too long, the result will be burnout and boredom. At some point, team members will consider whether to continue their involvement in the project. Interestingly, on doomed projects, this happens almost immediately when new members start by updating and distributing their resume.

An important question to resolve is how long to continue the project. This includes planning for disbanding, dissolving, or transitioning the team to a different kind of team under both normal and abnormal project completion circumstances.

These four team growth phases may be overlapped and/or performed iteratively at the project team level. This team growth lifecycle is also recursive in the sense that identified sub-teams will also go through this four phase process when they are formed. We now describe each phase of the team growth lifecycle.

Formation

The goals of team formation are to:

1. Staff the project with competent, talented professionals who collectively can become an effective, jelled, high performance team.

2. Make sure all crucial roles are covered by person(s) with the proper expertise and experience before they are needed.

3. Ensure that these roles get staffed by a systematic process of selection performed by a leader whose career depends on the success of the project.

4. Choose and communicate to the team a teamwork model appropriate to the situation and skills of the team.

Within any teamwork model selected, the following key role players are needed:

- Problem domain specialist
- Customer needs and expectations manager
- Product development project manager
- Chief system architect/engineer
- Software engineer
- External components acquirer
- Software quality engineer/tester
- Product delivery specialist
- End-user educator

For simplicity, the assumed product lifecycle model consists of these high-level phases:

1. Product and project definition
2. Development planning
3. Development
4. Product delivery
5. Product evolution

In a defined project process model, these phases may be overlapped and/or performed iteratively at the system level. Today's most popular commercial project process model is characterized as incremental and iterative development (IID). This project process model also is recursive in the sense that major subsystems and components also go through this process when they are identified.

Table 7.2 shows a simple mapping of the key team roles onto the five major product lifecycle phases. Each entry in the table briefly identifies the essential activities for each team role during each phase. The table provides a useful guide during formation.

TABLE 7.2 TEAM FORMATION—ROLES, PHASES, AND ESSENTIAL ACTIVITIES

Key team roles	Definition	Planning	Development	Delivery	Evolution
Problem domain specialist	Provide the wants, desires, needs and requirements	Contribute priorities and satisfaction assertions	Act as sounding board	Apply acceptance criteria	Use product and evaluate its value
Customer needs and expectations manager	Write vision and scope document	Contribute to the functional specification	Management of customer expectations	Coordinate product launch	Start definition of new version, collect user survey data
Product development project manager	Define project objectives, charter and organization	Draft functional spec, create project plan and schedule for development, set ship date	Track and control project, changes, issues, risks, etc.	Coordinate release process	Start definition of new version, and analyze user surveys
Chief System engineer/ architect	Provide technical advice to other roles on system architecture, design and technology alternatives	Map functional spec, and non-functional requirements onto one or more system structures	Define and control subsystem interfaces; ensure integratability with COTS elements	Resolve integration bugs, support release process as needed	Transition knowledge to lead maintainer, plan for next cycle

continues

TABLE 7.2 CONTINUED

Key team roles	Definition	Planning	Development	Delivery	Evolution
Software engineers (including "illity" specialists)	Provide technical advice to other roles on component architecture, design and technology alternatives	Estimate tasks, define detailed schedules, evaluate technologies, develop prototypes, contribute to design issues	Develop product and its elements, build internal releases, work with testers	Repair reported problems and bugs, bring documentation up to release standards	Fix bugs, start new cycle for next version, transition to maintenance/customer support
External components acquirer	Get components information as needed, establish relationships	Make contractual supplier development and delivery commitments, get more detailed information.	Acquire supplied parts and technologies when and as required	Ensure to the delivery team as needed	Ensure that maintenance agreements are in place for sub-products as needed
Quality engineer/ tester	Evaluate vision/scope document for quality and validation issues	Build QA and Test plans, contribute to design issues (quality, testability)	Execute tests and report bugs, track them to fixes; lead inspections and team reviews of requirements and design	Perform readiness tests for system configurations, alpha, beta and acceptance; ensure acceptability of product quality; stop shipment if necessary	Transition to maintenance as needed
End-user educator	Establish user education strategy	Build the user training plan, contribute to design issues (usability)	Create documentation and training materials	Deliver user training, elicit performance feedback	Continue as needed, start definition of new version
Product delivery specialist	Identify roll-out, delivery risks	Build roll-out and CM plans	Build CM system, operational support guidelines, final release schedule	Support alpha and beta sites, manage release and roll-out process	Start definition of new version

On an individual project, the key product author must play all of these roles simultaneously or find some support staff to do some of them. Ultimately, only he/she is responsible for the success of the project and product. For small team projects, individual team members may play multiple roles, either full time or part time, depending on each team member's capabilities and experience. It is important to be sure that all roles are covered by someone with the expertise needed. For large projects, these roles can be filled by entire sub-teams or functional business units—depending on the business organization and project size.

There are a number of useful teamwork metaphors available for a project to use as a pattern for how the team will function as it performs. Teamwork metaphors available include: peer team with leader, surgical team, chief-programmer team, skunkworks team, egoless programming team, integrated product feature team, search and rescue team, SWAT team, professional sports team, theater production company, and very large team of teams. All these team concepts require the roles listed in Table 7.2 and somewhat different collaboration patterns. The chosen metaphor should also take advantage of the leadership capabilities of the team members.

This chapter is primarily about team considerations, and therefore the subject of evaluating the credentials of potential team role players is not specifically treated here. In Figure 7.3, I have attempted to identify a framework which represents the major factors of individual software performance. These factors would apply to all software role players within a team. All the major factors should be explored when evaluating individuals. The variation in programming performance across individuals and tasks has been observed to be large and therefore it makes good sense to select the best and brightest and pay them what they are worth.

Exploratory studies have shown [6] that most software professionals use idiosyncratic approaches to development based on education and accumulated expertise from the applications/systems they have done. Because we do not yet know enough about the cognitive processes of software professionals, it seems inappropriate to attempt to control behavior at that level. We can, however, affect the experiential knowledge of individuals via education and use of individual improvement techniques to raise the level and reduce the variation in performance. In those situations, when the individual interacts with other team members in the project, and others in external organizations, it makes sense to model those behaviors.

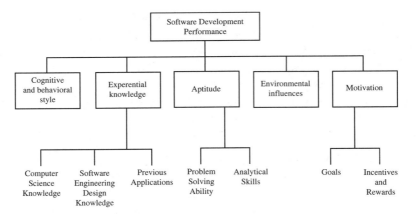

FIGURE 7.3 *Factors affecting individual software performance.*

The following sections describe the most crucial software team roles and provide guidelines for their processes and practices. In a sense, these are the *key process areas* (KPAs) of a role-based software team model, naturally aligned with the emerging roles and specialties of the field. Some of the role descriptions presented here are better defined than others because of the focused involvement of certain professional societies, and other institutional entities.

We start with a detailed discussion of the three crucial technical and project management roles (Software Engineer, Chief System Architect, and Project Manager), and then expand to discussions of the other roles.

The Software Engineer

Software development when performed by an individual is primarily a process of problem solving, learning, design, exploration, engineering production, and personal resources management.

Project and division general managers interviewed over the years consistently comment on how individual differences relate to project performance. Watts Humphrey [7] states that even experienced individuals produce code that has roughly 100 defects per KSLOC. It is a significant challenge to remove all those defects once they are introduced into the product.

I define a *professional software engineer* as an experienced practitioner who uses sound engineering principles, good judgment, and knowledge of the application domain to create working software systems that achieve given user objectives within stated economic, time, resource, and other constraints. A professional software engineer uses systematic, disciplined, and quantifiable approaches for the definition, development, delivery, operation, and evolution of a computer software system.

A software engineer is not someone who is certified to be knowledgeable about the technology of a specific software manufacturer (for example, Microsoft, Novell, SAP, and so on). In Texas, and perhaps soon in other states, software engineers are starting to be licensed to practice under the existing laws applied to other engineering disciplines. There is a hot debate going on as to whether this is a good idea. In any case, the body of knowledge, code of ethics, and the educational requirements for creating and growing good software engineers is slowly becoming defined.

For example, according to Parnas,[8] an apprentice software engineer graduating with a Bachelors degree in Software Engineering should know about the following topics:

- Mathematics (logic, calculus, statistics)

- Basic science (physics, chemistry, biology)

- Computer science fundamentals (computational principles)

- Electrical, computer, and general engineering topics (circuits, physical systems design)

- Software systems engineering (design approaches, programming)

- Software science topics of interest (AI, database methods, modeling)

And these software engineers will later become knowledgeable about such topics as:

- Application domain concepts, architectures, and component technologies

- Processes and best practices for successful development of high-quality software

- Software project planning and management techniques (estimation, scheduling) to the extent needed for effective management of his/her own work and team leadership.

Seen in that light, the essential process of a software engineer in a team context includes the following core tasks roughly performed in the following chronological order. The software engineer in a team will:

1. Participate in the formulation of a project's scope, business, and technical objectives that impinge on the development of the intended application (or subpart).

2. Analyze the intended application (or subpart) to determine and document the requirements to be satisfied.

3. Participate in the design of the computing system, determining which functions will be implemented in hardware or software, and selecting the basic components of the architecture.

4. Analyze the performance of a proposed design to make sure that the requirements can be met.

5. Plan and document his/her contributions to the overall system development as a personal work plan.

6. Design the software structure, including module identification, module interfaces, the structure of individual programs, and databases and document all design decisions.

7. Analyze the software structure for completeness, consistency, and suitability for the intended application.

8. Implement the software as a set of well-structured and well-documented programs and datastores.

9. Integrate new software with existing and/or off-the-shelf software.

10. Perform systematic and statistical testing of the software and integrated system.

11. Deliver the system (or subpart) through a disciplined approach to customers in an acceptable condition and known configuration.

12. Revise, enhance, and evolve the system (or subpart) so as to maintain its conceptual integrity, while keeping documents complete and accurate.

13. Record data and maintain/evolve his/her personal work plan as needed.

Within most teams, the individual software engineer takes responsibility for a designated subsystem or component, and performs the process within that restricted context.

Personal process improvement is accomplished primarily through planned education, training, career development, and systematic learning from experiences, mentoring, introspection and other sources.

Of course, the preceding steps actually represent the normal process of software engineering, during which an individual might spend most but not all of his/her time. The other portion (that is, the non-normal process) might be characterized by solving unexpected problems, redoing previous work, going to unplanned meetings, and other unanticipated types of activities. It is important for individuals to recognize and plan for the non-normal activities of software development, lest they be guilty of overly optimistic planning.

A joint task force of IEEE Computer Society TCSE and ACM Sigsoft has started work on defining the body of knowledge for a software engineer. At the time of this writing, a strawman version exists,[9] and there is also a committee of the IEEE Computer Society collecting job analysis survey data on this role. Clearly the eventual outcome of these efforts will further affect our notions of the individual software engineering process.

The Chief Software System Engineer/Architect

The *chief software system engineer/architect* (CSSE) has emerged as a crucial role in medium and larger size projects. In some organizations, he/she is known as team leader, key product author, chief architect, and so on. The CSSE should be the technical leader of the team.

The CSSE performs the 13 steps in the preceding section at the total system level, as well as, partitioning the technical work and ensuring that the individuals and/or subteams are performing quality work within the approaches chosen. The CSSE is usually responsible for system architecture issues, system level interface definitions, system modularity, and total system integratability.

He/she chooses the:

- System development technical approach

- System architecture

- How to define and control the interfaces

- Design criteria for selecting and/or building components

It is usually the responsibility of the CSSE to determine the technical design approaches, methods, techniques, and tools to be used on the project.

Approach to Software Development

Approach to software development is a technical strategy for achieving the development of a software system in a way that conforms to project goals and some project software process model. An approach can be expanded into a more detailed approach that includes certain methods, techniques, and tool sets.

A simple (highly abstract) example of an approach to software development is shown in Figure 7.4. The terms application concept, operational system, transformation, and verification are notionally defined. The figure is a dataflow diagram. There are many approaches that have been developed over the last 30 years. Well over 500 such approaches have been published in the literature, more are proprietary.

FIGURE 7.4 *Model of an approach to software development.*

In the '60s structured analysis/design and entity relationship approaches were dominant. In the '90s object-oriented approaches using Unified Modeling Language have dominated. In the next decade, new approaches inspired by distributed computing system design and JAVA thinking will emerge.

Current wisdom asserts that a given approach (and the detailed process model that conforms to it) might be more appropriate for a particular class of applications (application domain specificity) or for a class of system structures (structural specificity). This issue is related to the interaction of system structure with development approach and organizational structures. Hopefully, the choice of approach made by the CSSE is not limited to using the only approach known. See Chapter 9, "Select Tools to Fit the Tasks," of this book for more information.

A committee of the IEEE Computer Society has starting collecting job analysis survey data on this role. The eventual outcome of this effort will further affect our notions of this individual's process and knowledge needs.

The Software Project Manager

The larger the project, the more likely it is that management talent will differentiate success from failure. In some cases a project management team is needed. Also, the larger the project the more the need for a well-conceived project lifecycle model. The project lifecycle is primarily a management activity-based model, which can be blended with the selected technical software design methodology.

Software development in large projects is a collection of individual processes and also:

- A management challenge for resources balancing and conflicting goals satisfaction

- A cultural establishment process

- An organizational learning process

A large project process consists of identifiable subtasks distributed among subteams who must coordinate and integrate their work to achieve the project objectives. A large project process has several dimensions, including the flow of activities and artifacts over time, and the dynamic relationship of the system architecture to the project organization topology.

Software project management is concerned with an organized approach to planning and running the project in order to accomplish the stated goals and meet or exceed customer needs and expectations. This invariably involves balancing competing demands among:

- Scope, time, cost, and quality

- Customers (or users) with differing needs and expectations

- Identified and unidentified requirements and needs

The software project manager should be the management leader of the team. The fundamental abilities of a good software project manager are the ability to:

- Understand the complexities of a given situation so that a project can be planned.

- Observe behavior during execution and act so as to keep the project on plan or to modify the plan so that action and objectives are aligned.

- Organize and reorganize a project to carry out the plans.

- Measure, observe, and understand the significance of project activities so as to take effective adaptive actions as necessary.

- Act appropriately in difficult interpersonal situations in which they are intimately involved.

The essential process of the Software Project Manager is to:

1. **Initiate**. Define project objectives, charter, and organization.

2. **Plan**. Plan a workable scheme to accomplish the goals established—create the project plan and scope document.

3. **Execute**. Staff and coordinate people and other resources to carry out the plan.

4. **Control and inform**. Ensure that project objectives are being met by monitoring and measuring progress and taking corrective actions when necessary, control changes to scope and plans, ensure that customer expectations stay aligned with delivery realities during the development process.

5. **Deliver.** Coordinate the release of an acceptable system.

6. **Close**. Transition to maintenance/customer support, carryover additional requirements to the next product version if iterative process, bring the project to an orderly close.

Figure 7.5 is an overview of the Project Management Institute (PMI) Body of Knowledge [10] which when specialized with the knowledge of complex software and systems, becomes a powerful weapon in the fight to keep software projects from being unsuccessful. A more detailed project management process can be found in the Body of Knowledge in the SQI's Software Project Management Certificate Program,[11] which elaborates and conforms to the more general guidelines of the PMI. Also, a committee of the IEEE Computer Society has starting collecting job analysis survey data on this role.

The only traditional project support function missing from the top level of this model is the area of Software Configuration Management, and other aspects of product delivery, which are attributed in this essay to the product delivery specialist.

Project Management KPAs

FIGURE 7.5 *Project Management Body of Knowledge.*

Fashioning a good project lifecycle model is a worthwhile up-front investment that puts all project staff on the same page. Figure 7.6 shows an example of one that I have used with commercial clients that blends the traditional V model with the incremental, iterative development model. This model attempts to balance the need for management controls with the need for technical innovation and situation dynamics.

The keys to success of the Incremental V model are what happens at the control (which are also team synchronization) points. These are the formal mechanisms when management and development must jointly make explicit decisions to proceed to the next phase. Along with periodic management reviews and previews, these control points force the discussion of issues, risks, and alternatives. The meaning of each control point should be explicitly defined within the overall process.

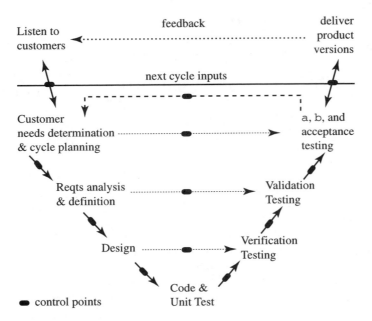

FIGURE 7.6 *Incremental V Project Process Model.*

Behind such a high-level model are concrete plans based on rigorous estimates and well-defined milestones that lead down the path to success.

The Software Quality Assurance and Testing (SQAT) Specialist

In the not too distant past, conventional industry wisdom was that you had to test software to make sure that it was just good enough for customer use. We have learned the hard way that projects which wait until testing to find out if they have quality are usually doomed to become runaways. We now understand the broader implications of producing quality software products.

The purpose of the SQAT role is to ensure that quality software is delivered to customers. To perform this role, "quality" must be defined and measured. The SQAT can be a customer advocate as well as, a disciplined and objective verifier of information. Several techniques are utilized by the SQAT. For example, the up-front definition of acceptance criteria focuses development prioritization, inspections are used to detect flaws before code exists, process audits are used to make sure that the team is following its defined process, and testing is planned and used to determine the presence of defects in the system. In many cases, SQAT is a focused subteam of the project team.

The SQAT performs the following tasks, usually done in the following order:

1. Identify quality issues and define project functional achievement and quality goals.

2. Write the project SQA plan including such things as: release criteria, testing goals, product reviews and audits, process evaluations, and so on.

3. Define and plan approaches for achieving special "illities" for some kinds of systems (for example, for high reliability systems, the approach to Software Reliability Engineering)

4. Plan the testing approach from the requirements—write the test plan.

5. Define and create the needed testing facilities.

6. Develop test strategy, scripts, and test cases.

7. Lead inspections, quality reviews, and audits of requirements, designs, code, test cases, and so on.

8. Perform (or ensure that the developers perform) adequate unit and subsystem testing.

9. Perform integration and system testing.

10. Perform staged release (alpha and beta) testing.

11. Perform final acceptance testing and stop shipment if unacceptable.

12. Collect and report software quality metrics and their trends.

13. Transition SQAT work products to maintenance.

As a result of SQAT activities during the development phase, identified problems and defects will be recorded, tracked, and dispositioned. Showstoppers are identified early and escalated as necessary.

Steps 5 and 6 may be done concurrently with software design and code development. Step 8 is typically done by the developers as code becomes available. Steps 9 through 11 are done by the SQAT or under his/her direction. Best practices for software QA and testing are employed within these steps.

The criteria for knowing when a software product is acceptable (for customer use) should be preestablished as the "software acceptance/release criteria" (see the project's SQAP). As approved and controlled changes are made to the requirements during development, these must also be provided to SQAT.

For more details of the SQAT role, see the Body of Knowledge developed by the ASQ Software Division [12] for its Certified Software Quality Engineer Program. In some other professionalism models, SQAT is considered a technical support role.

The Problem Domain Specialist

Writing code isn't the problem, understanding the problem is the problem.

The MCC studies in the '80s [13] discovered that the deep application knowledge required to successfully build most large, complex systems was thinly spread through software development staffs. Although individual staff members understood different components of the application, the deep integration of various knowledge domains required to integrate the system was either nonexistent or was concentrated in heads of just one or a few individuals.

Many forms of information must be integrated to understand an application domain. For instance, some one has to understand how the planned system will behave under extreme conditions, such as a jet fighter entering battle at night during bad weather, a telephone switch undergoing peak load on Mother's Day, or an automated factory with machines running at different speeds.

The domain specialist is someone who was typically once a user of similar systems. He understands such things as usage scenarios, application-specific algorithms, the structure of the tasks, objects and processes in the application domain, and even more esoteric bodies of knowledge about how different users might perform specific tasks.

There is a crucial relationship between the domain specialist and the CSSE that is expressed in Figure 7.7, which attempts to show how their bodies of knowledge must be integrated in the course of the project.

Software engineers may be knowledgeable in the computational structures and techniques of computer science, but many begin their careers as novices in the application domains that constitutes their company's business. As a result, software development requires a substantial time commitment to learning the application domain.

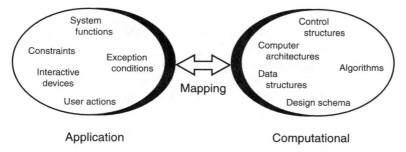

FIGURE 7.7 *Application and computational domains.*

The steps of the essential process of the application domain specialist are to:

1. Help build the problem domain model

2. Help identify different classes of system users, and their essential needs

3. Help build user/usage scenarios

4. Help document the wants, desires, needs, and requirements of intended users

5. Contribute priorities and satisfaction assertions

6. Act as sounding board and user advocate when needed

7. Provide user guidance to the developers

8. Help evaluate prototypes, and alpha/beta releases

9. Help determine and apply acceptance criteria

10. Use product and evaluate its value

The success of the product will be gated by the extent to which the domain specialist actually represents the interests of the target user population. Sometimes this role is supported and enabled by a User Representatives Group led by a trained user advocate.

The External Components Acquirer

Modern day computing systems are often constructed from a suite of preexisting components, along with custom developed software. It typically occurs that part of a product is composed of software modules (including plans, requirements, designs, code, tests, user documents, maintenance arrangements), which originate from outside of the development project.

It is necessary to establish the basic process for the acquisition of high-quality software components that are being developed for the project under contract, or purchased from other suppliers. The process of acquiring components must be rigorously and proactively managed to ensure that the delivered software meets the project's stated needs, and expectations (including schedule). For longer term relationships, it is expected that supplied software will be developed by the external organization using a process with demonstrated capability and repeatability that conforms to, or exceeds, the project's standards for software process maturity.

The external components acquirer must ensure that each such externally supplied software component:

1. Meets the stated needs and expectations

2. Conforms to defined requirements,

3. Is delivered in a timely (as expected) fashion

4. Is of the highest possible quality

5. Is within contracted cost/price limitations

6. Has integration considerations which are known

7. Is developed using a process with demonstrated capability

Software subproducts (that is, parts or components) are either purchased from a vendor, developed in-house by subcontractor personnel, custom developed by an outside source under specific contractual terms, or acquired by some other means. The following paragraphs describe these situations.

Any in-house subcontractor working on the project is expected to follow the software process on the project exactly as though he was a full-time company employee. This is a natural consequence of doing the contracted work on company premises.

When done off-site, subcontracted work is treated as a subsidiary software subproject. At the direction of the Software Project Manager, all phases, phase audits, and reports are included in the Statement of Work and enforced. Subcontracted work is accepted as phase products, under the same acceptance criteria as those for an in-house developed software product. The subcontract must always specify the success criteria required for acceptable delivery of software from the subcontractor (more than unenforceable and vague statements such as it must meet requirements or be user friendly).

A further consideration for long-term subcontractor relationships (partnerships) has to do with the general production processes followed by the subcontractor. In some cases, it is important for these subcontractors to develop software process capabilities similar or superior to those of the company. In any event, long-term approval of such a relationship comes from General Management, who relies on contractor assessments, past performances, and other information about the processes and products of the supplier being considered as one of the company's preferred software suppliers.

It is unrealistic to expect that vendor standard products would have been developed using the company's process; therefore, the primary (nonfinancial) issues are acceptance criteria and who is responsible for evolution and maintenance. Ideally, the individual vendor product under consideration is qualified for acceptance into the project's software process using the same criteria as a software product going out of its process to customers. Acceptance criteria would typically include documented Requirements, Design, Internal Implementation, Known Problems, Maintenance Plans, and Use. The systems test criteria for acceptance are developed and agreed to by the project's SQAT, and the vendor's SQA representative. When necessary, a specific systems test suite is developed and performed at the receiving company. The vendor contract must always specify the success criteria required for completion of purchase from the vendor.

Other sources of externally acquired software can be treated similarly. Such software might include some acquired from another part of the company (reused), from a customer, and/or from shareware sources off the Web.

For a single software component acquisition, the following process is performed by the component acquirer:

1. Software (and associated work products and services) that must be acquired externally is identified and defined (usually done in conjunction with the CSSE).

2. Sources for satisfying those needs are sought, product information is provided.

3. Qualified software suppliers are identified, evaluated, and selected using defined criteria.

4. Formal agreements with selected software suppliers are established (and maintained) in which they make development and delivery commitments.

5. Performance and results are monitored at agreed on interim checkpoints to ensure that delivered software will satisfy its intended requirements.

6. Ongoing communications are proactively done to allow for discussion of issues, problems, risks, and so on.

7. The software goes through a rigorous acceptance process.

8. Software is acceptable when and where it's delivered and received.

9. Support to the project to ensure proper operation is provided as needed.

10. Maintenance or evolution for the acquired software is arranged for, if needed.

Longer term software supplier relationships will include the performance of additional processes such as: supplier appraisal and certifications, supplier contractual terms that include conditions for product and process improvement, periodic performance evaluations, and the use of supplier performance metrics to make acquisition decisions.

It is crucially important that this process be applied to the acquisition of vendor supplied middleware products (for example, CORBA, DCOM) and infrastructure products (for example, Windows NT, Oracle), which are used as a platform for distributed enterprise applications.

Customer and Expectations Manager

Software projects frequently fail because the expectations for success are different (or unstated) between the developer and the customers. This is particularly true in custom project development situations, but is also true in commercial software packages. Because expectations can change over time, they also can diverge if no one is paying close attention. This role is responsible for being sure that a particular customer's expectations are understood and in fact met. The particulars of this role are heavily dependent on the type of business the company is in and the practices of upper management that affect the setting of customer expectations.

In a small company, this role is performed by marketing, account management, general management or even development management.

The customer needs and expectations management specialist performs the following. They will:

- Write the product vision and high-level scope document

- Contribute to functional specification

- Provide ongoing management of dynamic customer expectations

- Coordinate the product launch

- Start collecting information for the definition of the next new version

- Collect, analyze, and report user survey and customer satisfaction data

Here are a few different definitions of success that bear on establishing and evolving expectations:

- **Development success.** A project that is completed on time, on budget, and with all features and functions originally specified

- **Delivery success.** Producing and delivering a system of reasonable quality that satisfies the customer's needs

- **Ultimate success.** A satisfied or delighted customer using the product that feels that he got reasonable value for his money, and that wants more features or products in the future

Product Delivery Specialist

This role is responsible for the staged delivery of various versions of the product/system, to both external and internal customers (in many cases including the development team).

The product delivery specialist knows who has what versions of the system at any point in time (past and present), and controls the content, building, packaging, and installation of the release of the integrated whole system to various types of users and customers of the project.

The product delivery specialist performs the following activities:

- Identifying product rollout and delivery risk areas

- Establishing with the SPM, the process by which change requests and problem reports are initiated, recorded, reviewed, approved and tracked

- Creating the product rollout and CM plans, including which work products are to be placed under configuration control

- Establishing the configuration management library system as a repository for the software versions and baseline configurations

- Creating or acquire the CM system, and establish the procedure by which changes to baselines are controlled

- Defining, establishing, and managing the synchronized development build process

- Establishing guidelines for development module check in/check out policy

- Creating operational support guidelines

- Creating the final release schedule

- Providing installation support to alpha and beta sites

- Managing the system version release and roll-out process

- Create the reporting schemes by which the contents of the software baselines are documented, and allowing for periodic baseline audits to be conducted

End-User Educator

For a product of more than simple complexity, users must be taught how to use it effectively. Superior software companies realize that this is their responsibility. The product can assist by containing self-describing features and user friendly help commands, but these are not usually sufficient for jump starting the user's learning curve.

The end-user educator usually has a background in professional education and teaching, and experience in the application domain. They own the new product user-training plan.

The End-user educator:

- Establishes the user education strategy

- Builds the user training plan

- Contributes to product design issues for usability

- Creates user documentation and training materials

- Delivers user training sessions

- Elicits performance feedback from users

- Collects information about enhancements, problems, and so on

In many cases, this role requires a team. In some cases, this role is performed by a group of consultant organizations who have become knowledgeable about the external operation of the product.

Tying It All Together

We all know that the success of a software project depends more on the talents and effectiveness of the team than on such things as the technical methodology and tools applied. Therefore, team creation and composition should be treated as a major success factor. Aside from just basic competence, it does matter how these roles get staffed. Staffing a particular project depends on a number of factors that include delicately balancing this project with other business demands.

In one suboptimal situation that I have encountered, the project manager was not allowed to choose the members of his team. Instead, individuals were "loaned" or "assigned" to the project from other organizational units responsible for different areas of expertise—and not necessarily on a full time basis. In addition, the project had serious technical issues to be solved and an extremely aggressive schedule. If you have seen a project created this way, then you should recognize the signals of impending disaster. This kind of project and all others like it in the same organization are very unlikely to succeed—a problem which is normally beyond the ability of an individual project manager to solve. This is sometimes called "corporate insanity" because it involves doing the same thing over and over again, but expecting different results. Darwinian theory holds the promise that such businesses will not evolve over the long term.

Leadership is another crucial enabler. The key leadership roles are the Chief Architect and the Project Manager. They must be effective leaders.

Team Alignment

The goals of team alignment are to:

1. Ensure shared ownership, by the team, of the project's business objectives.

2. Create a context sensitive framework (including tools) for close and effective collaboration among team members.

3. Create the mechanisms to be used to facilitate team synchronization at the beginning and end of each product phase (for example, launch workshop, review).

4. Formally describe relationships among team members.

5. Have a rigorous task management scheme.

6. Create a defined code of conduct for team behavior.

7. Ensure that three levels of plans are aligned—at the project level, at the next phase level, and at the individual team member level.

Managing software development has been described as being similar to herding cats. The initial challenge is getting all the cats moving in the desired direction and then keeping them all moving in the desired direction. There are many stray cats in today's software teams, perhaps because they get easily distracted. When too many software cats stray, the result is team alignment problems, sometimes leading to project failure. The key is getting the team to work collaboratively on doing the right things in an effective way. This starts by getting the team all on the same page.

If we assume that each major product lifecycle phase requires a newly reconstituted (or constituted) team because of different skill needs, then it is important that we go through another iteration of the team lifecycle at the beginning of each product phase.

Assuming that rigorous project management is in place, each of these phases will be an individually chartered, planned, and tracked subproject of the over-all project, which is also chartered, planned, and tracked. The constitution of the team for each of these major phases will be different because of its different purposes. Definition and planning phases will be populated by a small, senior team. Development and delivery phases will have a much larger staff because that is where the bulk of development effort occurs. The evolution phase team will likely be much smaller and dependent on the product's maintenance strategy. The nature and mix of skills needed changes sufficiently from phase to phase so as to require that each team reform and resynchronize at the start of each phase. The end of each phase is also a good point at which the lessons learned from the previous phase can be used to positively affect what is done in the next phase or the next project cycle.

Shared ownership of the project business objectives by the team is a desirable way to get off on the right foot during the project definition and planning process. Ownership of the project development plan (and technical scope document) is a desirable way to get off on the right foot during the develop-ment project startup. Shared ownership is enabled by the team members signing the plan documents.

Coordination-based processes are as important as management hierarchical control models for team effectiveness. The goal is to create a context sensitive framework for close and effective collaboration among team members.

A small, co-located, dedicated team will have frequent and substantive dialogues about the issues that are impediments to success. As members of this kind of team are moved more than 100 feet away from one another, these dialogues break down. The challenge for virtual, dispersed teams is to overcome these breakdowns via process and teamwork mechanisms that support the kinds of dialogues that would occur in the co-located team. Such mechanisms might include: team review meetings, online dialogues (for example, in a Lotus Notes database), or planned socialization occasions.

For virtual teams of semi-independent experts, the following leadership issues require more attention: shared ownership of the project's business case, formally described relationships among team members, rigorous task management, and a defined code of conduct.

Mechanisms that can be used to facilitate team cohesion at the beginning of each product phase include:

- Phase launch and alignment team workshops

- Phase end team performance reviews

- Regular team synchronization, status, and issue meetings within phase

- Regularly planned social interactions that have the side benefit of facilitating communications

The alignment workshop identified previously can serve as the formal team mechanism for phase launch and for the previous phase lessons learned.

The Launch and Alignment Workshop

At the beginning of each major phase of the project, it is important for the team to:

- Define their goals

- Establish their roles

- Devise a phase development strategy

- Define a project phase process

- Produce a project phase plan

- Detail the plans for each team member

- Perform a risk analysis

- Agree on a team communication and reporting approach

A phase launch and alignment workshop is one way of accomplishing these objectives. An expanded version of this workshop should be used at the beginning of a new project.

Three levels of planning must be aligned (or realigned) as an outcome of the workshop—at the overall project level, at the next phase level, and at the individual team member level. These plans can then be fine-tuned and balanced as necessary. These plans establish the basis for team alignment during the performance of each phase.

A launch and alignment workshop is a co-located, behind closed doors meeting of all team members. It is a planned event, and is led by a trained teamwork coach.

The workshop process consists of the following flow:

1. Customer/management representatives describe the project/phase goals.

2. Q&A about the goals is performed by the team to ensure it understands them.

3. The team defines its goals and establishes its roles.

4. The team reexamines the overall project plan to see if adjustments are needed.

5. They define the strategy and process for the next phase.

6. They produce a phase development plan.

7. Team members produce a personal plan.

8. The phase development plan and the personal plan are aligned and balanced.

9. The team conducts a project and phase risk assessment. Risks are assigned for tracking.

10. The team agrees on the team performance metrics, which will be collected and tracked (for example, effort, size, defects, progress, quality).

11. The team prepares a management presentation.

12. The team presents and defends the plan to management.

13. The plan is reviewed and issues are resolved.

14. The team signs up to the plan.

During the workshop, the team members define their personal roles, define their own processes, produce individual and team plans, balance these plans, and assess and assign responsibility for identified project risks.

This works well for small to medium sized teams. For very large teams, a coordinated set of cascading workshops may be necessary.

Periodic Teamwork Performance Review (PTPR)

The notion of a "post project performance review" is familiar to most software professionals: at the end of a software development project, a report is written to document the good, the bad, and the ugly experiences, so that future projects can learn and improve. Unfortunately by the time the project finishes, most of the key technical team members have been reassigned to other projects or have moved on to greener pastures. If the project has dragged on for years, hardly anyone remembers what transpired in the early days of the project (when most of the fatal mistakes were made), and everyone is so burned out and exhausted that they have little or no interest anyway. As a result, the post project performance review process has been less than successful in many organizations.

We can apply the same incremental concepts to team performance evaluation that we apply to the modern product lifecycle. Instead of having *one* post project performance review at the end of the project, conduct *many* smaller grained reviews throughout the project. This works particularly well in those projects that use any variation of an iterative, incremental development lifecycle, because a version of the system is produced frequently throughout the project schedule. We call these periodic team performance reviews (PTPR), and they are done at least at the end of each lifecycle phase, and perhaps more frequently (for example, at major milestones).

There are several advantages to this approach. First, the PTPR only covers the activities that have transpired since the previous PTPR—that is, a phase or interval of work associated with the development of the current version. Thus, there's much more of a chance that everyone involved will remember the details of the positive and negative team experiences during this time period. Second, if the phase results have been reasonably successful, then everyone will be in a reasonably good mood, and the PTPR is more likely to be conducted in a constructive, friendly fashion. Third, the results of the PTPR can be applied to the next phase or period of the project and to the current team instead of just future projects and teams.

A PTPR focuses on evaluating the following areas from a team perspective:

- Team performance and project success indicators
- Things we did right
- Things we could have done better
- Things that we shouldn't have done
- Lessons learned to be applied to the next phase
- New practices, and so on to be introduced in the next phase

Performance

The goals of team performance are

1. To openly identify and discuss unknowns, issues, assumptions, decisions, and risks.

2. To use the defined team process for effective negotiation, collaboration, conflict resolution, consensus building, prioritization and decision making.

3. To use groupware tools to support the team's processes.

4. To collect, analyze, and use team data to improve overall performance.

During performance, it is crucial for the team to have ample opportunities to identify and discuss unknowns, issues, assumptions, decisions, and risks that are occurring. These discussions should be planned to occur at specific points in time, as well as, occurring continuously and spontaneously.

By analogy, this is why we have half-time and other time-outs during sporting events; to quickly evaluate performance *in situ*, discuss problems, receive valuable coaching advice, and make corrections in tactics, personnel, and so on, before continuing. There are only minor adjustments that can be made during the heat of the battle with teammates talking to one another in localized circumstances.

The goal of typical project management structures is to control the responsibilities, authority, and communications of a project team and not necessarily to coordinate the flow of technical information needed for making good design decisions.

These discussions can be facilitated by someone who is by nature a boundary spanner.[14] Boundary spanning activities translate information from the form in which it was used by one individual/team to a form that can be used by other individuals/teams. Boundary spanners reduce the amount of information lost or miscommunicated between different phases of development and different development team members (or subteams). Boundary spanners have good communication skills and a willingness to engage in constant face-to-face inter-action. Boundary spanners often become the hubs of information networks that assist the technical integration of the project.

The coordination activities of boundary spanners can be described as a collection of intersecting dialog spaces in an open system in which a node (for example, a programmer as a processor of information) may exist in several spaces simultaneously. As such, a programmer provides both formal work products and also crucial information based on experience and expertise.

The five crucial spaces of technical information that must be integrated by the team are

1. Feature and attribute negotiation

2. Application design

3. System problem diagnosis

4. Technology awareness

5. Component reuse

The dialogue in each of these areas is characterized by processes of negotiation, conflict analysis, issue formation, consensus building, and decision making. We observed that these spaces have different informational topologies, different loci of knowledge, and different diffusion rates. These spaces are typically not represented in the formal division of project labor, but are crucial to project success. A more precise definition of these dialog spaces could provide a stronger basis for the coordination and management of large projects.

Tools with mechanisms to coordinate the communication of technical informa-tion across the project team can provide an improvement in productivity and quality separate from that offered by most CASE tools. Software development groupware contains features such as: mediated topical discussion groups (for example, technology supported quality circles), integrated mail/scheduler/calendar, issue-based conflict resolution, decision support aides, strategic assumption surfacing aides, coordination data collection, and organizational design support tools (for example, containing reusable coordination protocols).

Current technology for facilitating team coordination in software development operates on the simple model of passive synchronization of programming level tasks through the check-in/check-out policies of centralized configuration management, plus by providing a passive, integrated project information base. It is assumed that effective coordination will occur by providing the team a shared information base within the software engineering environment. For example, the use of Lotus Notes as a team coordination mechanism is currently popular among software developers.

Conflict Management

I have often been asked the following questions about the behavior of software teams.

1. Is conflict a positive or negative factor in determining software team success?

2. What are the underlying causes of conflict in software teams?

The answer to the first question is that conflict can destroy a team or can become a major success factor if properly managed. The answer to the second question is much deeper and the following discussion will shed light on the answer to both questions.

Conflict behavior and interpersonal disagreement are considered to be normal aspects of group interaction, and are neither intrinsically good nor bad. Previous studies of groups engaged in solving complex problems have observed tendencies to avoid uncertainty and smooth over conflict. Such groups have also been found to retain unchallenged, invalid assumptions that reduced the quality of the resultant solution. Other studies have shown that conflict behavior increases the quality of group decision making by stimulating critical thinking, increasing group involvement and widening the search for alternatives. These results imply that a certain amount of conflict is beneficial for group problem solving—but *how much on my team* is unanswered.

When two people try to communicate with one another, we find a typical set of difficulties caused by emotional, personality and interaction style differences. In goal-oriented team situations, we see a number of areas in which conflict arises. Common general problems within a team are

1. Floundering

2. Overbearing or dominating team members

3. Reluctant team members

4. Acceptance of stated opinions as facts

5. Impatient rush to results

6. Attribution rather than substantiation

7. Crediting and discrediting

8. Wandering off on digressions, tangents and unrelated subjects

9. Combative feuding among members

10. Consensus versus authority-based team decision making style

There are known solutions for dealing with these kinds of problems. Good team leadership solves most of them. Good team meeting protocol can help solve these problems during meetings. Team ground rules (code of conduct) for proper behavior can help solve these problems outside of meetings.

In software development, conflict occurs more frequently when uncertainty exists—a common situation. Software subject matter areas in which uncertainty and therefore conflict will likely exist include

1. Climbing the team and individual learning curves

2. Competing, incomplete, inconsistent models of the problem space

3. Identifying and clarifying unknowns and missing knowledge

4. Difficulty in considering all the stated or inferred constraints

5. Choosing and using a good design process

6. Understanding of, and commitment to, project objectives

7. Identifying and resolving of issues—difficulty in tracking and returning to postponed issues

8. Decisions about functional scope—effectively prioritize system features

9. Decisions among competing models of the system architecture

10. Synthesis of a good design from knowledge fragments

11. Handling conflicting information from multiple sources

12. Communication breakdowns due to rapid change in project directions

These problems are harder to deal with. More than just good team leadership, or interaction ground rules are required. Relevant expertise and experience are invaluable.

Managed conflict is considered to be an essential part of the team process of developing complex computer software systems. This means that conflict (and the underlying reasons that cause it) must be systematically surfaced, identified, and resolved. The specific methods for doing so depend on the nature of the conflict and its underlying basis.

In the mid-1980s, our empirical studies team at MCC developed a method for observing software design teams and analyzing their conflict behaviors.[16, 17] We applied the method to the Leonardo Object Server Project, which we considered to be a typical leading edge, medium-sized software development effort. The results of that study were published as Diane Walz's Ph.D. dissertation at the University of Texas in 1988. For the Object Server team, a considerable amount of conflict behavior was observed, however it did not cause dysfunctionality. This was because the conflict was mild—nonagressive and nonpersonal—and was generally offered with substantiation. It was not used to hurt someone's feelings. On the other hand, I have personally observed team interactions whose sole purpose was to humiliate or discredit a team member; as well as team meetings best characterized as turf wars. These lead quickly to dysfunctionality.

As one result of our research, we proposed that a software development process must support at least the following components:

- The synthesis of relevant design patterns

- The integration of component knowledge into a complete design

- The coordination of mental models of the problem space and system design across the project team

Conflict management was seen as a key discipline for achieving the level of synthesis and integration needed for team success.

At the heart of many of these conflicts are found the basic human emotions of trust, fear and ambition; as well as, natural differences in personalities and interaction styles. The key is differentiating emotion-based conflict and miscommunications from honest technical differences of opinion based in different sets of knowledge and experience.

A simple conflict resolution process that works within the team process is

1. Deal with the emotional and personality issues first

2. Identify the underlying reasons for the conflict (for example, misunderstanding, someone failing to take responsibility, or difference of opinion)

3. Choose a conflict resolution technique appropriate to the situation (negotiate, collaborate, accommodate, compromise, or avoid)

4. Define ground rules and work out an agreeable solution

The preceding process works whether the conflict is between individuals or between different factions on a team. When the conflict is about a technical issue that is relevant to achieving the team's goals then I recommend that Issue Management Groupware be used to document the decision making process. Also, when teams are not face to face, which is very often the case, we still need some way to manage the conflict that is rising above the level of the cubicles or even across the ocean.

Software Team Groupware

One of the biggest problems of software teams, is achieving a group sense of what is and what is not known; and what is the current status of key decisions that are made along the path to designing and building a complex software system. As the size of the team increases, so does the importance of visibility into global knowledge. Effective coordination is impossible without some way of achieving a group level understanding of all the key issues. Many unproductive meetings can be spent rediscussing, rethinking, and remaking decisions.

Issue Management Groupware (IMG) is an approach to enabling the process of discussing and resolving the class of complex problems (issues) in a software development project. The purpose of IMG is to:

- Facilitate systematic exploration and resolution of issues by a software development team

- Provide a means of recording the exploration (rationale) as it occurs over time

The IMG model was an extension of the Issue Based Information System (IBIS) model developed by H. Rittel and W. Kunz in 1970, and the ISAAC model, which led to the development of gIBIS at MCC in the mid-1980s. An interactive groupware tool for IMG was built in 1990 at the Lockheed Software Technology Center.[18] IMG supports software team discussions and rational decision making using the key concepts shown in Table 7.3.

TABLE 7.3 KEY CONCEPTS IN IMG

Term	Kind of term	Definition
Discussion	Information Container	A set of issues, discussions, and their contextual information.
Issue	Statement	A simple question within the topic of a discussion. Issues can be factual, explanatory, conceptual, or instrumental.
Position	Statement	A simple statement that answers in whole or part a question raised in an issue.
Argument	Statement	A simple statement that contains a reason for accepting or rejecting a position.
Issue tree	Set of Statements and Relationships	An issue, the positions on that issue, and the arguments for or against each of the positions.
Participant	Person's Role	An individual who is active in, or strongly interested in, a discussion. Participants can create, revise, and delete IMG statements and can vote on positions.
Moderator	Person's Role	A participant of a discussion who monitors the discussion's progress, marking positions accepted and rejected, issues resolved, or discussions moot.

A *discussion* is the container of information generated by the discussion participants over time. Discussions can be nested to any depth—each depth dealing with more specific aspects of a large problem than the last. Each discussion has participants.

Participants within a discussion can:

- Explore problems by raising issues, stating positions on an issue, and arguing for or against positions

- Provide context for a discussion by providing background information, creating free format statements, sending notes, describing decisions, facts, assumptions and objectives, connecting contextual information to issues or discussions, and connecting issues to other relevant issues.

- Register preferences by voting for or against positions

- Manage change by revising or deleting statements or the relationships between them;

- Control discussion flow by creating subdiscussions or creating meta-relationships between issues.

In addition, participants acting as moderators also can accept or reject positions for the team, resolve or abandon issues, declare discussions "moot" (irrelevant), reopen issues and reverse acceptance or rejection of positions, and make decisions.

The discussion window shown in the Figure 7.8 is an example of a high-level graphical representation of a software team discussion about whether to build or buy the database subsystem of a larger software system. All the icons in the window are clickable and lead to more detailed information about the discussion. The documented decision was to buy the database subsystem, and the rationale for that decision is documented.

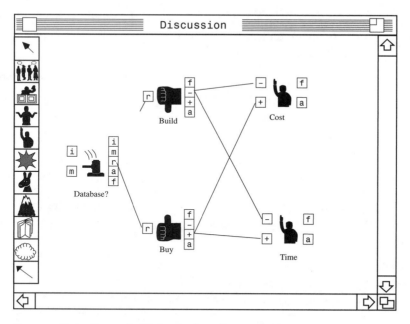

FIGURE 7.8 *Buy or build the database discussion in IMG.*

Software development groupware tools that support active issue exploration and resolution are still not generally available, but are sorely needed for large team projects. Current software engineering environment (SEE) technology does not facilitate certain types of teamwork. Groupware tools with issue management capabilities will enable the process sensitive SEEs to become "active" coordination assistant using the groupware medium and the team process.

Transition and/or Closure

The goals of team transition and/or closure are to systematically:

1. Transition people off the project when they are no longer needed, based on overall organizational core competency plans and personal growth plans

2. Capture important knowledge and work products from departing team members before they depart (or at least as a commitment to mentor)

3. Move the core team to one of the following planned alternatives:

   - An ongoing maintenance and support project once the product or system has been delivered

   - A new development project (including a new major version of this product)

   - A post mortem analysis project, if this development project is prematurely killed

There is a special set of considerations to be addressed when closing a project. In too many situations, competent software teams are completely disbanded by throwing all members to the wind, and/or letting them find better jobs in other companies. Perhaps in some situations it would be wiser to keep good teams together.

The easy way out is to use contract project workers who can easily be dismissed. Unfortunately, this has led to the short-sighted situation where key corporate knowledge is lost and we do not have enough senior people with the breadth and depth of knowledge necessary to staff the key roles in future projects.

The organizational context in which project teams are disbanded is crucial to long-term success. Disbanding a given project team is much easier if an organizational strategy exists for career and talent development. In that case, each project member will have an individual growth plan which will guide educational needs and the next assignments that they should take on in order to strive for their overall career goals, and organizational core competencies. With such a strategy in place, an organization will exhibit a culture of excellence that attracts and then develops talent into the most motivated and productive software engineering teams in the world. Investment in software systems talent growth will increase the organization's capability to engineer superior software and to leverage the benefits of improvements in both technology and process.

The People Capability Maturity Model (P-CMM) was created to enhance the readiness of organizations to undertake increasingly complex applications by helping them attract, grow, motivate, deploy, and retain the talent needed to improve their software development capability.[15] Key P-CMM practice areas include: recruiting, selection, performance management, training, compensation, career development, organization design, and team and culture development.

Evaluating Team Growth Effectiveness

Within a given project, in order to adapt or change the team's behavior, we must have ways of knowing how effectively the team is performing. There already exists a normal set of traditional software performance measures that focus on such areas as effort expended, system size growth, requirements change rates, development progress, productivity, and defect containment effectiveness. These are always used in high-process maturity organizations. See the Chapter 8 of this book for more information about using classic software measures.

In addition, we also need some kind of a team thermometer to help determine whether a software team is healthy (that is, not sick). There are three types of measures to help determine team health; these are anecdotal indicators, team attitude surveys, and the results of team growth practices assessments.

The model described in the previous sections begin to elaborate a maturity model for software team growth in which the four areas (formation, alignment, performance, closure) are like KPAs with goals, practices, organizational institutionalization factors, and so on. At this point we only have goal statements. When this model is fully defined, systematic assessments are possible.

Using a rating scheme similar to CMM-based appraisals, it is possible to determine the extent to which the team growth area goal statements are being satisfied on selected projects within a given organization. This would lead to a team growth capabilities assessment result such as shown in the Figure 7.9. Institutionalization of team growth capability requires organizational mechanisms.

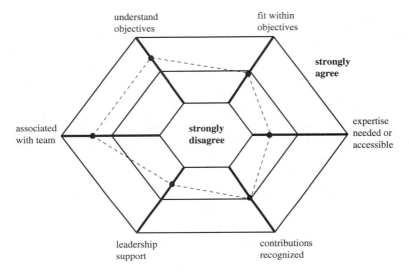

FIGURE 7.9 *Team growth capabilities profile example.*

A more detailed team growth best practices assessment would involve evaluating the extent to which the team is following the best practices of a defined team growth approach in support of the stated goals. Such an assessment method does not yet exist.

The software team growth maturity model is not the same as the software development capability maturity model, because it is in a different dimension. There is a potential relationship in that the organizational context established by a high CMM level creates a management infrastructure that makes growing high performance teams easier. However, it is not necessary or sufficient for a specific project/product.

A second measurement indicator involves regularly and more formally surveying the team about their attitudes. Team attitude survey measures derive from collected team responses to a standard team-ness questionnaire. The aggregated results are periodically displayed as a Kiviat diagram. An example of such a questionnaire is displayed here.

TEAM-NESS SURVEY QUESTIONS

1. I understand the direction and objectives of our team.
2. I know how my work fits within our team objectives.
3. I have the expertise to be successful, and I have access to the additional expertise needed.
4. I feel that my contributions are recognized within the team.
5. I have the leadership support to be successful.
6. I am pleased to be associated with this team.

The responses are from a Likert scale and range from one (strongly disagree) to five (strongly agree). The aggregated averages of the team are plotted on a Kiviat chart and the trends are tracked over time by the team itself (see Figure 7.10). Management and the team can take corrective action based on the results of these measures.

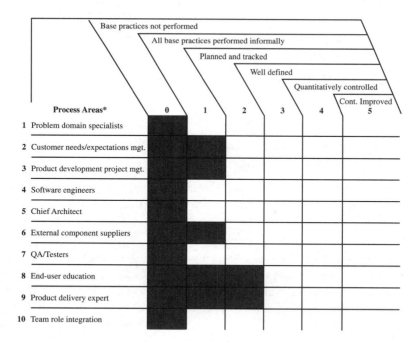

FIGURE 7.10 *Kiviat diagram for team-ness measures.*

In addition, anecdotal indicators derive from management by walking around techniques. These involve observing how the team identifies itself, how the team members describe the project they are on, what the team does when a member is failing in their obligations to the team, and what the team does in its casual time (for example, lunch).

Summary

The following team characteristics for success are worth repeating. The software team should have:

- Clear team purpose, mission, and/or goals

- A plan to guide schedules and progress indicators, and also for identifying resources needed

- Clearly defined roles and relationships

- Clear communications

- Reasonably balanced participation of the team members

- Established ground rules for individual and team behavior - a written code of conduct

- Effective interactions and meetings using the different skill sets of members

- A well-defined decision making process

- An awareness of and buy-in to the teamwork and development processes by all members

- An understanding of how to use the scientific approach (that is, using data, tools, and causal analysis to enable problem solving and decision making)

Over the course of my 30 years in the software industry, I have seen too many dysfunctional teams leading to unsuccessful projects. In many cases, such teams cannot cope with the inherent difficulties of software development (that is, complexity, changeability ,and conformability) because they have not been grown to do so. In the previous sections of this essay, specific advice was given to facilitate the growth of a given software project team through the identifiable stages of formation, alignment, performance, and dissolvement.

Once that advice has been assimilated within a specific project team, we can broaden the goal to creating an organizational capability for the systematic growth of high performance software teams. To accomplish that, we must address organizational infrastructure issues. Organizations that cannot effectively create, manage, and dissolve teams find themselves unnecessarily limited by rigid or functional organization structures, or they find themselves constantly reorganizing in an attempt to find the right structure. This limits their ability to compete and successfully manage complex software development projects.

Therefore, creating the organizational infrastructure to systematically enable effective, high performance teams should be high on the senior executive's list of things to do. In addition to the normal personnel staffing and management functions, this creates the need for a staff level role called the software teamwork coach, who provides consulting, advising, and assistance to emerging project software development teams.

The software teamwork coach must have excellent people skills, technical skills, and teaching skills. The teamwork coach:

- Focuses on the team's process, that is, how decisions get made rather than what decisions get made

- Assists the team in structuring themselves to achieve the required work

- Assists the team leadership with group process improvements

- Uses and teaches the principles of TQM and scientific methods

- Assists the team with data collection and analysis activities, so that the team can see what conclusions may or may not be drawn from the data as collected

- Helps team members extrapolate data into meaningful trends and graphics so that problems may be solved and they may be explained to outsiders

- Assists the team with intervention techniques when needed to correct teamwork problems

- Assists the team with presentation styles and techniques

- Assists the team with use of effective meeting processes

- Teaches team members how to use various techniques, tools and methods when needed

The value of a good teamwork coach is more at the front end of a project than at the back end.

From the SEI's process management point of view, a mature organizational software development process is characterized as being: defined, documented, supported, trained, practiced, enforced, measured, tailored, and continuously improved. Although this may be necessary, it is not sufficient for effective, high-performance teamwork.

In addition, a team process is effective when it helps the team: define and plan a project, control what can be controlled and quickly identify and deal with what cannot be controlled, overcome unexpected or unplanned events, understand what everyone else on the team is doing, monitor real progress or lack thereof, accelerate learning by providing a framework for introspection, evaluation and change, and ensure a successful project outcome. A team process is not effective when it becomes: shelfware, fatware, a bureaucracy, cast in concrete, a hindrance to communications, a shield that hides the truth about progress, or an obstacle to learning from the valuable experiences of past performers and performances.

Furthermore, the team process should be

- Owned by the performers
- Fashioned from previous experience-based processes for both the project at hand, and with consideration of wider applications
- Well-aligned with objectives (for example, user, business, product, project)
- Measurable, evolvable, and improvable
- Used in professional, systematic and disciplined ways
- An enabling framework for the inclusion and use of good practices, methods, techniques and tools
- Compatible with the organization's culture
- Well-integrated with other processes around it
- Complete (essential activities are covered)
- Defined to the degree necessary to enable its effective use
- Of good overall process quality
- Better than your competitors' processes—in business critical ways (for example, time to market, high quality and/or predictability)

A team process must be a living process, because of the dynamics of the situation. Things can change daily, and sometimes hourly, on a software project. A major advantage of applying a defined team process is improved collaboration and teamwork resulting from a clear, agreed upon, definition of activities, roles, and dependencies. A defined team process increases visibility and lessens misunderstandings. As in any engineering discipline, the adherence to any well-defined process will require a significant amount of control, tracking, measuring, record keeping, and reporting. Some software cowboys have been unwilling in the past to do this, and perhaps they should be put out to pasture. There is also the need for a suitable set of tools to minimize the burden of some of the more clerical activities.

High-performance software teams are characterized as having: a clear, elevating and achievable project goal (and related objectives), a results-driven team structure, competent team members, a team spirit, and commitment to success. They demonstrate a collaborative working environment in which experts can thrive, and there are standards of excellence, external support and recognition, principled leadership, and traditional team values such as loyalty, trust, shared experiences and beliefs. High-performance software teams are no accident—success is designed into their growth process and thus they consistently produce superior results. We want effective, excellent, high-performance teams producing superior software on mission critical system projects. This is what we must try to achieve on every software development project in which we are involved, to turn dismal success rates into a winning record for the new millennium.

When growing high-performance software teams becomes the norm, we will have good players, a good playbook, practice sessions, and good coaching that leads to the routine production of superior software. Hopefully, this essay has given the readers a better framework for looking at their own development team growth processes and asking some hard questions.

References

1. Paulk, M., Weber, C., Curtis, B. and Chrissis, M., The Capability Maturity Model: Guidelines for Improving the Software Process, ISBN 0-201-54664-7, SEI Series on Software Engineering, Addison-Wesley Publishing Company, 1995.

2. Malcolm Baldrige National Quality Award Materials, see www.asq.org.

3. Humphrey, W. Managing the Software Process, SEI Series on Software Engineering, Addison-Wesley Publishing Company, 1989, ISBN 0-201-18095-2.

4. Grady, R. Practical Software Metrics for Project Management and Process Improvement, Prentice Hall Publishing, 1992, ISBN 0-13-720384-5.

5. Yourdon, E., Death March Programming, Dorset House Publising, 1998.

6. Guindon, R., Krasner, H., and Curtis, B., Breakdowns and Processes During the Early Activities of Software Design by Professionals, in Software State-of-the-Art: Selected Papers, pp 455-475, edited by DeMarco and Lister, ISBN 0-932633-14-5, Dorset House Publishing, NY, NY, 1990.

7. Humphrey, W., An Introduction to the Personal Software Process, SEI Series on Software Engineering, Addison-Wesley Publishing Company, 1998.

8. Parnas, D., 1998, Basic Knowledge Needs for Practicing Software Engineers, UT Computer Sciences—distinguished lecture series in software engineering, Dec., 1998, on the Web at www.cs.utexas.edu.

9. Guide to the Software Engineering Body of Knowledge—Strawman, IEEE Computer Society and the ACM SWECC, see www.swebok.org and www.computer.org/tab/swecc.

10. A Guide to the Project Management Body of Knowledge, Project Management Institute, 130 South State Rd., Upper Darby, PA, 19082, ISBN 1-880410-12-5, 1996.

11. University of Texas Software Quality Institute—Software Project Management Certificate Program, see criteria online at www.utexas.edu/coe/sqi.

12. American Society for Quality—Certified Software Quality Engineer Program, see online at www.asq.org/sd/swqweb.html.

13. Curtis, B., H. Krasner, and N. Iscoe. (1988). A Field Study of Large Software Projects, in Communications of the ACM, Vol 31. No. 11, November, 1988.

14. Krasner, H., B. Curtis and N. Iscoe, Communication Breakdowns and Boundary Spanning Activities On Large Programming Projects, in the Empirical Studies of Programmers, Ch. 4, pp 47-64, ISBN 0-89391-461-4, Ablex Publishing, 1987.

15. Curtis, B., W. Hefley, and S. Miller, The People Capability Maturity Model, CMU/SEI-95-MM-02, Software Engineering Institute, Carnegie Mellon University, 1995.

16. Walz, D., Elam, J. and Krasner, H.. A Methodology for Studying Software Design Teams: An Investigation of Conflict Behaviors in the Requirements Definition Phase, Proceedings of the 2nd Workshop on Empirical Studies of Programmers, Ablex, Inc. December, 1987.

CHAPTER 8

Use Realistic, Effective Software Measurement

Shari Lawrence Pfleeger, President, Systems/Software, Inc., Washington, DC

What Problems Can Measurement Address?

Having worked on many software projects, you know that each one is different from the one before. How do we understand these differences? How do we apply our understanding to the critical problems that arise during the development or maintenance process? Ultimately, we want to control the many software activities and product characteristics with which we deal, and to predict what will happen later in this project as well as on future projects. Measurement can help. Software measurement is the quantitative assessment of any aspect of a software engineering process, product, or context; it aims to enhance your understanding and to help you control, predict, and improve what you produce and how you produce it.

In this sense, measurement serves the same role in software development as in any other science or engineering discipline: it enlightens and enables us to develop theories; apply them; evaluate them; and ultimately use them to improve our products, processes, and resources. Chemists and physicists, for example, measure properties of matter to understand how matter is created and evolves, and then chemical engineers use the measurements to help guide their activities. Initial, crude attempts to measure matter were refined as understanding improved and the supporting technology allowed. In the same way, software measurement helps us measure properties of software-related processes, products, and resources, so that we can understand how software is created and evolves. As we learn more and more about software development, we refine, improve, and perhaps even expand our measurements. That is, we go from understanding to predicting to changing and improving.

In this chapter, we look at how to use measurement to be more effective developers and maintainers. Along the way, we point out several guidelines for using measurement wisely. That is, by using examples of how to define and use measures, we suggest how measurement can be made an essential part of good software development and maintenance.

Using Measurement

Software measurement is not new. We have measured aspects of software since the first compiler counted the number of lines in a program listing. As early as 1974, Donald Knuth was using measurement data to demonstrate how FORTRAN compilers could be optimized, based on actual use of the language rather than on theory. Many of us, especially those developers involved in large projects with long schedules, like to use measurements to help us understand our progress toward completion. Similarly, managers look for measurable milestones to understand whether a project is healthy and will meet its effort and schedule commitments. And customers, who often have little control over software production, use measurement to help them decide if the products are of acceptable quality and functionality. At the same time, measurement helps maintainers with decisions about reusability, reengineering and replacement of legacy code.

We can see evidence of measurement's assistance throughout the popular and research literature. Ed Weller,[1] for example, describes how metrics helped to improve the inspection process at Honeywell. Wayne Lim [2] discusses how measurement supports the reuse program at Hewlett-Packard, helping project managers to estimate the number of times a module will be reused as well as to predict how much money and effort will be saved from reuse. Michael Daskalontanakis [3] reports on the use of measurement to improve processes at Motorola. In each case, measurement is useful in making visible what is going on in the code, in the development processes, and in the project team.

For many of us, measurement has become standard practice. Just as we now take operating systems, databases, and compilers for granted, some of us also take certain measurement practices for granted, as in the following:

- Counting lines of code to get a sense of how the system is growing in size as it is maintained and upgraded

- Using structural complexity metrics to target our testing efforts

- Using defect counts to help us decide when to stop testing

- Using failure information and operational profiles to assess the reliability of our code

We must be sure, however, that the measurement efforts are consonant with our project, process, and product goals; otherwise, we risk abusing the data and making bad decisions.

Abusing Measurement

To see how, suppose that you measure program size using lines of code or Halstead measures (a set of measures based on the number of operators and operands in a program). In both cases, common wisdom suggests that module size be kept small, as short modules are easier to understand than large ones. Moreover, as size is usually the key factor in predicting effort, small modules should take less time to produce than large ones. However, this metrics-driven approach can lead to increased effort during testing or maintenance. For example, consider the following code segment:

```
FOR i = 1 to n DO
READ (x[i])
```

It is clear that this code is designed to read a list of n things. To prevent errors, however, it is better for programmers to terminate input using an end-of-file or marker rather than using a count. If a count ends the loop and the set being read has more or fewer than n elements, an error condition can result. A simple solution to this problem is to code the read loop to look something like the following:

```
i = 1
WHILE not EOF DO
        READ (x[i])
        i:= i+1
END
```

This improved code is still easy to read but is not subject to the counting errors of the first example. Suppose that the general notion of "smaller is better" had been turned into a measurement-based rule that restricts software size. On some projects, strict limits on the size of modules might have led a programmer to choose the first code example over the second, in order to meet size restrictions. The result would have been code that is more difficult to test and maintain. This abuse of measurement leads to our first guideline:

Guideline 1: Measurement Is a Means, Not an End

Another abuse occurs when measurement is not tied to the development or maintenance process. That is, it is dangerous to measure aspects of development or maintenance without first knowing what we will do with the measures after we have them. For example, a measurement usually makes sense only when we first associate it with one or more models. One essential model tells us the domain and range of the measure mapping; that is, the model describes the entity and attribute we are measuring, the set of possible resulting measures, and the relationships among several measures (that is, that productivity is equal to size produced per unit of effort). Models also can distinguish prediction from assessment; we need to know whether we are using the measure to estimate future characteristics from previous ones (such as effort, schedule or reliability estimation), as opposed to determining the current condition of a process, product, or resource (such as assessing defect density or testing effectiveness).

Models also can guide us in deriving and applying measurement. A commonly used model is the Goal-Question-Metric paradigm. This approach uses templates to help us derive measures from our goals or our users' goals. Then, from each goal, we generate the questions whose answers tell us whether we have reached our goal. The template encourages us to express goals in the following form:

> Analyze the [object] for the purpose of [purpose] with respect to [focus] from the viewpoint of [viewpoint] in the environment [environment]

For example, an ABC Corporation's manager who is concerned about the extent to which code is reused may express the goal of "reusing code" as the following:

> Analyze the project for the purpose of understanding with respect to reusing code from the viewpoint of the project manager in the ABC Corporation.

From this goal, we can generate several questions, such as the following:

- Which code components are reused without change?
- Which code components are reused with some modification (for example, less than 30 percent but more than 0 percent)?
- Which code components are written as new?
- How much of the system is new? Modified? Reused?

The questions then suggest metrics that should be used to find the answers. In our example, we might want to count lines of code, and then designate how many lines of code are in each of the three categories (new, modified, and reused). This top-down derivation assists managers and developers, not only in knowing which data to collect but also in understanding which kind of analysis is needed when the data are in hand.

Some practitioners encourage a bottom-up approach to metrics application, where organizations measure what is available, regardless of goals. Other models are based on a particular kind of goal, such as quality or business goals.

Notice that, by using models or goals tailored to your particular project or organization, you may end up with goals, questions or even metrics different from those on other projects—even projects producing the same or similar software! That difference is your assurance that you are understanding and solving your problems, not someone else's.

If your organization is interested in software quality for its standalone software products, for example, you may decide to measure it in terms of defects found during development; but my organization, also interested in quality, performs more maintenance than development. Because we sell a product that is very expensive to fix once it is out in the field, we may prefer to measure quality in terms of failures—that is, problems our customers see. It makes no difference to us if we find one or one hundred defects before delivery; one failure in the field can mean the end of a product line. Moreover, our product contains embedded software that is invisible to the user unless the product fails. Consequently, our managing director understands quality in terms of failures in the field, not in terms of defects per thousand lines of code. So although quality is a key goal for both your organization and mine, our evaluation process is very different.

Guideline 2: Use Different Strokes for Different Folks

You also can measure as part of a case study or experiment for software engineering research. That is, you measure (and often manipulate) one or more factors; then, researchers monitor the factors' effects on key variables in development products or processes. Your organization, for example, may build software using two different techniques: one a formal method, another not; then, you evaluate the resulting software to see whether one method produced higher quality software than the other.

Experimentation models are essential to this research. Such a model describes the hypothesis being tested, the factors that can affect the outcome, the degree of control over each factor, the relationships among the factors, and the plan for performing the research and evaluating the outcome. Consequently, the measurements support the hypothesis-testing and lead to a better understanding of how software development really works.

Guideline 3: Don't Measure in the Dark

Measurement, as any technology, should be used with care. Any application of software measurement should not be made on its own. Rather, it should be an integral part of a general assessment or improvement program, where the measures support the goals and help to evaluate the results of the actions. For that reason, we look next at what measurement can mean to your particular project.

Applying Measurement Sensibly

The things we want to study are entities in the real, empirical world. Each entity has one or more attributes; that is, we describe an entity by its characteristics so that we can distinguish one entity from another. A measure is simply a mapping from the real, empirical world to a mathematical world, where it may be easier to understand the attributes and their relationships to one another. We want the measure to capture in the mathematical world the behavior that we perceive in the empirical world. Where we often have difficulty is in interpreting the mathematical behavior and making judgments about what that means for the real world behavior.

Examining the Measures Themselves

None of these notions is particular to software development. Indeed, measurement has been studied for many years, beginning long before computers were around; however, the issues of measurement theory are very important in choosing and applying metrics to software development.

Guideline 4: Pay Attention to the Way in Which You Measure

To see why it's important to be aware of the way in which you measure, consider that one of the basic principles of measurement theory is the existence of several scales of measurement: nominal, ordinal, interval, and ratio. As we move from left to right in that list, each scale captures more information than its predecessor. A nominal scale puts items into categories; for example, we can identify programming language as one of Ada, COBOL, FORTRAN, or C++. The number of categories gives a sense of how widely dispersed the data are, and we can count the number of items in each category. We cannot say, however, that one category is in any sense better or bigger than another; that is, we cannot order the categories. For that, we need an ordinal scale. Ordinal measures involve a ranking that preserves order; for example, we can consider categories of software failures, and assign to each failure a severity, such as minor, major, and catastrophic, where major is more severe than minor, and catastrophic is more severe still.

An interval scale defines a distance from one point to another, so that there are equal intervals between consecutive numbers. This property permits computations not available with the ordinal scale, such as calculating the mean. Because no absolute zero point is established in an interval scale, however, ratios do not make sense and care is needed in making comparisons. For example, the Celsius and Fahrenheit temperature scales are interval, so we cannot say that today's 30-degree Celsius temperature is twice as hot as yesterday's 15-degree temperature. Thus, the scale with the most information and flexibility is the ratio scale, which incorporates an absolute zero, preserves ratios and permits the most sophisticated analysis. Measures such as lines of code or numbers of defects are ratio measures, and it is for this scale that we can say that A is twice the size of B.

Measurement types are described in more detail in Fenton and Pfleeger's book, *Software Metrics: A Rigorous and Practical Approach*.[4] They are important to the way you use measures because each scale permits only certain types of admissible calculations. For example, you cannot compute a meaningful mean and standard deviation for a nominal scale; such calculations require an interval or ratio scale. Thus, if we are unaware of the scale types we use, we are likely to misuse the data we collect.

At the same time, we want to be sure that the metrics we use are actually measuring what they claim to measure. For example, sometimes we measure the "complexity" of a design or code by using the cyclomatic number, a property of the control flow graph of a program. Many researchers are careful to state that cyclomatic number is a measure of structural complexity, but it does not capture all aspects of the difficulty we have in understanding a program. Few researchers have studied programs from a psychological perspective, trying to apply notions about how much we can track and absorb as a way of measuring the complexity of code. So it is important for us to be sure that the measures we are using are valid; that is, that they tell us what we really want to know.

To validate a measure, we must prove that the measure captures mathematically the characteristic we are observing in the real world. In other words, we must show that if H is a measure of some property, such as height, and if we perceive that the property of A is larger than that of B, then H(A) is larger than H(B). For example, if H is a measure of height, and Bill is taller than Bob, then we must show that H(Bill) is larger than H(Bob). Such a proof must by its nature be empirical, and it is often difficult to demonstrate. Moreover, we must pay attention to whether we are measuring something with a direct measure (such as size) or an indirect measure (a compound such as defects per thousand lines of code), and what entity and attribute are being addressed.

Suppose that we are interested in measuring software quality. We can measure software development products directly, by looking at how many defects have been found (in the code, the requirements, the designs and the test plans, for example), and how many changes or fixes have been made. We also can measure quality indirectly, by tracking how much time it takes to test or maintain a system. If we choose an indirect approach, we risk using a measure that is not capturing what we really want to know. Testing or maintenance time, for example, may be a function not only of quality but also of system availability. Moreover, developers understand better what the measurements mean if measures are direct and clearly related to how to how the problems are fixed. In other words, measurement is best when behavior or action is clearly tied to changes in the measures.

Guideline 5: Be Simple and Direct

Measurement theory and validation should not distract us from the considerable difficulty of measuring software in the field. We often try to relate measures of an artifact that we would like to behave like a physical object (software) with behaviors (psychological and organizational) that do not follow physical laws. For example, consider the *capability maturity* (CMM) level as a measure. The maturity level is designed to reflect the practices that an organization is using in its software development process. It is purported to be a predictor of the organization's capability to produce high-quality software on time. From one perspective, the CMM level is a valid predictor of development capability only when an organization at level *n always* creates better software than an organization at level *n-1*.

Suppose that we run a formal, well-designed, and tightly-controlled experiment where level 1 and level 2 organizations develop software, however. We examine the results and find that there are differences in the resulting software quality (measured as delivered faults) in favor of level 2 organizations, and the results are statistically significant at the $p < .001$ level.

If our experimental design is well-controlled, then most people would agree that we had successfully rejected the null hypothesis (that there were no differences between levels). As in any other science, we could then justifiably conclude that we have convincing evidence that level 2 organizations develop software better than level 1 organizations. Does this say that all level 2 organizations develop software better than level 1 organizations? No; it says only that the means of the quality distributions of the two organizations are sufficiently separated based on their dispersions. We can conclude that the two organizations really do represent two different populations, one of which generally develops higher quality software. However, we can probably find examples of level 1 organizations that build some software better than some level 2 organizations. The experiment shows only that level 2s are better than level 1s most of the time, usually under similar conditions.

Thus, a measure like the CMM can be useful as a predictor without being valid in the sense of measurement theory. The standard techniques we use in other scientific disciplines to assess association by analyzing distributions can be applied even to heuristics like the CMM to yield valuable information about the relationships among the factors that affect software development. In other words, even when something is not a strict measure according to the measurement theorists, it can be useful in practice to help us anticipate what is likely to happen most of the time.

Models and Measures

As software engineers, we tend to neglect models; however, models act as useful organizing principles for the analysis we do and the techniques we use. We have much to learn from other scientific disciplines, where models act to unify and explain, so that apparently disjoint events are placed in a larger, more understandable framework. This lack of models in software engineering is symptomatic of a much larger problem: lack of systems focus. Few software engineers understand the need to define a system boundary or to explain how one system interacts with another. Thus, research and practice have a very long way to go in exploring and exploiting what models can do to improve software produces and processes.

To understand the importance of models, let us complicate further the preceding CMM example. Suppose that we compare a level 3 organization that is constantly building radically different and more challenging avionics systems with a level 2 organization that continues to build versions of a relatively simple COBOL business application. Obviously, we are comparing sliced apples with peeled oranges, and the domain, customer type, and many other factors moderate the relationships we observe. This situation reveals problems not with the CMM as a measure, but with the model on which the CMM is based. In other words, we begin with simple models that provide useful information. Sometimes those models are sufficient for our needs, but at other times we must extend or make more detailed the simple models in order to handle the more complex situations we find in reality. It usually is better to begin with a simple model of cause and effect, and then collect data to determine whether the variables and their relationships produce acceptable descriptions of behavior and good estimates of dependent variables. If they do not, or they explain only part of the variation, the next step should involve measurement to expand our understanding. Again, this approach is no different from other sciences, where simple models (of molecular structure, for example) are expanded as we understand more about the factors that affect the outcomes of the processes we use and study.

Guideline 6: Change Your Measures and Your Models as You Understand More About Your Situation

Measuring Process

For many years, computer scientists and software engineers focused on measuring and understanding only code. In recent years, however, software process issues have received a great deal of attention, as we have come to understand that product quality is evidence of process success. Process measures can include large-grain quantifications, such as the type of process used or the CMM scale, as well as smaller-grain evaluations of particular process activities, such as test or inspection effectiveness.

Process measurement relies, to some extent, on current research. Some process researchers have developed process description languages that can be used in describing and measuring a process. If the process is expressed in a particular process language, for example, a count of the language's tokens tells us about the size of the process; the connections among the tokens and the number of tokens used tell us about the process complexity. We can use this information to compare and contrast projects, or to understand how processes and projects become more or less complex over time.

We also can look at existing processes and use measurement to help us understand and improve them. Many recent studies, for example, have examined the effectiveness of inspections and reviews. We can inspect or review a variety of documents: requirements, designs, code, and test plans, for example. We also can perform the review in many ways: using a checklist, looking for particular types of problems, or comparing several document perspectives to make sure that a product is complete and consistent. At the same time, we can measure how many problems are found, what types they are (such as user interface, database, algorithmic), and how much time it takes to find each one. If reviews involve both individual and team scrutiny, we can examine how much the team effort contributes to the total problem discovery, and in what way. Thus, measurement supports our understanding of how reviews work; we can use measurement information to tailor the review process and make it more effective for our particular situations.

The reuse community provides good examples of process-related measurement as it tries to determine the impact of reuse on quality and productivity. Lim, for example, modeled the reuse process at Hewlett-Packard and suggested measurements for assessing reuse effectiveness. In Italy, Favaro used business investment concepts to evaluate the impact of reuse on a company's bottom line. Pfleeger and Theofanos combined process maturity concepts with a goal-question-metric approach to suggest metrics to instrument the reuse process. Similarly, an Italian research group evaluated a large system reengineering project. As a banking application's millions of lines of COBOL code were reengineered, a very extensive set of measurements was kept over a period of years to track the impact of the changes made. These measures included the structure of the system, the number of help requests, the number of change requests, and more. Measurement enabled the team to evaluate the success and payback of the reengineering process.

When you are measuring aspects of process, you should be aware of some common problems. First, large-grained process measures require validation, which is difficult to do. Second, project managers often are intimidated by the effort required to track process measures throughout development. Individual process activities usually are easier to evaluate, because they are smaller and more controllable. Third, regardless of the granularity, process measures usually require an underlying model of how they interrelate; this model often is missing from process understanding and evaluation activities, so the results of other peoples' investigations are difficult to interpret. That is, unless you can be sure that your process is like the one you are reading about, you cannot be sure that the results apply to your situation. Nevertheless, investment in process measurement has the potential for offering big benefits. In other words,

Guideline 7: Model and Measure the Process When You Can

Measuring Products

Products, being more concrete entities than processes and resources, are easier to measure, so it is not surprising that most measurement work addresses product issues. Our customers are interested in the characteristics of the final product, regardless of the process used to produce it, so they encourage product assessment, too. As a result, we measure faults (in specification, design, code and test cases) and failures as part of a broader program to assess product quality. We sometimes use a quality framework, such as the one shown in Figure 8.1, to suggest ways for us to describe different aspects of product quality, distinguishing usability from reliability from maintainability, for example.

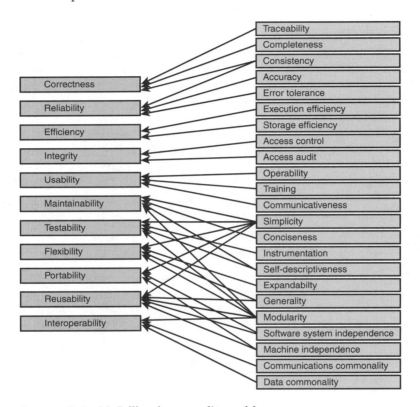

FIGURE 8.1 *McCall's software quality model.*

Failures are the most visible evidence of poor quality, so predicting and assessing reliability are important to us and our customers. There are many reliability models, each focused on using operational profile and time-to-next-failure data to predict when the next failure is likely to occur. These models are based on probability distributions, plus assumptions about whether new faults are introduced when old ones are repaired. Figure 8.2, for example, shows how different models give very different results in predicting reliability for a single data set. At a given point on the x-axis, a particular model predicts a certain median time to failure, as indicated on the y-axis. In this example, the predicted median time to failure 100 is more than four times for the most optimistic model as it is for the most pessimistic model. For a product with tight reliability requirements, knowing which model is correct is vital to the success of the product!

Clearly, more work is needed for us to learn how to build good models. We must make our assumptions more realistic, as well as assist users in deciding which model is most appropriate for a given situation.

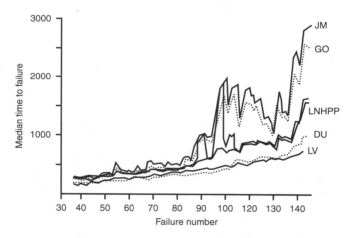

FIGURE 8.2 *Performance of several popular reliability models on a single dataset.*

In general, there are models that are accurate most of the time, but there are no guarantees that a particular model will perform well in a particular situation. For that reason, we recommend that you build models to reflect the characteristics of your own organization and products, rather than using one that has worked well for someone else.

Guideline 8: Build Models that Reflect Your Own Situation

Because most developers and customers cannot want to wait until delivery to determine if the code is reliable or maintainable, some practitioners measure faults, hoping that the number of faults found will act as evidence of delivered code quality and likely reliability. Counting faults as a surrogate reliability measure has several drawbacks, however. First, if many faults are discovered during review and testing, is that an indicator of good or bad quality? We can argue that finding many faults early means that there are even more faults remaining in the code. We also can argue that finding many faults means that reviewing and testing have been particularly thorough. Second, we must recognize that not every fault leads to a failure. Each of us has seen examples of faults that will never lead to a failure, sometimes simply because the faulty code is never executed!

An IBM researcher revealed the dangers of assuming that faults represent failures. [5] Ed Adams used IBM data to show that 80 percent of the reliability problems in the OS-360 operating system were caused by only 2 percent of the defects. That is, had we counted faults and considered one fault to be much like another, activities focused on removing those faults might have done very little to improve the overall system reliability. When measuring faults and failures, it often is more useful to use that data to understand the nature of software quality problems, rather than focus on global counts. This understanding will, in the long run, help us to decide which defects are likely to cause the most problems, and to prevent such problems before they occur.

We also can measure earlier life-cycle products. For example, although requirements are often recorded as English-language sentences, we can record measures such as the number of requirements, perhaps segregated by type of requirements. These measures enable us to compare (albeit roughly) one system with another, to see if they are the same or different. We can also measure the readiness of requirements, in the following sense.

Suppose that a set of requirements is given to the design team. The designers are asked to rate each requirement from 1, meaning "We understand this requirement completely and can do a design for it," to 5, meaning "We don't have a clue about what this requirement means, and there is no way we can even begin to do a design." If we draw a histogram of the number of requirements in each category, we get a subjective but useful sense of whether this system is ready to move from the requirements stage of development to the design stage. If the profile looks like picture (a) in Figure 8.3, then the project can move on to design. If the profile looks more like (b), however, then it is probably appropriate to continue working on requirements—clarifying understanding within the development team and with the customer. There is very little objective requirements measurement in actual practice, reflecting the fact that serious measurement of requirements attributes is just beginning. Nevertheless, subjective measures can be powerful in revealing readiness and improving understanding.

Notice that the requirements readiness measure also can be used by the test team to decide if the requirements are ready for use in developing system and acceptance tests. Some developers insist that metrics be objective. This example, however, shows that subjectivity does not always diminish utility; waiting for the "best" metric may mean passing up good measurement opportunities.

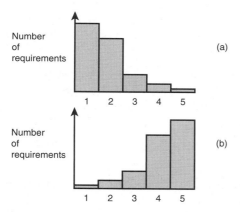

FIGURE 8.3   *Assessing requirements readiness.*

Guideline 9: Using Some Metrics Is Better than Using No Metrics

As software development activities move from the fuzzy, real-world require-ments to the more concrete, mathematically-based artifacts, measurement becomes easier, so it is no surprise that more metrics are available for use with designs and code. In particular, researchers and practitioners have several ways of evaluating design quality, in the hope that good design will yield good code. For example, one design measure is based on the fan-in and fan-out of modules. Another uses notions of internal and external complexity to build a measure of overall software design complexity that predicts where faults are likely to be in the code. But many of the existing design measures focus on functional or procedural descriptions of design; many researchers are now extending these types of measures to object-oriented design and code.

The fact that code is easier to measure than earlier products does not prevent controversy in code measurement. Debate continues to rage over whether lines of code are a reasonable measure of software size. The U.S. Software Engineering Institute has produced a framework that organizes the many decisions involved in defining a lines of code count, including reuse, com-ments, executable statements and more. Its report makes clear the necessity for knowing your goals before you design your measures. Another camp prefers to measure code in terms of function points, a technique developed at IBM; a function point purports to capture the software's functionality from the specification in a way that is impossible for lines of code.

Both sides have valid points, and both have attempted to unify and define their ideas so that counting and comparing across organizations is possible; however, there are many issues still to be resolved. The problem for practitioners and customers is that they have no time to wait for resolution; they need measures now that will help them understand and predict likely effort, quality and schedule.

These concerns lead to several common-sense guidelines for choosing and using measures. First, remember that several measures may be better than one. If one size measure has pros and cons, for example, try measuring size in two or three ways (as long as you are not adding unnecessary burden to the developers' and managers' jobs). Then look at trends in all of the measures to make sure that they have the same indications.

Suppose that user interface code is growing in lines of code, and user-interface-related function points are growing at the same rate. These measurement trends may be highlighting a problem with gold-plating. That is, the customer may be adding fancy interface requirements as the developers are scrambling to get the system coded and tested. The development team can use the dual measures to request a moratorium on requirements changes until the initial system is complete. The double measurements give the developers' argument added weight.

Guideline 10: Measure Twice, Act Once

Second, it is important to remember that code measures can provide instant and important feedback to developers as they examine their designs and code. For example, unusual measures of complexity or size can raise red flags, allowing developers to rethink their strategies and perhaps redesign. A delay in this feedback, however, dramatically reduces the utility of the measures. A static metric analysis of a programmer's code, for example, does her no good if the results are reported two days after the code is analyzed; she may have changed the code substantially by the time she gets the feedback, so the metric results are irrelevant. Quick measurement feedback can aid not only design and development decisions but also testing and maintenance choices.

Guideline 11: Keep the Metrics Close to the Developers

Third, remember that the developers are busy getting the system written and running. They rarely have the luxury of extra time to record and analyze metrics. At the very least, make sure that the time required to capture data is exceeded by the time saved in taking the actions suggested by the measurements. For example, it may take a project manager 15 minutes to analyze weekly fault and failure data from his system, but that analysis may save testers and maintainers hours of time, so the 15-minute investment is well-worth the time spent.

Moreover, the more you can automate the measurement capture and analysis activities, the better. Static code analyzers can generate size and structure measures automatically, and analysis packages make assessment and trend analysis simple and quick.

Guideline 12: Capture as Much as You Can Without Burdening the Developers

Not all measurement can be automated. For example, the requirements readiness measure is intrusive but useful. Often, developers are reticent to collect measurement data; they see no potential benefit. If developers are forced to supply measurement data, they may be sloppy or inaccurate because they are in a hurry to get back to their "real work." In such cases, it is better to begin a measurement program by finding receptive developers who have a clear problem to solve. Often, they welcome measurement, and they are eager to advertise its benefits if the measurement-based effort is successful.

Guideline 13: Start with the People Who Need Help; Then Let Them Do Your Advertising for You

Suppose that an organization's director mandates a measurement program. We can poll the various projects to see which ones are experiencing what kinds of problems.

We may find a group that is maintaining a system, finding and fixing dozens of problems each month. Because many of the problems are severe and must be fixed quickly, the maintenance team is working overtime to clear them. Measurement may offer some help to this team. We can perform the following tasks:

- Track the categories of failures and faults to see which ones are causing the most problems.

- Perform root-cause analysis to determine where the fault was "injected" in the system.

- Determine how to fix the process to prevent the faults from occurring.

- Use the fault and failure data to suggest preventive maintenance, including redesigning so that the system will "fail soft" when a fault is triggered.

- Measure some static properties of the design and code, such as depth of nesting, use of inheritance, and cyclomatic number; then look for unusual circumstances that might be the source of some faults.

These problem-solving steps should be supplemented with measures of progress or success. For example, we can track the decrease in faults and failures over time, the resulting increase in reliability, and the decrease of overtime or hours to fix each maintenance problem. Armed with this quantitative success story, we then can suggest to other organizations that measurement can help them in similar ways.

Measuring Resources

For many years, some of our most insightful software engineers have encouraged us to look at the quality and variability of the people we employ for the source of variation in our products. Some initial measurement work has been done. An IBM study, for example, found that a developer's surroundings (such as noise level, number of interruptions and office size) can affect the productivity and quality of his or her work. Likewise, several studies suggest that individual variation accounts for much of the difference in code complexity; for example, work at ITT showed that the average time to locate a defect in code is not related to years of experience but rather to breadth of experience.[6] However, relatively little attention is paid to human resource measurement, as developers and managers find it threatening.

More attention has been paid to non-human resources: budget and schedule assessment, and effort, cost, and schedule prediction. A rich assortment of tools and techniques is available to support this work, including the COCOMO model, embellishments of the original function points model, and many proprietary tool-based models. However, no model that works satisfactorily for everyone, in part because of organizational and project differences, and in part because of model imperfections. Many researchers have demonstrated how tailoring models can improve their performances significantly; it is more important to follow consistently a particular modeling technique than to use a model developed for someone else's data and situation.

Moreover, some models are better than others at capturing key aspects of a project. It often is useful to make estimates using several different modeling approaches; then we can combine the results into a larger model that is more accurate than any of its component models. That is,

Guideline 14: Use Multiple Models, Tailoring Each to Your Particular Situation

Storing, Analyzing, and Reporting the Measurements

Researchers and practitioners alike often assume that once the metrics are chosen and the data collected, the measurement activities are done. The goals of measurement—understanding and change— for example, are not met until the data are analyzed and change is effected. It is helpful to have a tool to store and analyze the data, even if it is an application built from a spreadsheet or database management system. More sophisticated tools are available, but they are not always necessary.

The choice of tool depends on the use to which the measurements will be put. For many organizations, simple analysis techniques such as scatter charts and histograms provide useful information about what is happening on a project or in a product. Others prefer to use statistical analysis; regression and correlation, box plots, and measures of central tendency and dispersion are informative and helpful.

More complex still are classification trees; they can be applied to problems of determining which metrics are the best predictors of quality or productivity from among a large collection of metrics. For example, if module quality can be assessed using the number of faults per module, then a classification tree analysis can generate a decision tree to illustrate which of the metrics collected predict modules that have more than a threshold number of faults. Figure 8.4 shows an example classification tree. According to the tree, past history for this product suggests that if a module is between 100 and 300 lines of code and has at least 15 decisions, then it is likely to have a significant number of faults. Likewise, if it is more than 300 lines of code, has not been the subject of a design review, and has been changed at least five times, then it is likely to have a significant number of faults.

Such analysis helps us to understand the nature of our systems, and to focus our review and testing efforts. For example, if this project has a tight schedule for testing and it is clear that the entire system cannot be tested thoroughly, the testers may decide (based on the tree) to test first these two categories leading to likely faults. Then, if time permits, the remainder of the system can be tested.

Process measures are more difficult to track, as they often require traceability from one product or activity to another. In this case, databases of traceability information are needed, coupled with software to track and analyze progress. Practitioners often use their configuration management system for these measures, augmenting existing configuration information with measurement data.

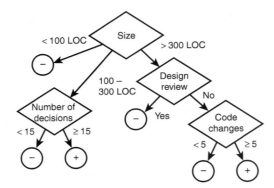

FIGURE 8.4 *The classification tree (from Pfleeger, 1998).*

In storing and analyzing large sets of data, it is important to choose analysis techniques that are appropriate to the data. Population dynamics and distribution are key aspects of this choice. When sampling from data, it is essential that the sample be representative, so that the judgments made about the sample can be assumed to apply to the larger population. At the same time, it is equally important to be sure that the analysis technique is suitable for the data's distribution.

Often, practitioners use a technique simply because it is available on a statistical software package, regardless of whether the data are distributed normally or not; as a result, we use invalid parametric techniques instead of the more appropriate nonparametric ones, and we risk generating bogus results. Although some of the parametric techniques are robust enough to be used with non-normal distributions, we must take care to verify this robustness.

As noted earlier, the statistical techniques also must be appropriate to the measurement scale. Measures of central tendency and dispersion differ with the scale, as do appropriate transformations. Nominal data that describe categories can be analyzed using mode and frequency distributions but not means and standard deviations. Ordinal data, where an order is imposed on the categories, permit medians, maxima, and minima for analysis. However, not until data are interval or ratio can means, standard deviations, and more sophisticated statistics be employed.

Guideline 15: Make Sure the Analysis Is Appropriate to the Data and Their Distribution

Another major problem with measurement data is their presentation to those who need to understand and use them. Metrics are chosen based on business and development goals; they are then collected by developers but presented to customers who are not experts in software development. Moreover, customers want a "big picture" of what the software is like, not a large vector of measures of different aspects. Hewlett-Packard, for example, has been successful in using Kiviat diagrams (sometimes called radar graphs) to depict multiple measures in one picture, without losing the integrity of the individual measures. Similarly, Contel used multiple metrics graphs to report on software switch quality and other characteristics.

Guideline 16: The Presentation Should Be Appropriate for the Audience and the Problem

Data analysis and reporting often are part of a larger effort to examine the empirical basis for software engineering. Sometimes we use what is easily available and easy to use, regardless of its appropriateness; in part, this situation is the fault of researchers, who have not taken steps to describe the limitations of and constraints on techniques as they are put forth for practical use. The measurement community has yet to deal with the more global issue of technology transfer. It is unreasonable for us to expect practitioners to become experts in statistics, probability or measurement theory, or even in the intricacies of calculating code complexity or modeling parameters. Instead, we need to encourage researchers to fashion results into tools and techniques that are easily understandable to and applicable by practitioners.

We need not wait for sophisticated tools and techniques, though. Instead, we must recognize that we often focus on the average instead of the unusual. That is, we know quite well what usually happens on our projects, especially when we have a great deal of experience in building the same kind of product with the same kind of people using the same kinds of techniques and tools. What we do not understand as well is what to expect when we change a major variable: the application domain, the development technique, or the team dynamics, for example. In other words, it often is not the average case that causes problems; it's the unusual case—the outliers. Thus, it is essential that we take a careful look at the data, searching for patterns or trends to help enlighten us.

Guideline 17: Look at the Data to Understand It Before You Jump In and Run Statistical Tests

Consider the scatter diagram in Figure 8.5. An analyst rushing to apply a statistical technique might look for a line whose behavior approximates that of the dots. The solid line labeled "linear fit" is what might result from a linear regression. If we look more carefully at the dots, however, we see that three have behavior distinct from the others; they may be *outliers*. If we omit those three and search for a line to approximate the behavior of the rest, we might get the nonlinear fit represented by the dashed line.

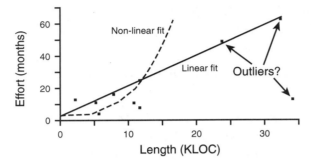

FIGURE 8.5 *Analyzing a scatter diagram.*

What distinguishes the outliers from the rest? Only a more careful analysis will tell us. The outliers might represent the three modules coded in an object-oriented language, while the other modules are procedural. Or the three modules were coded by the newest, least experienced members of the team. Or the modules might represent the user interface, while the rest are more traditional, data manipulation modules. The reason is not apparent from the initial measures, but the measures make more visible the patterns that are important to making the project a success.

Steps to More Effective Measurement

As we have seen, there are many useful, practical ways to measure, and practitioners can start measuring today. So why aren't all practitioners using measurement? One reason is that researchers, practitioners and customers are not communicating with one another. Each is driven by a different set of goals.

Researchers, many of whom are in academic environments, are motivated by publication; in many cases, highly theoretical results are never tested empirically. New metrics are defined but never used; new theories are promulgated but never exercised and modified to fit reality. At the same time, we practitioners want short-term, useful results.

Our projects are in trouble now, and we are not always willing to be a testbed for studies whose results will be helpful on the next project, not the current one. Moreover, practitioners are not always willing to make data available to researchers, for fear that the secrets of technical advantage will be revealed to their competitors. Customers, who are not always involved as development progresses, feel powerless. They are forced to specify what they need and then hope that what they want is what they get. It is no coincidence that the most successful examples of software measurement are the ones where researcher, practitioner and customer work hand in hand to meet common goals and solve common problems.

Thus, it is essential that researchers and practitioners pay careful attention to the measurement needs of our customers. We must base our activities on customer goals. As practitioners and customers cry out for measures early in the development cycle, we must focus our efforts on measuring aspects of requirements analysis and design. As our customers request measurements for evaluating commercial off-the-shelf software, we must derive product metrics that support decisions about purchasing off-the-shelf software. And as our customers insist on higher levels of reliability, functionality, usability, reusability, and maintainability, we must work closely with other software engineers to understand the processes and resources that contribute to good products. Measurement can be useful, easy-to-use, and effective, but until measurement is a mainstream software engineering activity, our delivered code will be good in theory but not in practice.

Further Reading

There are many places where you can find more information about the theory and practice of software measurement, and we have listed some of them here.

Books

D. Card and R. Glass, *Measuring Software Design Complexity*, Prentice Hall, New Jersey, 1991.

S. D. Conte, H. E. Dunsmore, and V. Y. Shen, *Software Engineering Metrics and Models*, Benjamin Cummings, Menlo Park, California, 1986.

T. DeMarco, *Controlling Software Projects*, Dorset House, New York, 1982.

J. B. Dreger, *Function Point Analysis*, Prentice Hall, New Jersey, 1989.

N. Fenton and S. L. Pfleeger, *Software Metrics: A Rigorous and Practical Approach*, second edition, PWS Publishing, New York, 1997.

R. B. Grady, *Practical Software Metrics for Project Management and Process Improvement*, Prentice Hall, New Jersey, 1992.

R. B. Grady and D. L. Caswell, *Software Metrics: Establishing a Company-Wide Program*, Prentice Hall, New Jersey, 1987.

T. C. Jones, *Applied Software Measurement: Assuring Productivity and Quality*, McGraw Hill, New York, 1992.

K. Moeller and D. J. Paulish, *Software Metrics: A Practitioner's Guide to Improved Product Development*, IEEE Computer Society Press, Washington, DC, 1993.

P. Oman and S. L. Pfleeger, Applying Software Metrics, *IEEE Computer Society Press*, Washington, DC, 1996.

Journals

IEEE Software (March 1991, special issue on measurement; July 1994, special issue on measurement-based process improvement; January 1996, special issue on software quality on trial; March 1997, special issue on measurement)

IEEE Computer (September 1994, special issue on product metrics)

IEEE Transactions on Software Engineering

Journal of Systems and Software

Software Quality Journal

IEE Journal

IBM Systems Journal

Information and Software Technology

Empirical Software Engineering: An International Journal

Key Journal Articles

V. R. Basili and H. D. Rombach, "The TAME project: Towards improvement-oriented software environments," *IEEE Transactions on Software Engineering*, 14(6), pp. 758-773, 1988.

C. Billings, J. Clifton, B. Kolkhorst, E. Lee and W. B. Wingert, "Journey to a mature software process," *IBM Systems Journal*, 33 (1), 1994, pp. 46-61.

B. Curtis, "Measurement and experimentation in software engineering," *Proceedings of the IEEE*, 68(9), 1980, pp. 1144-1157.

B. A. Kitchenham, L. Pickard and S. L. Pfleeger, "Using case studies for process improvement," *IEEE Software*, July 1995.

S. L. Pfleeger, "Lessons learned in building a corporate metrics program," *IEEE Software*, May 1993.

S. L. Pfleeger, "Experimentation in software engineering," *Annals of Software Engineering*, 1(1), 1995.

S. L. Pfleeger, B. Curtis, R. Jeffery and B. A. Kitchenham, "Status report on software measurement," *IEEE Software*, March 1997.

S. S. Stevens, "On the theory of scales of measurement," *Science*, (103) 1946, pp. 677-680.

Conferences

Applications of Software Measurement, sponsored by Software Quality Engineering, Inc., held annually, usually in Florida and California on alternate years. Contact: Software Quality Engineering, Jacksonville, Florida, USA.

International Symposium on Software Measurement, sponsored by IEEE Computer Society (1st in Baltimore, 1993, 2nd in London, 1994, 3rd in Berlin, 1996, 4th in Bethesda (MD) in 1998, 5th in Florida in 1999); proceedings available from IEEE Computer Society Press. Contact: Prof. James Bieman, Colorado State University, Fort Collins, Colorado, USA.

Oregon Workshop on Software Metrics Workshop, sponsored by Portland State University, held annually near Portland, Oregon. Contact: Prof. Warren Harrison, Portland State University, Portland, Oregon, USA.

Minnowbrook Workshop on Software Performance Evaluation, sponsored by Syracuse University, held each summer at Blue Mountain Lake, NY. Contact: Prof. Amrit Goel, Syracuse University, Syracuse, New York, USA.

NASA Software Engineering Symposium, sponsored by NASA Goddard Space Flight Center, held annually at the end of November or early December in Greenbelt, Maryland; proceedings available. Contact: Frank McGarry, Computer Sciences Corporation, Greenbelt, Maryland, USA.

Organizations

Australian Software Metrics Association. Contact Prof. Mike Berry, School of Information Systems, University of New South Wales, Sydney 2052 Australia.

Quantitative Methods Committee, IEEE Computer Society Technical Council on Software Engineering. Contact: Prof. James Bieman, Department of Computer Science, Colorado State University, Fort Collins, Colorado, USA.

Centre for Software Reliability. Contact: Prof. Bev Littlewood, CSR, City University, London, England.

Software Engineering Laboratory. Contact: Prof. Victor Basili, Department of Computer Science, University of Maryland, College Park, Maryland, USA.

SEI Software Measurement Program. Contact: Anita Carleton, Software Engineering Institute, Carnegie Mellon University, Pittsburgh, PA, USA.

ami (Applications of Measurement in Industry) User Group. Contact: Ami User Group, South Bank University, London, England.

International Society of Parametric Analysts. Contact: J. Clyde Perry & Associates, P.O. Box 6402, Chesterfield, Missouri, 63006-6402 USA.

International Function Point Users Group. Contact: IFPUG Executive Office, Blendonview Office Park, 5008-28 Pine Creek Drive, Westerville, Ohio 43081-4899 USA.

References

1. Edward F. Weller, "Using metrics to manage software projects," *IEEE Computer*, pp. 27-34, September 1994.

2. Wayne C. Lim, "Effects of reuse on quality, productivity and economics," *IEEE Software*, 11(5), pp. 23-30, September 1994.

3. Michael K. Daskalantonakis, "A practical view of software measurement and implementation experiences within Motorola," *IEEE Transactions on Software Engineering*, 18 (11), pp. 998-1010, 1992.

4. Norman Fenton and Shari Lawrence Pfleeger, *Software Metrics: A Rigorous and Practical Approach*, second edition, PWS Publishing, New York, 1997.

5. Edward Adams, "Optimizing preventive service of software products," *IBM Journal of Research and Development*, 28(1), pp. 2-14, 1984.

6. Bill Curtis, S. B. Sheppard, P. Milliman, M. A. Borst and T. Love, "Measuring the psychological complexity of software maintenance tasks with the Halstead and McCabe metrics," *IEEE Transactions on Software Engineering* SE-5 (2), pp. 96-104, 1979.

CHAPTER 9

Select Tools to Fit the Tasks

Anthony I. Wasserman, Software Methods and Tools

What's the Issue?

Software tools support software development and maintenance, whatever the process may be. Each organization has its own process, whether or not it is well-defined, and this process often varies among projects and among different groups within a company. The development process, and hence many of the tools, are different for an embedded system than for a client-server application providing shared access to a database. Similarly, the process and tools are different for a complex, business-critical application, such as electronic funds transfer, than for small, departmental level applications. Finally, the tools needed to evolve or maintain a system are typically different from those used for the original development. The nature of applications influences the degree of control needed over the process, the types of tools that are needed, and the demands on software performance and reliability.

Most tools are specialized for specific tasks, such as modeling requirements, testing a piece of code, or version control. Tools may be classified as *horizontal*, covering the entire process, or as *vertical*, covering a specific phase of the process. Typical vertical tools are modeling tools, test generators, and compilers. Typical horizontal tools include project management and documentation tools.

The collection of tools, combined with the platform(s) on which it is used, is a central part of the software development *environment*, which also includes organizational aspects and physical workspace.

The key issue for development organizations, then, is to create a productive development environment, making the best possible match between tools and tasks, while balancing numerous business and technical considerations.

Why Is It Important?

Tools can make a big difference in developer productivity. While some tools can be a drag on productivity because of a steep learning curve or a major impact on existing processes, other tools can produce huge savings in development time, such as automating most code generation for a graphical user interface.

This difference in productivity is separate from improvements that may be obtained from adhering to a well-defined software process, as advocated by the Software Engineering Institute, among others. Note that it is possible to have a well-managed process without obtaining the productivity gains available from a judicious choice of effective tools. In practice, many organizations give primary emphasis to their tool set, giving less attention to software process improvement issues.

In this chapter, I offer some practical guidance in tool selection and use. I first review the various tasks in software development and maintenance, then describe types of tools used for these tasks, discuss mechanisms for integrating tools, cover some of the business issues in tool selection, and give pointers to additional resources.

Software Development and Maintenance Tasks

It's important to think of tools and environments in relation to the development and maintenance tasks being performed. These tasks can range from project planning and requirements gathering through regression testing of a release candidate and deployment of the release version of the application with its documentation.

Project Planning

Project planning is a critical first step that goes hand in hand with understanding the requirements for a project. Project planning involves estimating the resources needed (such as time, money, people, space, equipment, tools) for a project and attempting to resolve those against existing resource constraints. Resource constraints might be "firm" delivery dates, staffing shortages, or limited budgets for equipment and tools.

In such cases, project planning must involve making appropriate tradeoffs and deciding if it is feasible to accomplish the planned objectives with the available resources. Historical data, such as metrics from previous projects, are valuable here. If estimated available resources fall far short of estimated resource requirements, then it is desirable to modify the project requirements and/or the delivery dates rather than embarking on a "death march"[3] that is likely to yield unsatisfactory results.

Aspects of project planning include risk analysis, cost estimation, initiation of project management, staffing assignments, and equipment and tools acquisition.

Requirements Gathering and Problem Analysis

Requirements gathering involves understanding the desired features and functions of a system from many different perspectives. Understanding the requirements for a software product include, among other things, analyzing the features of competing products, talking to prospective buyers of the product, planning to conform to various standards and quasi-standards, becoming aware of future plans of other software vendors on whom the product depends (such as an operating system or database vendor), defining platform requirements, and establishing price and release date requirements.

Requirements gathering, as with many other software tasks, is an iterative process. Major requirements are identified at an early stage and are subsequently refined as the project proceeds. Refinement may add more detail to the existing requirements, add new requirements, or eliminate some of them as a result of resource constraints. In many situations, simulations and user interface prototyping are important steps of requirements gathering. A user interface prototype is often useful to give a potential user a better sense of the system's intended behavior. However, it's not until users can actually work with a prototype that they come to understand what the system will eventually do and how it will look.

Requirements are frequently enumerated, often in a hierarchical manner, so that they can be linked to the overall system design and implementation. Requirements should be written in a way that makes them as precise as possible, so as to minimize misunderstandings and to facilitate testing the resulting system for conformance with the requirements.

The result of requirements gathering is a specification that describes the expected behavior of the system under development.

Design

System design covers a broad range of topics, ranging from joint hardware/software design to software architecture (including database design) to the logic of individual program units. Whereas requirements gathering occurs in the problem domain, design occurs in the system domain. Thus, one of the critical tasks of the design process is to transform external requirements into software structures. This task involves transforming requirements to system activities, data, and/or events. Design also entails analyzing tradeoffs for performance, including realtime event handling, memory and processor utilization, and system security and reliability.

Software architecture includes making decisions about distribution of program units and data among processors and storage units, as well as specifying interfaces among program units and external application programming interfaces (APIs). Program units may be connected with proprietary interfaces or by widely followed mechanisms, such as Microsoft's Open Database Connectivity (ODBC), Microsoft's extended Component Object Model (COM+), or the Object Management Group's CORBA model.

There are a growing number of domain-specific software architectures. Many applications, for example, developed for the World Wide Web rely on a multi-tier architecture, where one tier is a Web browser that displays HTML, XML, and/or Java applets to the user, another tier is an application server that dynamically generates the pages served to the browser, and yet another tier is a database server used for secure transactions. Application of these domain-specific architectures greatly simplifies the design process and allows for modularization of the development effort.

Reuse and components also are key aspects of design. In addition to reusable assets that an organization or individual may have developed, there are also third-party sources for "standard" software architectures, numerous components for common software functions, and frameworks for generic applications, exemplified by IBM's San Francisco project. Scripting languages assist in "gluing" together different programs into a coherent system. Organizations moving to component-based development find that it affects their design process.

Implementation: Coding and Debugging

Implementation refers to creating and debugging an executable program that meets the requirements specified for the system using the design information. Implementations can be accomplished in many different ways. For many years, procedural programming languages (3GLs), such as FORTRAN, COBOL, C,

C++, Ada, or Java, have been used. Each of these languages includes a set of predefined library functions or classes for many common operations. Java's libraries are quite extensive and serve as a generally available set of components that can significantly reduce the amount of original code to be written.

Nonprocedural languages (4GLs) were first used successfully beginning in the early 1970s, and these have proliferated widely since then. The SQL data definition and manipulation language is perhaps the best known instance of a nonprocedural language. SQL statements are embedded in many languages, including the widely used PowerBuilder and Visual BASIC 4GLs. These 4GLs can create client-server architectures, providing for an ODBC connection from a client program to a relational database on the server. These 4GLs support the visual development of a graphical user interface that runs on the client machine, along with any processing logic, including SQL statements, needed for database processing.

Implementation also includes documenting the system for its users and for maintainers of the system. External documentation includes printed user and reference guides or their electronic equivalents. User-visible program documentation includes online help, such as tutorials, examples, movies, and online assistance. Internal documentation includes design documentation, as well as program comments within individual program units and files.

Finally, implementation includes packaging the complete system for release. While the complete system may simply be an executable file, it is more common for the system to be a collection of files grouped together by an "installer" program, a separate executable program that provides the end user with installation options and then installs the desired options on the end user's system. From a user perspective, the installation process is the first thing that a user sees when installing a new piece of software, so the organization and implementation of the installation program is a vital piece of the system.

Testing and Quality Assurance

Testing and *quality assurance* (QA) is a continuous activity, occurring in parallel with the other tasks described here. For each major task, it's possible to identify a complementary task aimed at validating the task. An important goal is to find problems, including omissions and errors, as early as possible, because that sharply reduces the cost of finding and fixing such problems at later stages of development or after deployment.

Many organizations have a QA group that works in parallel with the development team. As the requirements are developed, the QA group works on acceptance tests that can be used to see if the finished system meets the requirements. The QA group also may review the requirements for consistency, completeness, and precision so that the requirements are clearly understood by those responsible for the design and implementation. This step is particularly important in those organizations where the design and implementation will be outsourced or done by contractors, possibly at geographically remote locations.

As the design is completed, the QA group may lead a design review to validate the software architecture, the database design, or other design decisions. Unspecified or incomplete interfaces are particularly problematic, because they interfere with the capability to isolate pieces of the system and support independent implementation of various subsystems. Reviews can also identify areas of unwanted dependencies between program units, such as extensive use of global data, message passing of control information, and so on. At this stage, QA activities also can include the creation of test cases for the eventual integration of program units, as well as generating sample databases for database applications.

As the implementation proceeds, the programmers typically do routine debugging. However, the QA group is responsible for thoroughly testing the program outside the development environment. Testing activities may include creating sets of test cases that exercise a high percentage of lines of code or logical branches within a program unit, as well as simulating the behavior of program users with a broad variety of correct and incorrect inputs. The QA activity also involves reviewing user-visible documentation (including online assistance) to make sure that it is complete and consistent with program behavior.

The goal is to find as many errors as possible before the program is released to its eventual users. Many of the same notions apply if the program is to be embedded in a hardware device; in that situation, testing is even more important, because it is much more difficult to fix errors when the program is part of a control device, such as an automobile braking system, or a standalone unit, such as an electronic toy or a personal digital assistant.

Ongoing Evolution

Many software systems have a long lifetime. They are changed to fix identified bugs, updated to work with new versions of operating systems or databases, and enhanced based on user feedback, competitive considerations, industry standards, or research results. (The size of efforts to remediate programs for the year 2000 is an excellent illustration of this point.)

The result of such evolution is a series of versions of the program or a family of programs. With the exceptions of fixing minor bugs and porting source code to a different platform, most maintenance and enhancement tasks go through all the phases of development, from requirements gathering through implementation and testing.

Besides the tasks associated with those other phases, maintenance also involves gaining an understanding of the structure and behavior of the program(s) being modified. It often is necessary to visualize the various software and data components, such as a database schema or a program calling or message passing structure.

Coordination

Coordinating all the different tasks is an important task in and of itself. This statement is true not only for large projects involving many people over months or years, but also for small projects, including those where all of the work is being done by a single person. Projects must keep track of their status with respect to the original project plan, updating the plan as needed to reflect the current state of the project.

Large projects need multiuser coordination, including access control, check in and checkout of various software artifacts (design models, code, test data, test results, and so on), and logging of meeting results and decisions reached by telephone conversations, email, or whiteboard sessions. Configuration management is especially important to coordinate not only the pieces of the program (or program family), but also the associated documentation, build scripts, and related information that can help in the ongoing maintenance tasks.

Tiny projects also need some coordination, such as problem tracking, logging of project time, and version control. Such coordination is important even for an individual software developer, who often finds it necessary to revert to a previous version of a program unit or a document.

Accurate design and program documentation is a critical aspect of coordination. Documentation is particularly important for the ongoing maintenance of systems; unfortunately, it often is neglected during the development process. If documentation for a system is missing or incorrect, it becomes necessary to examine the existing program directly, or to use design recovery (reverse engineering) tools that can help those responsible for ongoing program development.

Coordination also involves keeping metrics on the work. Tracking of errors, identified and fixed, overall productivity by function points or lines of code, and similar measures all help to improve future estimates and projects, as well as to provide some overall measures of quality.

Projects, Tasks, and Tools

The preceding set of tasks appears quite imposing, particularly for projects of modest size. In fact, even small projects incorporate most, if not all, of these tasks, though some are given very limited attention. Ignoring these tasks often leads to problems or to additional work, even when a single person is doing all the work. Large and complex projects may go well beyond the tasks identified here, and may impose a disciplined process for performing the tasks.

The set of tools needed for a project also is closely related to the size and complexity of the project. Many simple systems are built with only a collection of programming tools or an integrated development environment in a 3GL or 4GL. These integrated development environments incorporate program editing, language processing (interpretation and/or compilation), debugging, and often version control.

As another example, many applications for the World Wide Web are created with specialized Web application development tools that provide HTML page design capabilities, an application database designer, and packaged routines that carry out the desired database insertion, update, retrieval, and deletion operations. These tools work with an application server that executes the resulting program, and require very little coding. For specialized applications, such as building a Web-based storefront for electronic commerce, it often is possible to use a prepackaged solution that incorporates an application server with some template-based components, leaving the developer with little custom code to be written.

Tools and Environments

As the previous example shows, the nature of software development has changed significantly, particularly over the last few years. The driving factors for these changes have included changes in the economics of computing, the transition to object-oriented technology, advances in user interface technology, the emergence of the World Wide Web as a key deployment platform for many applications, and the dominant role of Microsoft Windows as a development platform, as well as a deployment platform. Software development tools have correspondingly evolved to reflect these changes.

These next sections enumerate a broad range of software development and maintenance tools, covering the various tasks for many different types of applications.

Horizontal Tools

As noted previously, tools may be classified as *horizontal*, covering the entire software development process, or as *vertical*, covering a specific phase of the process. Tools for project and product management, including documentation, are the primary horizontal tools.

Documentation Tools

Documentation tools are used throughout the development process. Besides a basic word processor, documentation capabilities often are found within other tools. For example, programming tools may include a "pretty printer" that formats source code (3GL or 4GL) to enhance its readability, and may also include mechanisms for generating comments within the source code. Tools for requirements analysis and design may include templates that support the output of structured documents, such as those required by various government agencies. These documents are usually formatted so that they can be viewed and edited with a word processor.

Version Control

Version control can be applied to many different artifacts in the software development process, not just code. Requirements documents, UML models, Web pages, and user documentation also exist in multiple versions, so it is useful to have a version control tool that can be consistently applied to all of the different items that need it.

Configuration Management

Configuration management refers to managing all the different pieces that comprise a system, not just the source code. A configuration management tool should be able to store source and object code, scripts, analysis and design documents, test cases, test results, and anything else needed to re-create the items that comprise a system. Configuration management is tied closely to version control, because there are typically different versions of the different artifacts and the configuration management tool must associate the correct version of each artifact with a specific configuration.

Project Management

Project management involves project scheduling, resource allocation, problem tracking, status review, and more. Project management tools support allocation of people to budgets and to projects, linking of project information to and from spreadsheets and databases, calculation of critical paths, display of information in Gantt charts and other formats, and the capability to analyze changes in resource allocations. Problem tracking often is associated with quality assurance and testing, but it is also essential to project management as a key indicator of project status.

Cost Estimation

Cost estimation tools typically include models of existing system development projects, either as formulas or datapoints. A cost estimation tool works from an empirical knowledge base, working with user input to forecast the size, scope, staffing requirements and resources for a project. Cost estimation tools are often integrated with project management tools.

Process Management

Process management is closely related to project management, with the added notion that it is important to make certain that the organization follows a defined process within the overall context of the project. Process management tools may identify key process areas, such as those identified by the Software Engineering Institute, and may simply be checklists or templates.

Vertical Tools

To a large extent, the vertical tools needed for a project are highly dependent on the project itself. The tool needs for a small system being created by an individual for a small group are quite different from those needed for an automobile braking system or for an Internet-based electronic commerce system. For example, the following description of requirements analysis tools is suitable for large systems, where many people and many groups must coordinate work over months or years. For a small system being developed by a small team for a small audience, simple documents or models are sufficient.

Requirements Analysis

Requirements analysis focuses on understanding the perceived needs for a system from a variety of different perspectives, taking into account all the constraints on development. Thus, tools for requirements analysis must provide a way to collect requirements from different stakeholders, along with mechanisms to elicit those requirements and to track adherence to those requirements throughout development.

One type of requirements analysis tool can take a text document and save each paragraph or data item as an object that can be managed and tracked. For example, individual requirements can be linked to parts of a system model, to test cases that check to see that the requirement is met, or to program units that implement the requirement. The requirements tool can then generate traceability and completeness reports.

User interface (UI) prototyping tools also can play an important role in requirements gathering. UI prototypes are a highly effective way to give potential end users a way to conceptualize the features and functions of a system, even at the earliest stages of development, and thereby provide a way for those users to gain a better understanding of the system that allows them to express their own wishes.

Modeling tools are used throughout the analysis and design phases of a project. The most common form of modeling is database modeling, in which the application data is represented as a set of entities and relationships. For many years, data flow diagrams were used as part of Structured Analysis as a way to illustrate a hierarchy of system functions, data flows, and data stores. Structured Analysis was complemented by Structured Design, which showed a hierarchy of modules, along with data and control information passed among them.

UML (Unified Modeling Language) has now become a standard notation for system modeling, and is supported by many different tools. UML is a complex, formally defined notation that includes eight different types of diagrams, which are used to represent such things as the structure and relationships of objects, interactions among objects according to time sequences or responses to events, and deployment of components on processors and devices. Among the diagram types are use case diagrams and scenario diagrams, which are particularly helpful during requirements analysis.

Finally, test case generation tools are used to validate the resulting system against the requirements. The automated creation of test cases helps make requirements testable, consistent, and unambiguous.

Design

Design tools show the architecture and interfaces of software systems, and may also show the logical structure of individual program units. You can use database modeling tools to create logical models of a database and to generate the database schema in the form required for a specific database management system.

You can use UML modeling tools to create class, sequence, state, activity, component and deployment diagrams. Operations defined in class diagrams can be refined in state and activity diagrams. Component and deployment diagrams can be used for creating the architecture of distributed systems, showing the allocation of various system components to processors. At the component level, it is possible to model existing components and design patterns as a way to reuse designs and design fragments.

Specialized tools support domain-specific architectures, such as that provided by a Web application server or a client-server system, where a client program provides a user interface to a database residing on a server. In other words, these tools eliminate much of the design process by providing a proven architecture especially well-suited for that type of application. Other architectural models come from standard or common mechanisms, such as CORBA and Microsoft's COM+. Some UML modeling tools can be directly associated with a design framework, thereby addressing the transitions between analysis, design, and implementation.

Programming

For many developers, the only "essential" tool is the *programming environment* (or integrated development environment, or IDE). This tool provides, at a minimum, editing, program interpretation and/or compilation, debugging, and linking and loading capabilities to produce an executable program. IDEs may also incorporate components and libraries appropriate to the development language. For example, Java IDEs include an implementation of the Java Foundation Classes. Development tools for client-server systems usually include a forms builder, a database designer, and connectivity mechanisms to allow the application on the client machine to communicate with the database on the server machine. Development tools for Internet/Intranet applications may include an HTML editor (with syntax checking, pretty printing, and previewing), a form designer, a database designer, a link checker, and more.

Many commercial IDEs address the needs of small developers as well as large development teams. It is quite common for an IDE to come in multiple versions, ranging from a Learning Edition or a Standard Version for individual developers to an Enterprise Version intended for large scale development projects. The Enterprise Version is likely to include built-in version control, support for distributed architectures, and database connectivity routines, none of which are included in the low-end versions. Most IDEs also support "build management," pulling together the various pieces of a program that are part of the released software.

The tools needs of the programmer don't stop with the IDE. For example, additional debugging tools often are needed to examine program behavior at execution time, checking for memory leaks, references to locations outside a defined data structure, and so on.

Realtime and embedded applications need cross-platform support, including emulators for debugging the application on the development platform.

For applications that will be released to a wide user community (including, but not limited to software products), it's important to include online tutorials, examples, and help. There are specialized tools for creating help files, as well as tools for capturing screen images and user sessions, editing images, and editing movies and sound. For many Web applications, the application has little traditional "source code," but requires extensive use of graphics design tools. Many software products are licensed, so the toolkit for such products also must include a tool to support license validation during installation and/or runtime license checking.

As noted, the released "product" usually is more than just a single executable program. Not only are modern programs delivered in pieces, with separate runtime libraries and components, but they also include help files, tutorials, examples, and more. Accordingly, the programmer needs tools that can assist in building an installer, a specialized program that will manage the proper installation of the application program and related material on the user's computing environment. It also usually is helpful to have a compression tool that can reduce the size of the installer.

In short, programming goes well beyond the IDE for almost any programming language.

Testing

Testing is a particularly complex activity, because there are many aspects of a program to be tested, from its conformance to the requirements to its proper execution for a variety of possible inputs and conditions. Testing should evaluate the performance of the program: memory and processor utilization, transaction volumes, and behavior under load, such as many concurrent users. Load testing is particularly important for Web applications, and can be used with load balancing routines to see how a website would perform under heavy load.

Execution profilers can help to pinpoint inefficiencies in programs, displaying information that helps the tester see where the program is spending its time. Such profiles often are helpful in evaluating off-the-shelf products, such as object request brokers and database management systems, where there can be substantial performance differences among similar products, depending on the other execution characteristics of the program. Similar tools are also available for database performance testing and tuning.

Different tools are needed for these different tasks. A test management tool keeps track of many different aspects of testing, including test planning, test case development, and manual and automated test case execution. Managing the test data makes it easier to perform regression tests when the program has been modified.

A *test coverage tool* is used to determine the thoroughness of the test data set for a given program. It's desirable to create test cases that cause as many as possible of the paths through a program to be executed. At the level of individual program units, logical branch testing is important. When various components are assembled, it's important to test various function calls and messaging mechanisms.

Capture and playback tools can be used to test common scenarios of user behavior, including erroneous user inputs. These tools also are valuable for regression testing, as well as for creating demonstration scenarios in online help.

Web applications need link testing tools to make certain that users won't encounter broken links when they use the hyperlinks embedded in the application website. Given the dynamic nature of the World Wide Web, it's essential to check external links regularly. Web applications also may need to be tested with multiple versions of multiple browsers on multiple platforms if they are going to be used by a wide user community.

While this is only a partial list of the various kinds of testing tools that might be useful, it serves to illustrate the value of suitable tools in making the testing activity as efficient as possible.

Maintenance

Because many maintenance projects involve analysis, design, programming, and testing, many of the tools described in the preceding paragraphs are applicable to maintenance tasks. In addition, it is valuable to have tools for understanding existing systems. Reverse engineering tools, for example, allow the developer to visualize the organization of an existing system or database.

Tool Integration

Supporting all the different tasks of a software project requires a collection of tools that must work together. Therefore, you must pay attention to how tools are (or can be) integrated with one another. There are at least five different types of tool integration as documented by Wasserman: data integration, control integration, presentation integration, platform integration, and process integration.[1]

Data Integration

Data integration refers to the ways in which tools share data with one another. Data integration between two tools can occur in numerous ways, including explicit message passing or pipes, use of an intermediate file, or use of a database (object base). The first alternative implies an explicit connection between the tools, in which the user of the two tools makes certain that the first tool sends data to the second tool. The second alternative implies an agreement between the two tools whereby the second tool is told (or knows) where to find the data supplied by the first tool. The same situation holds for the third alternative, although the use of a database may reduce the need for the second tool to be aware of the file structure(s) used by the first tool. The latter two alternatives also allow participation by more than two tools (which may or may not be desired).

Control Integration

Control integration refers to the capability for tools to initiate and respond to actions in another tool. Control integration between tools can take place in different ways. Direct notification can occur through remote procedure calls caused by the execution of a code segment in a tool. Notification also can occur through the use of a time-activated mechanism, such as the UNIX cron daemon. Triggers in a database or object management system also can activate tools based on access to or modification of an item in a database or an object. Still another approach involves using a message server for notification.

Presentation Integration

Presentation integration refers to consistency of the user interface among different tools and to adherence with user interface conventions for the underlying platform.

Platform Integration

Platform integration refers to the capability of tools to interoperate in the same "virtual operating environment," which may encompass several different platforms. In other words, the user should have direct or indirect (via another tool) access to all the tools from a single location, typically the user's "desktop," with transparent access across a possibly heterogeneous network.

Process Integration

Process integration refers to the extent to which tools are related to any tools that control the software development project or process.

All but the last of these forms of integration are shown in Figure 9.1, which shows a model of an idealized development environment, in which various horizontal and vertical tools are available and integrated with one another. This model is a variant of the "toaster" model developed by ECMA and subsequently incorporated in the National Institute of Standards and Technology model for software engineering environments.

There are several observations to be made about this model. First, the tools are accessible from a single interface, although access to specific functions and tools may be controlled. Second, there is a data integration mechanism, a shared repository, through which tools share data. Historically, the repository has been a file system, although some integrated environments have successfully used a DBMS as part of the shared repository. (The first of these was Software through Pictures, circa 1985.[2] Third, there is a control integration mechanism, through which tools can send messages and initiate actions in other tools. Finally, all these items are placed in a virtual operating environment to show that the various tools may be hosted across a network.

Finally, this model does not show the nature of the integration, which can range from "loosely" to "tightly" connected. Informally, a loose integration between tools A and B is one where tools are "integrated" by standard systemwide mechanisms, such as cutting and pasting of text or sharing of text files. In other words, the tool builders haven't created any mechanisms aimed specifically at integrating A and B. A tight integration, by contrast, is one where the tool builders have agreed on specific interchange mechanisms, such as a shared repository, message passing, or remote invocation, and have done specific engineering work to implement that integration. Such an integration may or may not use industry-standard mechanisms, and typically must be custom-built for each pair of tools (and often for new releases of tools).

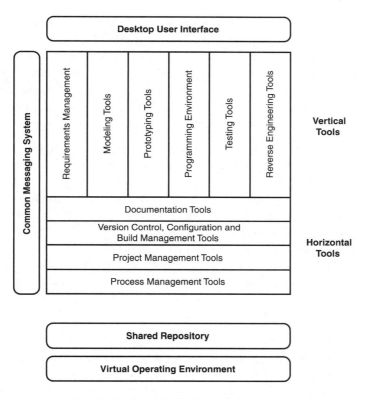

FIGURE 9.1 *Idealized model of integrated development environment.*

Tool Integration Is Hard

While the preceding model is attractive, it doesn't represent any real-world environments. There are numerous reasons why tools are not more closely and completely integrated with one another or around a common set of integration mechanisms.

First, integration capabilities are not always a goal when a tool is built. For a long time, integration among tools was not a market requirement, so tool suppliers focused exclusively on the features and functions of their own product(s). When they integrated their tools with products from other suppliers, it usually was on a point-to-point basis, often creating an integration that would not work properly when subsequent versions of the integrated products were released.

Second, different tools may have different underlying platform requirements. For example, two different tools may rely on two different DBMSs for storage support. The DBMSs, in turn, may require two different versions of the underlying operating system or file system. In this case, the two tools would have to be installed on two different machines running two versions of an operating system, a situation that goes against the system administration goal of having the same system software on every machine in an environment.

Third, tools may not have a suitable architecture to support integration. They may not be sufficiently "open," or may have an architectural mismatch with other tools. An open architecture provides access to the features and functions of a tool under program control, such as from another program. Among the features of an open architecture are published APIs, message formats, file formats, and database schemas. The APIs and the messaging mechanism typically provide program access to tool fragments, such as specific tool functions, or to data in the tool's internal storage structures. The file formats and database schemas can provide lower level access to the tool's storage mechanism. By contrast, a "monolithic" tool can only be used as an indivisible piece, and is not well-suited for integration.

In addition to being open, tools can be customizable. Customization could include the capability to change menus, toolbars, messages, graphical symbols, and more. For example, some modeling tools are based on "meta CASE" technology, where almost every aspect of the tool's behavior can be modified by the tool supplier, the user, or a third party without access to the source code.

An open architecture is illustrated in Figure 9.2. There are application programming interfaces to several different parts of the tool, along with message passing to a message server that then can communicate with other tools. The tool itself is split into layers, with the implication that different layers may execute on different processors. Of course, a more complex tool may have more layers.

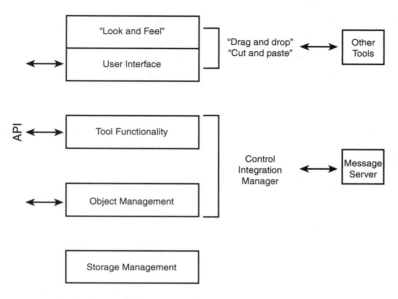

FIGURE 9.2 *Aspects of an open architecture.*

Tool Integration in Practice

For practical tool selection purposes, however, a different perspective may
be more helpful. This perspective reflects the different strategies for tool
integration that can be found among commercially available tools. There are
six different categories to be considered, which are explained in the following
sections.

Best-of-Breed Do-It-Yourself Integration

In this situation, the tool buyer selects tools freely among all suppliers and
arranges for the desired integration to be done, perhaps internally with help
from the vendor(s), or more likely under contract to the vendor or a third
party. There is no assurance that the integration will continue to work if the
tool buyer installs new versions of any of the integrated products.

Best-of-Breed with Point-to-Point Integrations

In this situation, two or more vendors have agreed to integrate their products,
typically by passing data statically or dynamically. A good example of this situation is the source code output of a modeling tool that can be used by specific
IDEs or rapid application development tools. Another example is the capability
of a test case generation tool to work with the data formats of a requirements

traceability tool. In some cases, cooperating vendors have announced that they will support such integrations through successive releases of their respective products, but this integration may not be ready at the time that the new release is available. This situation may create an undesirable dependency on the vendors of the integrated products.

Prime Integration Mechanism with Conforming Tools

In this situation, the tool buyer selects an integration mechanism, such as CORBA IDL, COM+, or the Microsoft Repository, then imposes a requirement on all key tool suppliers, prior to purchase, that they support the chosen mechanism(s) as a standard part of their product. It should be noted that tool buyers rarely take such a position and rely on the tool supplier to decide which mechanisms (if any) to support.

Prime Tool Supplier with Tool Integration Partners

In this case, the tool buyer identifies a prime tool supplier and relies on the supplier's partners for complementary tools. Many tool suppliers have such programs, though with varying efforts in validating the tool integrations, controlling the way that tools are integrated, or imposing delivery schedules on the integrations. Much of the burden falls on the tool buyer to understand what mechanisms are used for tool integration and who, if anyone, provides technical support for the integration.

Prime Tool Supplier with Multiple Product Lines

In this situation, the tool buyer selects a prime tool supplier, and works, insofar as possible, with other tools from that supplier, depending on that supplier to perform and support the integrations among its various tools. While this sounds like a good idea, it doesn't always work as well in practice because the various tools may be been built independently of one another and are available from a single source only as the result of corporate mergers and acquisitions. Different products may be maintained and supported by different groups in different geographical settings, serving to make this situation very similar to the preceding one.

Prime Tool Supplier with Dynamic Integration Mechanisms and Integration Partners

In this case, a tool supplier provides both a set of tools and a set of mechanisms that can be used by other suppliers to integrate with those tools. The best example of this situation today is Microsoft, which offers the Visual Studio family of development tools. The "enterprise" level of this family includes built-in "out of the box" integration with a modeling tool and a version control tool. The environment also supports three of the basic integration mechanisms noted previously. Data integration is provided through Microsoft Repository, which allows conforming tools to maintain multiple versions of individual objects. The Microsoft Repository includes a Unified Modeling Language Model, with the goal being the ability to exchange UML models among various UML tools. (Achieving this goal will require that suppliers of UML modeling tools agree to support the UML model of Microsoft Repository.)

Control integration is provided through Microsoft's Component Object Model services (COM, DCOM), which incorporates message passing and remote procedure invocation mechanisms.

Presentation integration is provided through the Windows platform standard, which provides for a standard desktop user interface.

All these mechanisms are open, but proprietary. Because they are open, any tool supplier can decide to adhere to them and use them as the way to integrate with other tools. Because they are proprietary, Microsoft (in this case) has the right to modify them as desired, although it is decidedly not in their interest to do so with great frequency.

Given Microsoft's extremely strong position in the marketplace, it's fair to say that Microsoft can provide a powerful "center of gravity" for tool integration, thereby leading to well-integrated environments for Windows-based tools. In other words, suppliers of Windows-based tools may find it necessary to integrate with other tools through these mechanisms as a prerequisite for success in the marketplace.

One also could imagine a variant of this case where the integration mechanisms are non-proprietary industry standards, but such a solution seems unlikely in the near future. Instead, there are "bridges" that communicate between the Windows mechanisms and others. A good example of such a bridge is a COM-to-CORBA bridge.

Tool Selection

Organizations must try to select a collection of tools that meets the needs of the organization, improves the quality of the software, and increases the productivity of the organization. The tool selection process must study both the characteristics of individual tools, as well as how they fit into an overall tool environment using the integration approaches described in the preceding section.

Decisions regarding tools cannot be made in a vacuum. The choice of tools for any project is influenced by current tools, project size, organizational standards, platform(s), planned programming language(s), the nature of the application, budgets, and personal preferences, among other things. Furthermore, most organizations already have an inventory of existing tools and staff members who are knowledgeable about specific tools.

In today's world, there are so many tools from so many different vendors that it is quite difficult to be aware of all of the different tools that address a specific development task. Many tools have a significant learning curve, so it is rarely practical to introduce a new suite of tools for a project, particularly when trying to meet tight schedule constraints.

Here is a short list of tool selection criteria. Note that many of the criteria are more directly related to the tool supplier than to the tool itself, reflecting issues that are important for businesses adopting a tool that will be used for a long time and be important for the success of their software development efforts. Overlaying these individual tool issues are the aspects of integration previously described. In practice, it is not always feasible to select the individual best tool in each category, but to make those choices in the context of a specific preferred tool, vendor, or product suite.

Suitability

Suitability refers to the extent to which the tool's functions and features support the software development task that it must support. For example, there are many different tools for version control, but an organization might want to have a version control solution that is combined with a configuration management system and a problem tracking tool. A standalone version control system would therefore be unsuitable for that project.

Tool suppliers frequently provide feature checklists for their own products that can serve as a basis for evaluating a set of competitive products. You should obtain these lists from several candidate vendors, combine the checklists, and then shorten the list to those functions and features that are most important for your organization.

It's important to avoid "analysis paralysis," evaluating too many comparable tools against too many features. In general, an evaluation should be limited to a maximum of five tools in a particular category. It's also important to avoid thinking that each organization is unique with respect to tool needs. Evaluation is often accelerated by talking to other users of a tool and by reading independent product reviews.

Tool Integration Support

As noted previously, most organizations are assembling a collection of tools, often from more than one supplier. Therefore, you must consider how individual tools integrate with other tools, and to select a set of tools that plays well together. To do so, you must understand the tool integration mechanisms of the individual tools or tool suites, and the extent to which that tool's supplier supports integration with other preferred tools.

This process often entails difficult tradeoffs, because a specific tool may be superior when compared to other tools supporting the same task, but may not work well with other selected tools. The goal is to create the best overall tool support for the software development process, which is not necessarily the same as selecting the best tool for each task in the process.

Installability

The tool selection process should include a test installation of the tool on a machine in the environment where it will be used. Such installations are quite common, because many tool vendors make trial versions of their product available over the World Wide Web. Installation should be a straightforward process, and should follow established conventions for the platform on which it is to be installed. It's important to be aware of unusual requirements, such as changes to system libraries. Tools should "tread lightly" on the overall environment, making it as easy to uninstall the tool as to install it. It's not a good sign if tool installation requires assistance from the tool supplier, particularly if the tool is going to be deployed to numerous users.

Tool Usability

Usability is a subjective measure, but is nonetheless a central issue in tool selection. Three aspects of usability dominate the evaluation. The first of these is the user interface. The tool interface should, of course, conform to standard user interface guidelines for the platform on which it runs. The capability to support standard GUI features, such as cut-and-paste or drag-and-drop, shows that the tool builder considered inter-operation with other tools on that platform. Other GUI considerations, such as number of menus, length of menus, fixed and floating toolbars, customization of menus and tool bars, error notification, and user feedback during long operations, often are a matter of personal preferences. Nonetheless, they are important to consider, because seemingly minor annoyances during an evaluation process will turn into major aggravations when you use that tool on a regular, long-term basis.

A second aspect of usability is ease of learning. Tools that support complex tasks often are of necessity complex themselves. Nonetheless, the complexity of learning to use a tool should be appropriate to the complexity of the task and the frequency of use. Tutorials, examples, standard help screens, and contextual help can combine to ease the learning curve. There also are numerous independently published books for popular tools.

The third aspect of usability is the match between the user task and the tool. Ideally, a tool should provide a logical mapping from the task at hand to the automated support steps. Accordingly, it's important to view the tool not simply as providing a set of features and functions, but enabling a task to be performed efficiently and effectively.

Finally, the usability testing should include the people who will be the real users of the tool, not just the specialized tool evaluation group.

Tool Quality

The tool evaluation process should pay careful attention to the quality of the tool. In general, your evaluation process should attempt to use the same non-trivial example(s) across all of the tools in a category. If multiuser and/or multisite support is needed, for example, then that feature should be explicitly tested as well. Similarly, client-server or n-tier deployment of a tool should be tested if appropriate. Distributed development settings are particularly hard to test, and the user environment is likely to be different from those tested by the tool supplier. Any bugs, crashes, or other anomalies should be carefully documented for the tool supplier. A high frequency of problems should, almost without exception, lead to rejection of the tool, as should problems that are viewed as "show stoppers" by the evaluation team. For other problems, it is useful to see which of these are already known by the tool supplier and to learn the plans for correcting them. Exploring these questions often gives some insight into the tool supplier's development and maintenance processes.

Tool Maturity

Some organizations are comfortable selecting a newly released (or soon to be released) product, perhaps from a young company, while others will only choose a more mature tool from an established company. This situation reflects the amount of risk that the organization is willing to accept.

In today's highly competitive tool marketplace, products often are brought to market with a subset of the planned features and with less testing than normally desirable. While this statement is particularly true for new companies, it applies for established tool suppliers as well. (One established supplier numbered the release of its new product 4.0, so that potential customers would be misled into thinking the product had been in use for some time.)

It's important to distinguish between reality (what's in the product now) and promised features, which may or may not materialize in the timeframe where they are needed. Organizations that select a new product must be prepared to spend extra time in installing updates (euphemistically known as "service packs") and new versions.

Tool Support

Product support often is overlooked in tool evaluation activities. However, you should pay careful attention to the levels of support that are available for a tool and to determine the responsiveness of tool suppliers, and then to match the available service to an organization's anticipated needs. Tool support ranges from do-it-yourself, online lists of FAQ's and product updaters, to 24x7 toll-free telephone support from knowledgeable support engineers. Tool suppliers often offer several different levels of support.

It's also important to understand the tool supplier's response to problem reports, not only for serious problems that cause the tool or the user's system to crash, but also for those problems where the tool does not perform as stated and adversely affects the organization's capability to use the tool effectively. Most tool builders perform triage on problem reports, classifying them by level of severity. However, it is important to understand whether serious problems will be immediately addressed, or whether they will simply be considered for fixing in a subsequent release.

Finally, it's valuable to understand the tool supplier's future plans for any tool that is viewed as essential to an organization's development environment. It also should be recognized that the large number of mergers and acquisitions involving software tool suppliers means that a new owner may change those plans.

Product Training

Because tools often have a significant learning curve, you must consider the ways in which tool users will learn how to use a tool effectively. One approach might be called "deep end of the pool," where each user is expected to learn the tool from the tutorials, examples, and user guides (if any) provided by the tool supplier. While this approach minimizes out-of-pocket costs for training, it often is more costly in the long run, because tool users will take longer to learn to use the tool, and may never learn some of the short cuts or tricks. Most tool suppliers offer both public classes and on-site classes in the use of their tools, and there are often independent training sources for the most widely used tools.

Pricing, Licensing, and Related Business Issues

Business issues play a significant role in tool evaluations, and cannot be overlooked. While pricing is often the first consideration, licensing issues can make a major difference in the overall price. Tool suppliers vary widely in licensing strategies. Some tools are licensed to a specific machine, while others are licensed for a number of concurrent users. Some tools allow a user to install the tool on more than one machine, with the restriction that the user can only use one of those machines at a time. Such an approach would allow use of the tool on a desktop machine in the office, and on a portable computer while away from the office, thereby reducing the overall license cost. Other business issues arise with multisite, and particularly multinational projects, as well as with site and organizational licenses.

Supplier Viability

Finally, when working with commercial tools, you should recognize that tool suppliers can go out of business or can be acquired by another company that decides to discontinue specific tools or product lines. Tool buyers can protect themselves up to a point by establishing an escrow agreement that provides the buyer with access to the tool's source code in such cases.

Of course, access to the tool's source code isn't a very satisfactory solution because that shifts the burden of tool enhancements onto the buyer's organization. As a result, you should consider the status and prospects for a tool supplier when making key decisions about tools, and to align the results with the tool buyer's acceptance of that risk.

What Next?

The goal of this chapter has been to indicate the broad range of tools that are available, the issues associated with building an integrated environments, and some guidelines that can be used to evaluate tools and their suppliers.

In summary, tool selection and use can be very complex, particularly for complex projects that need extensive tool support. Even within a single organization, it's common to find substantial differences in the tools being used for a specific project, based on the nature of the project.

Tool selection is further complicated by the rate at which tools evolve and new tools appear. There are research publications on tools and environments in some conferences, such as the annual International Conference on Software Engineering and the Conference on Advanced Information System Engineering, as well as in *IEEE Software*. There are relatively few books on tools and environments in general; most tool-related books describe the use of a specific version of a specific tool.

A dominant portion of the work on tools is done as product development by commercial tool suppliers, rather than as research by academic institutions and research laboratories. In general, information on the resulting products is not described in the research literature. As a result, keeping track of information on tools and environments requires following the places where these commercial developments are announced, reviewed, and demonstrated.

Among the best sources for such information are trade publications, trade shows, and sites on the World Wide Web, including vendor sites. As with tools themselves, these resources change frequently.

On the World Wide Web, the author's Software Methods and Tools website at `http://www.methods-tools.com` provides annotated tools listings, along with links to supplier sites. There are also lists of developer resources, including newsletters and trade publications. Other good sites are developer.com (`http://www.developer.com`), the Developer's Exchange (`http://www.devx.com`), and the Programmer's Directory (`http://www.programmersdirectory.com`), which include extensive resource information on software development technologies.

Part of the Microsoft website is devoted explicitly to developers and to Microsoft technologies (`http://msdn.microsoft.com/developer/default.htm`). The Cetus site (`http://www.cetus-links.org`) has thousands of links, mostly to object-oriented technology and products, but very little descriptive material about the links. For those looking for tools that support a specific programming language, the Software Methods and Tools developer resources page (`http://www.methods-tools/html/developer_resources.html`) is a good starting point, containing selective annotated links for numerous languages.

There are several sites that describe tools for building websites and Web-based applications. Among them are c|net's Builder.com site (`http://www.builder.com`), Songline Studio's Web Review site (`http:// webreview.com`), and Mecklermedia's Web Developer (`http://www.webdeveloper.com`).

Most tool suppliers provide extensive information about specific tools at their own websites. In many cases, it is possible to download trial evaluations of specific tools, in addition to viewing the tool supplier's sales materials.

Among the trade publications with extensive coverage of tools and components are *Component Strategies, Application Development Trends, Java Report, C++ Report, Java Developer's Journal, Visual Basic Programmer's Journal, Windows Developer's Journal*, and *Software Development*. Many of these publications have complementary websites with partial or complete content. There also are print and Web-based newsletters that cover these topics, including Cutter's *Application Development Strategies* (http://www.cutter.com/ads/) and *Component Development Strategies* (http://www.cutter.com/cds/) and *Javaworld* (http://www.javaworld.com).

There are dozens of trade shows that highlight commercially available tools and environments. Trade show topics are heavily influenced by market trends, so the following list should be viewed as representative of current events. Software Research sponsors Quality Week (http://www.soft.com), which combines reviewed research presentations with experience reports and a commercial exhibition. Software Quality Engineering sponsors the STAR conferences (http://www.sqe.com). Other commercially sponsored trade shows include:

> Miller-Freeman's Software Development Conference
> (http://www.sdexpo.com)
>
> Embedded Systems Conference (http://www.embedded.com)
>
> UML World (http://www.umlworld.com)
>
> SIGS Publications' Component Development Conference
> (http://www.componentdevelopment.com)
>
> Conference for Java Development (http://www.javadevcon.com)
>
> Sun Microsystems' JavaOne (http://java.sun.com/javaone)
>
> Fawcette's VBITS Conference (http://www.fawcette.com)

Web application development is a topic at Internet World (http://www.internet.com), Miller-Freeman's Web Design and Development Conference (http://www.mfweb.com), and c|net's Builder.com live (http://www.builder.com). Some of the larger user group meetings, such as Oracle Open World (http://www.oracle.com), also include tool exhibits.

References

1. Wasserman, Anthony. "Tool Integration in Software Engineering Environments," in *Software Engineering Environments*, ed. F. Long. Lecture Notes in Computer Science, vol. 467. Berlin: Springer Verlag, 1990.

2. Wasserman, Anthony and Peter Pircher. "A Graphical, Extensible Integrated Environment for Software Development," *ACM SIGPLAN Notices*, vol. 22, no. 1 (January, 1987), pp. 131-142. (Proc. ACM SIGSOFT/SIGPLAN Symposium on Practical Software Development Environments).

3. Yourdon, Edward. *Death March*. Englewood Cliffs, NJ: Prentice-Hall, 1997.

Note

This title is not cited in the text, but is a valuable reference for the reader of this chapter:

Brown, Alan W., David J. Carney, Edwin J. Morris, Dennis B. Smith, and Paul F. Zarrella. Principles of CASE Tool Integration. *New York: Oxford University Press, 1994.*

Addendum

The body of the chapter has intentionally omitted names of specific vendors and tools. This addendum gives examples of tools in the various tool categories discussed in the chapter. Keep in mind that products and vendors come and go, and that the leading tools in a category change over time. The tools in the following list are intended to be representative of tools available at the time of publication.

Category	Tool Name	Vendor (URL)
Requirements Analysis	DOORS	Quality Systems and Software (www.qssinc.com)
	RequisitePro	Rational Software (www.rational.com)
Modeling	Rational Rose 98I	Rational Software (www.rational.com)
	Software through Pictures	Aonix (www.aonix.com)
	System Architect 2001	Popkin Software (www.popkin.com)
Programming		
Ada	ObjectAda	Aonix (www.aonix.com)
	Rational Apex	Rational Software (www.rational.com)
BASIC	Visual Basic	Microsoft (msdn.microsoft.com/vbasic)
C++	Visual C++	Microsoft (msdn.microsoft.com/visualc)
	C++ Builder	Inprise (www.borland.com/bcppbuilder)
Java	Visual Café	Symantec (www.symantec.com)
	JBuilder	Inprise (www.borland.com)
4 GL	PowerBuilder	Sybase (www.sybase.com)
4GL	Delph	Inrpise (www.borland.com/delphi)

Category	Tool Name	Vendor (URL)
Debugging	BoundsChecker	Compuware NuMega (www.numega.com)
	Insure++	Parasoft (www.parasoft.com)
Web Development	SilverStream	SilverStream (www.silversteam.com)
	Apptivity	Progress Software (www.apptivity.com)
Testing and Test Management	Rational TeamTest	Rational Software (www.rational.com)
	TestWorks	Software Research, Inc. (www.soft.com)
	Astra SiteTest	Mercury Interactive (www.merc-int.com)
	Silk	Segue Software (www.segue.com)
	TestBytes	Platinum Technology (www.platinum.com)
Project Metrics	SLIM	Quantitative Software Management (www.qsm.com)
Configuration Management	PVCS	Merant (www.merant.com)
	ClearCase	Rational Software (www.rational.com)
Project Management	Microsoft Project	Microsoft (www.microsoft.com/project)
Cost Estimation	Foresight	Price Systems (www.pricesystems.com)
Documentation	DocExpress	ATA (www.docexpress.com)

All product names are trademarks of their respective holder.

Index

Symbols

V

validating measurements, 217-219

validation, user validation (traditional versus UCD), 49

variations, 33

vendor-led user groups, users of CBSE, 150

vendors of tools, 265

verification, 118

version control, 245

vertical tools, 237, 246

capture and playback tools, 250

design tools, 247-248

maintenance, 250

programming environment tools, 248-249

requirements analysis, 246-247

test coverage tool, 250

testing, 249-250

UI prototyping tools, 247

virtual threads, 96

visual designers, software development team, 63

W-Z

Walkthrough, evaluating usability, 76

waterfall design methodologies, 70

waterfall life cycle model, software development, 58

Web application development, 264

Web application development tools, 244

websites for tools, 263-264

Wills, Alan Cameron, 140

workshops, launch and alignment workshops, 191-193

World Wide Web (WWW)

libWWW, 91-92

testing tools, 250

Are You a Potential Author?

The Software Quality Institute (SQI) at the University of Texas at Austin has entered into an agreement with Macmillan Technical Publishing to sponsor a series of professional books. These books will focus on multiple issues, including software development, management, integration into other industries, and business, with an overall emphasis on quality. The series will be published by Macmillan and marketed internationally through major bookstores.

The emphasis, as with all SQI efforts, is on real-life problems that have strategic solutions based on actual experience. This book series, like our seminars and certificate programs, is created by practitioners for practitioners.

We are looking for books written by software professionals who have "been there and done that."

Do you have a specific expertise that you would like to write about?

Do you know of other potential authors who you would like to recommend?

Is there a "hot" topic that you would like to see discussed in a book?

To submit a proposal to SQI, complete the form on the Software Quality Institute home page at:

http://www.utexas.edu/coe/sqi/bookproposal.html

The SQI editorial board will evaluate the proposal. If the editorial board recommends publication, the author(s) will then contract directly with Macmillan Technical Publishing for publication rights. SQI will receive a small royalty for titles published by Macmillan Technical Publishing in the proposed series.

We believe that this series presents significant opportunity for authors of titles directed toward an audience of software professionals. We look forward to your participation in this important venture and to an early expression of commitment.

If you would like more information about Macmillan Technical Publishing, please contact Alan Bower, Executive Editor, at 317-817-7473 or through email at abower@mcp.com.